The Booksellers Association's Guide to Starting and Running a Bookshop

The Booksellers Association's Guide to Starting and Running a Bookshop

An introduction to bookselling practice and organisation

MALCOLM BRECKMAN

MALCOLM STEWART BOOKS

AUTHOR'S NOTE

In 1980, under the pen name of M. Knightley, I wrote *Your Own Bookshop* in the Kingfisher Business Guides series. The present book borrows freely from the earlier one but is so thorough a reworking and extension of it – broader in scope, more detailed in treatment and about three times as long – that it seems reasonable to present it as a completely new title rather than a new edition of an old one.

Malcolm Breckman
August 1988

First published 1988 by Malcolm Stewart Books,
2 Vines Avenue, London N3 2QD

British Library Cataloguing in Publication Data

Breckman, Malcolm, *1937–*
The Booksellers Association's guide to starting and running a bookshop : an introduction to bookselling practice and organisation.
1. Great Britain. Bookselling – Manuals
381'.45002'068

ISBN 0-904132-74-9

Printed in England by Billing and Son Limited, Worcester

CONTENTS

TABLES AND FIGURES

TABLES

FIGURES

FOREWORD

One sign of how attractive the prospect is of running one's own bookshop can be seen by the considerable number of people who contact the Booksellers Association each year in their search for information on the subject. Some have prior bookselling experience, and some have been involved in other retailing sectors, but many come with a deep enthusiasm for books and no sales or business knowledge.

The Booksellers Association exists to promote and protect the interests of booksellers, and we strive in many ways to create a vital and healthy book trade. One of our responsibilities is to encourage new bookshops to open in Britain and Ireland, but it is no less our duty to ensure that those beginning to run their own bokshops do so with a good understanding of the perils and pitfalls – as well as the pleasures and rewards – which await them.

Malcolm Breckman's *Starting and Running a Bookshop* is a marvellous introduction to the subject. The book successfully fills a gap in the market, which for many years has cried out for a well-informed, comprehensive and readable text on the steps to be taken prior to opening one's own bookshop. Although the book is primarily aimed at those who wish to run their own business and need to know all about the trade and the workings of a bookshop, it is also a book anyone employed in bookselling will find illuminating. It roots the reader in the bookselling world and provides a clear picture of the functions and workings of a bookshop as well as of the issues and debates central to the selling of new books. And, most importantly, the enjoyment of owning a bookshop is kept prominent, even amid the discussion of the more routine aspects of business which must be absorbed.

While *Starting and Running a Bookshop* has been written and published independently, the Association is delighted to adopt it as its own recommended text on the subject – though not all the views it contains, of course, are necessarily those of the Association. We hope that everyone who begins thinking of running their own bookshop will start their planning by reading this book. It offers the best possible introduction to the business of selling new books.

Tim Godfray, Director
The Booksellers Association of Great Britain and Ireland

ACKNOWLEDGEMENTS

Reflecting upon Dr Johnson's observation that booksellers are generous and liberal-minded, I believe that the many people who have helped me with different aspects of this book might consider themselves best thanked, not by figuring in a list of close-set names, but by knowing they had in some way contributed to a book intended to be useful to future trade colleagues. To the extent that the book fulfils that purpose, I am indebted to all who have helped me; to the extent that it falls short, the responsibility is mine.

So my general thanks to those members of the Booksellers Association who allowed me to visit their shops, pick their brains and seek their advice; and to the elected officers and permanent staff of the BA who answered my questions, fed me with information, commented on the draft manuscript and suggested corrections and improvements; and to the publishers, wholesalers and providers of services to the trade who helped me to understand their particular roles on the bookselling stage.

I will depart from nameless gratitude only so far as to acknowledge my debt to Andrea Livingstone, the BA's Assistant Director, who has served as the main link between the BA and myself, and who has watched over the book, with kindness and concern, from start to finish.

Malcolm Breckman

INTRODUCTION

Book trade people love books. It's what brings most of them into the business in the first place. While most of the population never buy books at all, few of those who do buy them ever lose that sense of excitement on crossing the threshold of a good bookshop. And many have doubtless felt, however fleetingly, that it would be rather nice one day to have a bookshop of their own. Business and pleasure combined. A seductively romantic dream. You may have dreamt it yourself.

With a bookshop of your own you need your share of romance to sustain you through the trials of what can be a very difficult business. But more than that, you need an honest appreciation of – and even enthusiasm for – the realities of the trade and the quite unromantic demands it can make upon you. You'll almost certainly spend more time reading invoices and statements than novels and biographies, and discussions with customers will tend to be about prices or delayed orders rather than the finer points of literary style.

While the present guide should satisfy the curiosity of anyone wanting to peek behind the bookselling scenes, it is primarily addressed to people, not at present in the book trade, who are thinking of starting up – or taking over – a bookshop dealing in new books. It aims to give an insight into the workings of the trade, and to direct the attention of prospective bookshop owners to the things they must know about and the problems they will have to solve.

This is not a textbook, still less a blueprint for success. It is more a guided tour of the bookselling trade, pointing out its character, organisation, practices, preoccupations, achievements, failures, risks and opportunities. It shows you the broad highway of major bookselling trends, the niches where small newcomers might find a home, the possible costs and rewards of a bookselling business, old cupboards complete with skeletons, and new technology brimming with promise. Put your ear to the wall and you may catch the odd phrase in long-running trade quarrels; and the sharp-eyed may even glimpse some dirty linen a-washing. The intention throughout is to be truthful rather than diplomatic. If you're thinking of risking your money and devoting your working life to the business, you've a right to expect a picture of how the trade really is, not a theoretical construct of how we might wish it to be.

Chapter 1

Books

Bookselling is a commercial and not a literary activity. If you're thinking of getting your own bookshop, that has to be understood. Of course you love books and reading; of course you value books as the repositories of knowledge and wisdom, as the expression and inspiration of the human spirit and the artistic imagination; of course you believe that society as a whole and the individuals within it are enriched and civilised by the literature available to them; of course you regard the ability to read with pleasure and understanding to be among the greatest gifts each generation may bestow upon its children. If you didn't subscribe to these views, you wouldn't be attracted to bookselling; most other retail commodities, from fruit and veg to diamond tiaras, offer a better money-making prospect than books. But while bookselling plays a crucial role in the maintenance and encouragement of literature and literacy, the role is not artistic or pedagogic, but marketing and distributive; and a bookseller's success is measured in cash.

SUBJECTS

What is true of bookselling is true also of books. Most of them are not 'literature'. Even fewer are the bestselling novels that most people think of whenever bookselling is mentioned. Look at Table 1 overleaf. This shows the number of titles published in 1987, classified by subject. Fiction is certainly the largest single class, yet if you work it out you'll see it accounts for less than 12 per cent of the total. Put that another way: nearly 90 per cent of new books published are *not* fiction.

The figures, as is the way with figures, can be misleading. Merely

TABLE 1 Source: *The Bookseller*, 8 January 1988

SUBJECT CLASSIFICATION OF TITLES PUBLISHED IN 1987 *Total Published 54,746*

(a) alphabetical order		(b) numerical order	
269	Aeronautics	6389	Fiction
456	Agriculture & Forestry	5014	Children's Books
408	Architecture	4451	Political Science & Economics
1573	Art	3345	Medical Science
133	Astronomy	2028	Religion & Theology
628	Bibliography & Library Econ.	2015	History
1880	Biography	1904	Law & Public Administration
811	Chemistry & Physics	1898	Commerce
5014	Children's Books	1881	School Textbooks
1898	Commerce	1880	Biography
167	Customs, Costumes, Folklore	1604	Engineering
837	Domestic Science	1573	Art
1226	Education	1412	Literature
1604	Engineering	1355	Travel & Guidebooks
627	Entertainment	1254	Natural Sciences
6389	Fiction	1226	Education
1032	General	1118	Sociology
596	Geography & Archaeology	1032	General
270	Geology & Meteorology	929	Mathematics
2015	History	919	Sports & Outdoor Games
260	Humour	837	Domestic Science
460	Industry	812	Psychology
700	Language	811	Chemistry & Physics
1904	Law & Public Administration	758	Poetry
1412	Literature	700	Language
929	Mathematics	628	Bibliography & Library Econ.
3345	Medical Science	627	Entertainment
277	Military Science	596	Geography & Archaeology
394	Music	578	Philosophy
1254	Natural Sciences	460	Industry
451	Occultism	456	Agriculture & Forestry
578	Philosophy	454	Trade
189	Photography	451	Occultism
358	Plays	408	Architecture
758	Poetry	394	Music
4451	Political Science & Economics	358	Plays
812	Psychology	354	Stockbreeding
2028	Religion & Theology	277	Military Science
1881	School Textbooks	270	Geology & Meteorology
78	Science, General	269	Aeronautics
1118	Sociology	260	Humour
919	Sports & Outdoor Games	194	Wireless & Television
354	Stockbreeding	189	Photography
454	Trade	167	Customs, Costumes, Folklore
1355	Travel & Guidebooks	133	Astronomy
194	Wireless & Television	78	Science, General

counting titles ignores the fact that some titles sell in their hundreds of thousands while others barely sell at all. You can see from Table 2 on page 17 that fiction certainly outsells any other category. Even so, across the trade as a whole, it accounts for little more than a third of shop sales.

NUMBERS

To stock one copy of each new book or new edition published in Britain you would need to buy about 60,000 books a year with a retail value well over a million pounds. Something like 160 new titles are issued or old ones re-issued for every single day of the year. Yet even if you took one copy of every new title into stock in your first year in the book business, you would still be missing about 380,000 other titles, representing books still in print though published in earlier years. To have just one copy of each of the 440,000 books in print in Britain, you would need about ten miles of shelving and a stock investment of several million pounds.

Paradoxically, if you did indeed take all these books into your shop, you would have more customers grumbling about the inadequacy of your stock than marvelling at its comprehensiveness. With only one copy of each title, you would unavoidably be out of stock of the most popular titles most of the time – and these, by definition, are the very ones your customers most want to buy. Once you had sold your single copy of *The Guinness Book of Records* to the first customer who asked for it, you would have to disappoint other customers who wanted the same title until the arrival of replacement stock.

Only an exceedingly wealthy library or one, like the British Library, with a statutory right to a free copy of every new publication, can possibly implement a policy of stocking one of everything. A bookshop can never stock more than a selection of available titles, and it often stocks multiple copies of many of them. Which titles to stock and in what quantities are matters of trading policy, commercial judgement, stock control and available space and finance.

A 4,000 sq ft branch of one of the major bookselling chains may have 30,000 titles and a stock of £150,000 at retail prices. A small independent bookseller with a shop of 700 sq ft may have 5,000 titles and a stock of £28,000 at retail prices. Beware of generalising from these figures; there can be wide differences in stockholding and stock investment even between shops which, to the casual observer, might seem rather similar. The important points to grasp are that no bookshop stocks more than a fraction of the titles available, and even the largest bookshops miss more titles than they stock.

Just consider: a shop with as many as 30,000 titles has less than one in fifteen of the titles in print, and a shop with 5,000 titles has barely one in ninety.

The number of titles bookshops typically have on their shelves as a proportion of the number of titles available may seem derisory. But compare the stock range offered by a small bookshop with that offered by neighbouring retailers in other trades. Does the sweetshop offer 5,000 varieties of sweets? Or the fishmonger 5,000 different fish? Or the radio and TV dealer 5,000 different models? And what sweetshop customer, asking for an 80p bar of Tasti Toothrot and being told that it wasn't stocked, would have the temerity to say that he would like to place a special order for a bar and how soon could he have it please? Yet bookshop customers traditionally expect that if they want an unstocked book, the bookseller should be able to get it for them, no matter how obscure the title, unknown the publisher or low the price. Most booksellers think so too.

FOUR HUNDRED AND FORTY THOUSAND TITLES IN PRINT

If you find it difficult to believe that there are 440,000 titles in print, check this year's edition of *Whitaker's Books in Print* (see page 22) for the most recent figures. And bear in mind that these figures represent only the totals of books published in Britain. Books published in the USA, Canada, Australia and other English-speaking countries are not included unless stocks are held by a sole agent in the UK; also left out, of course, are the publications of non-English-speaking countries.

Furthermore, some books are unintentionally left out of the count. While regular publishers ensure that their books are listed in *Whitaker's Books in Print*, as it is in their commercial interest that they should be, there are many books published by organisations and individuals whose primary business is not that of publishing, and a certain number of these titles – though how many is anybody's guess – escape the notice of the list compilers. A biscuit factory, for example, may publish a history of the firm to celebrate its centenary year; an amateur botanist may publish a flora of his native parish; a frustrated poet may pay the local printers to produce a slim volume of his work; and none of these titles, nor possibly thousands like them, may ever be known to the compilers of book lists.

TABLE 2 Source: *Lost Book Sales*, 1980

PERCENTAGES OF BOOKS BOUGHT, CLASSIFIED BY SUBJECT *1679 Customers*

(a) alphabetical order %		*(b) numerical order* %	
2	Agriculture	34	Fiction
2	Art	17	Children's Books
4	Biography	6	Domestic Science
17	Children's Books	4	Biography
6	Domestic Science	3	Natural Science
1	Engineering	3	History
2	Entertainment	3	Language
34	Fiction	2	Art
3	History	2	Sports and Games
3	Language	2	Travel
2	Law	2	Entertainment
2	Medical Science	2	Medical Science
3	Natural Science	2	Law
2	School	2	Agriculture
2	Sports and Games	2	School
2	Travel	1	Engineering

NB No other subject was named by more than 1% of the sample.

Titles

Talk of *titles* in this context is slightly misleading as different editions of the same title are counted as different titles in trade bibliographies. A novel, for example, published in both hardback and paperback editions adds two, not one, to the number of titles published. As far as the trade is concerned, the difference between one edition and another is as complete as that between two entirely different books: different editions of the same title may have different prices, be subject to different trade terms, appeal to different sections of the market and even be on the lists of different publishers.

Books

Numbers are also swollen by titles which may not be universally regarded as *books* at all, but rather as *pamphlets* or *leaflets* or *booklets*. There is no agreed definition of *book*. A 1964 UNESCO conference decided that it was a *non-periodical printed publication of at least 49 pages exclusive of the cover pages*. On this definition, there could be no such thing as a 48-page book, however impressive its content and appearance, while a 50-sheet list of names and addresses of objectors to the construction of a new motorway, run off on a spirit duplicator and stapled together at the top left corner, would constitute a book. A wider-ranging definition, used for the purpose of the Copyright Act (see page 31), says that *the expression 'book' includes every part or division of a book, pamphlet, sheet of letterpress, sheet of music, map, plan, chart or table separately published.*

Fortunately, booksellers have no need for a precise definition. We all know a book when we see one and most of the time that's all that matters. It's worth remembering, however, that books come in a variety of shapes, sizes and styles of production, and that not everything listed in a trade bibliography will necessarily match your own idea of what a book is. Does *The Highway Code*, for example, typically come to mind when the conversation turns to books? Probably not. But in 1987 it made frequent appearances in the trade's bestseller lists.

We may not all agree on what we mean by 'books' but one thing is beyond dispute: there are an awful lot of them.

THE PROBLEM OF PROLIFERATING TITLES

Non-booksellers might suppose that the book trade's huge product range is a cause for rejoicing rather than complaint: the more books there are, the greater the bookseller's choice of what to stock, the greater the public's choice of what to buy. Yet within the trade, the vast and continuously increasing number of titles is widely deplored.

This is what the Publishers Association was saying in its Annual Report as long ago as 1959:

> . . . British publishing, by all the evidence, is still suffering from chronic over-production. The number of new books and new editions issued during the last year established a fresh record of 22,143 titles. This is an alarming total in relation to the size of our book-reading public, even allowing for the high percentage of copies that are exported. As the average sale per title drops, as it is bound to do unless the public can be induced to spend far more money on books than it does at present, the need to charge still higher retail prices is intensified.

The word *chronic* was well chosen. Thirty years on, over-production continues at an accelerating rate, as you can see in Table 3. (The seeming discrepancy, by the way, between Tables 1 and 3 is explained on page 27.) In 1987, for example, the total of new titles and new editions was heading towards three times the number described as alarming in 1959. And the consequences warned of follow inevitably. As more titles become available, fewer

TABLE 3 Source: *The Bookseller*, 8 January 1988

NUMBER OF NEW TITLES AND NEW EDITIONS PUBLISHED EACH YEAR SINCE 1947

Year	Total	Reprints and New Editions	Year	Total	Reprints and New Editions
1947	13,046	2,441	1968	31,420	8,778
1948	14,686	3,924	1969	32,393	9,106
1949	17,034	5,110	1970	33,489	9,977
1950	17,072	5,334	1971	32,538	8,975
1951	18,066	4,938	1972	33,140	8,486
1952	18,741	5,428	1973	35,254	9,556
1953	18,257	5,523	1974	32,194	7,852
1954	19,188	5,846	1975	35,608	8,361
1955	19,962	5,770	1976	34,434	8,227
1956	19,107	5,302	1977	36,322	8,638
1957	20,719	5,921	1978	38,766	9,236
1958	22,143	5,971	1979	41,940	9,086
1959	20,690	5,522	1980	48,158	10,776
1960	23,783	5,989	1981	43,083	9,387
1961	24,893	6,406	1982	48,307	10,360
1962	25,079	6,104	1983	51,071	12,091
1963	26,023	5,656	1984	51,555	11,309
1964	26,154	5,260	1985	52,994	11,740
1965	26,358	5,313	1986	57,845	13,671
1966	28,883	5,919	1987	59,837	14,185
1967	29,619	7,060			

copies of each are sold. In expectation of lower sales, publishers print fewer copies, the unit cost per copy therefore rises and so necessarily does the price in the shops. Higher prices lead to lower sales, doubtless tempting publishers to produce yet more titles to compensate for the declining profit of each, thus putting a further twist in the spiral – a process that has continued with scarcely a blip for over forty years.

So what?

You may think that all of this is the publisher's lookout: if publisher X's book is too expensive, the customer may choose publisher Y's book instead – either way, the bookseller makes a sale. But that's true only to the extent that different titles are regarded by the customer as alternatives; often it's the unique book that the customer requires and nothing else will do. Someone wanting to buy Uncle George a gardening book for Christmas may be quite happy to choose whichever of your stock of gardening titles is attractive and looks to be good value. But if Uncle George comes in to buy a book for himself, he may well require the specific title recommended last week by the visiting speaker at the local gardening club. And if when he sees it, he thinks it over-priced, he may make no purchase at all. A significant number of sales are thought to be lost this way (see page 214).

SPECIAL ORDERS

As a bookseller, you have another problem. The size of your stock is constrained by space and finance: you can't stock more titles merely because more titles are available. Every increase in the number of titles published leads to a precisely similar increase in the number of titles you haven't got in stock, and this in turn – though not in so precisely mathematical a way – leads to an increase in the number of special customer orders relative to sales of books from off the shelves.

And special orders are a problem of their own – dealt with more fully on page 216. All that need be noted here is that a special order may be for a book produced by any one of about 13,000 publishers – assuming we're just talking of UK titles – with only a small number of whom you are likely to have existing supply arrangements. Wholesalers, invaluable in other ways, barely dent this particular problem as the largest of them deal with no more than a hundred or so publishers and stock no more than about 40,000 titles.

SOME TRADE TERMINOLOGY

When discussing the availability of books, it is helpful to include in one's vocabulary some of the more precise terms favoured by the trade – *in print*, *out of print*, and so on. These are known as *answers* (see also page 124).

A book is said to be *in print* if unused copies are available in the publisher's warehouse for sale to the trade – or sometimes, to the chagrin of booksellers, for sale direct to the public. The sole source of ultimate supply of any particular title is the publisher of that title, and when he has no more copies left the book is said to be *out of print* (OP).

The term is commonly misunderstood by the general public, and sometimes misused even by the trade. It should not be used when a book is merely temporarily out of stock while, for example, further supplies of bound copies are awaited from the binders – in this case the book is said to be *binding* (BDG). Nor should it be used when a reprint is taking place or is definitely planned – in which case the book is said to be *reprinting* (RP). A book is only out of print when the complete print run has been sold out or otherwise disposed of by a publisher with no present intention of printing further copies.

Consider the implication of this. A book is either in print or out of print; there is no gradual transition from one state to the other. When a book goes out of print it does so literally in a moment.

Imagine two booksellers in the same town, telephoning the same publisher on the same afternoon, each wanting to order six copies of a given title. Bookseller Anne phones in at three o'clock; the publisher checks his stock, finds he has exactly six copies left, and accepts the order. Bookseller David phones in fifteen minutes later; the publisher is very apologetic but regrets to say that the title is OP. So about a fortnight later when Anne is just putting her newly arrived stock of the title on display, David is turning customers away with the regretful assurance that the title is no longer available. If any of these disappointed customers visit Anne's bookshop, they are likely to conclude – understandably but unjustly – that David must be either untruthful, indifferent, ignorant or incompetent. David for his part is likely to conclude precisely the same things about the publisher if he discovers that Anne has just taken delivery of the very title reported OP two weeks ago. Much ill will is generated, and no one to blame.

The thing to remember is that when a book goes OP, that does not mean that all copies of it simultaneously vanish from the shelves of stockholding booksellers or wholesalers; it means only that the publisher has sold out. Indeed, a frantic game of 'hunt the last copy' not infrequently takes place when a book, suddenly in demand, is reported unavailable by the publisher. Booksellers rush to their phones and try all the wholesalers they can think of, but only the quickest have any luck. By the time most booksellers have realised the position, the wholesalers too are reporting the title unavailable. Some booksellers who only ever use wholesalers as suppliers of last resort have then been known unfairly to complain that 'wholesalers never have what you want'.

Titles are going out of print every day just as new titles are being published every day. Not only are there about 160 titles available today that were not available yesterday, there are also about 115 titles that *were* available yesterday that are now out of print.

BIBLIOGRAPHICAL TOOLS OF THE TRADE

Title availability is in a continuous state of flux, and keeping track of it is one of a bookseller's major tasks. Fortunately, a number of bibliographies are published, and although they become increasingly unreliable as the days pass – indeed all of them, in varying degrees, are out of date the moment they're published – you can't seriously run a bookshop without them.

There are two quite distinct bibliographical needs: (a) to confirm the availability, price, publisher and so on of specific titles; and (b) to evaluate available titles to decide which to take into stock. Although there is some overlap between the bibliographies serving these different needs, we are in this chapter mainly concerned with tracing specific titles. The business of evaluation is considered later (page 104).

The only certain way to know if a book is in print is to ask the publisher, though, as we have seen, the information he gives one moment may be wrong the next; and as we have also seen, even if a publisher reports a book OP or otherwise out of stock, copies may still be available in wholesalers' warehouses. Nevertheless, the main object of a search is usually to identify the publisher to whom a direct enquiry may be made if necessary, and from whom the book will probably have to be ordered.

MAIN BIBLIOGRAPHIES

Most of the book trade's basic bibliographies are published by J. Whitaker & Sons Ltd. The three main ones are alternatives to each other, containing more or less the same information presented via three different technologies: print, microfiche and electronic data storage. Which of the three you use will probably be determined by what you can afford, but as a serious bookseller you *must* have one or other of these Whitaker bibliographies as your prime work of reference.

The only British bibliographies which vie in comprehensiveness with Whitaker's are those provided by the British Library Bibliographic Services, but these, though considered below, are more suitable for libraries and for scholarly research than for the small independent bookseller.

Whitaker's Books in Print (WBIP)

PRICE £115 IN 1988

Published each autumn as a set of four volumes totalling nearly 8,000 pages, *WBIP* lists books available in Britain in a single alphabetical sequence under author, title and subject where a subject word forms part of the title. Thus *First Steps in Botany* by Daisy Chain is indexed under *Chain, First* and *Botany*; another book on botany called *Summer Delight* by Herb Robert is indexed only under *Robert* and *Summer*. Each entry gives author, title, publisher, size, number of pages, whether illustrated, price, whether net or non-net (see page 60), month and year of publication, binding style unless the usual cloth boards – ie an ordinary hardback – and ISBN (see page 34). *WBIP* also contains a directory of about 13,000 publishers, a numerical listing of publisher ISBN prefixes, a list of series names and their publishers, and a bibliography of some hundreds of titles on the book trade.

A major weakness of *WBIP* arises from the delay between the time it goes to press in March and the time it goes on sale in September. The six-month gap means that it's probably giving misleading information about the availability of some 51,000 titles by the time it reaches the bookseller – that's an estimate of the total of new titles omitted and OP titles included. During its twelve-month life it becomes increasingly misleading at the rate of about 275 titles a day. Even titles which remain in print may have their prices changed; that happens to more than 80,000 titles a month – yet another headache for booksellers.

Until the 1988 edition, by the way, *Whitaker's Books in Print* was called *British Books in Print* (*BBIP*), and you may still find the old name used in the trade from time to time. It is interesting to note that Whitaker dropped the old name because around 30 per cent of the titles listed are foreign by origin, largely American at present, and the intention is to extend the coverage to include even more English-language material of European origin. So it was felt that to retain 'British' as part of the title would be misleading.

Whitaker's Books in Print – on microfiche

ANNUAL SUBSCRIPTION £426 + VAT IN 1988

WBIP – on microfiche is published monthly. Instalment terms are available. Like the hard copy version, it aims to be a complete listing of all books published in Britain. In the first week of each month, subscribers receive a set of 84 fiches, each month's set superseding all previous sets.

Some subscribers sell their old fiches month by month to other booksellers. The going annual rate in early 1988 for one-month old fiches was about £180–£200. The main marketplace is the Business Supplies column of *The Bookseller* (see page 25).

The delay between updating and publication of the fiches never exceeds three weeks, so the current month's fiches are never more than seven weeks out of date. The hard copy version of *WBIP*, by contrast, is never *less* than twenty-six weeks out of date. This means that any sets of fiches less than six months old are more up to date than the hard copy *WBIP*, even on the day it's published. Hence the active market in cast-off fiches.

The monthly fiches include titles due for publication in the next two months; and twice a year, subscribers receive special fiches listing titles due for publication in the following six months. Prices of books which continue in print are also updated. Another difference from the hard copy version is that titles stocked by named wholesalers are flagged in the listing – though only if the wholesalers concerned pay to have their titles marked in this way. Not included in the fiches are the bibliography of book trade titles and the series listing found in the hard copy version. These differences apart, the listings are in the same format in both versions.

The fiches, each measuring 15 cm × 10.5 cm, contain printed information at a reduction of 48× and are therefore unusable without a microfiche reader. Suitable readers cost in the range £205–£225 (1988 prices). Microphax Ltd, one of the suppliers of microfiche readers, offers a 10 per cent discount to members of the Booksellers Association.

Bookbank

ANNUAL SUBSCRIPTION £980 + VAT IN 1988

Bookbank contains similar updated information to *WBIP – on microfiche*, though its coverage of forthcoming titles is greater since the two-month-ahead cut-off is not applied when selecting records from the database. It also retains recently OP titles on the list, signalling them as such. *Bookbank* is published monthly as a CD-ROM. Instalment terms are available.

CD-ROM stands for Compact Disc – Read Only Memory. It's basically a compact disc, looking just like an audio compact disc for a record player, but 'playable' only on special equipment linked to a computer. Each month's disc supersedes all previous discs.

With the appropriate equipment, the information on the disc may be accessed in various ways. You can search for specific titles not only by author, title and keyword but by virtually any word – or even part-word – included in the entry. Look for *penguin*, for example, and you're presented with a list of all books with *penguin* in the title, together with all books published by Penguin Books. Limit your search to *Penguin.pub.* and you only get titles published by Penguin Books. Look for *Dickens – Charles and Penguin.pub.* and you get a complete list of Penguin's Charles Dickens titles. Look for *$nucleic* and find all titles which contain the word *nucleic* or its derivatives – *ribonucleic*, *drug-nucleic*, etc. Try *computeri?ed* and find titles including that word, whether the spelling ends *-ised* or *-ized*. You can choose from a huge variety of access paths to the information on the disc.

But it's not as a look-up database that *Bookbank* justifies its cost. Its potential only starts to be exploited when it is linked into other computerised systems handling stock control, ordering and so on. More about this in later chapters.

The hardware you need to use *Bookbank* is an IBM PC compatible computer with 640 Kb of memory and a minimum of 7 Mb of free space on the hard disc, a monochrome or preferably colour monitor, a CD-ROM drive (sometimes called a player) and a printer. All can be used for other purposes than *Bookbank* – word processing, accountancy, other CD-ROMs, etc – so the substantial cost of the hardware should not be attributed to *Bookbank* alone.

Note that Whitaker incorporates a protection device in the CD-ROM designed to render superseded discs unusable – in the jargon, the discs are said to *time out* – in this way preventing the establishment of the sort of secondhand market that flourishes for *WBIP – on microfiche*.

BACK-UPS TO THE MAIN BIBLIOGRAPHIES

The main bibliographies have to be supported by other reference material. The need is most obvious in the case of *WBIP* which is always out of date for between six and eighteen months. But even the fiches and the CD-ROM can be seven weeks out of date, and since titles hot off the press are frequently the ones most in demand, the bookseller needs the very latest information.

The Bookseller

ANNUAL SUBSCRIPTION £57 IN 1988

This is the weekly journal of the book trade, published by Whitaker. It is essential reading for anyone seriously engaged in the book trade. The reason for including it here among the bibliographies is that in addition to its news and coverage of book trade activities, it also lists the week's new publications: these may run to thirty pages or more of three-column small print.

An entry in *The Bookseller*'s Publications of the Week section is the first confirmed public record to the trade at large that a title has been published. You can see in Figure 1 overleaf what an extract from the listing looks like. This is the standard Whitaker format.

The thoroughness and accuracy of the list is dependent upon the quality of the information which publishers send to Whitaker's Book Lists Editor. Some publishers are less prompt than others,

FIGURE 1 Source: *The Bookseller*, 29 May 1987

EXTRACT FROM *THE BOOKSELLER*'S PUBLICATIONS OF THE WEEK

ɔ2 3
(5.87)
ɔ3 033 2
Pub.
ɔ253 024 3
. Linford
ırge Print
7089 6399 4
ntation of
0 Wiley (4.87)
0 471 90915 7
ınson,Richard
ıwin Pbs. (5.87)
0 04 327105 7
n.of 6e.
Press Pub.
0 907069 73 8
m.of 2e.
Press Pub.
0 907069 72 X
om
0 86003 544 1
') Com
0 86003 646 4
ıl of Systems,
ı) D4.400.
d Ho. (5.87) Pol
0 917253 66 3
y.
5.00 Avero
0 907977 23 5
24. Ill. £10.95
0 86051 393 9
Ill. Dragon Bks.
0 583 30922 4
icinsci,Andrzej
eon A &
ılson (5.87)
17 439149 8
d Their
ɔlogy &
Viley (4.87)
'51 2728 4
ih,
Var.
ˀ66 8

Poe 1 87...

Skeel, Rowland. Handbook of Cancer Chemother..., C8.406. 2r.e.of "Manual of Cancer Chemotherapy". pbk £14.95 Little,Brown : Longman (5.87) Med 0 316 79573 9

Skilbeck, Jennifer. Protection of Property Rights in the Ideas Market. IC8.100. Thames Essays S. pbk £8.00 Gower Pub.Co. (5.87) Law 0 566 05341 1

Skills and Vocationalism: The Easy Answer (Ed. Holt, Maurice)
M8.224. £22.50 Open U.P. (5.87) Edu 0 335 10290 5
M8.224. pbk £7.95 Open U.P. (5.87) Edu 0 335 10289 1

Skin Clues of Systemic Diseases, Handbook of (Jacobs & Anhalt) sC8.123. pbk £7.36 Lea & Febiger : Quest-Meridien (4.87) Med 0 8121 1095 1

Skin Troubles, New Self-help for (Chaitow) sC8.96. Self-help S. pbk £1.50 Thorsons (5.87) Med 0 7225 1504 9

Skorzeny, Peiper and: "Ardennes,1944" (Pallud) C4.64. Ill.(some col.). £5.50 Osprey (5.87) Hist 0 85045 740 8

Skoyles, Edward & Skoyles, John. Waste Prevention on Site. D8.216. 48ill. £25.00 Batsford (5.87) Ind 0 7134 5380 X

Skoyles, John. *See* Skoyles,Edward & Skoyles,John.

Skrine, Sir Clarmont Percival. Chinese Central Asia. D8.416. Ill.M. n.e. £22.00 Oxf.U.P.(E.Asia) (5.87) Hist 0 19 583843 2

Skyscrapers (Michael) D4.32. Col.ill. How it is Made S. bds £5.95 Faber (5.87) Chi 0 571 14730 5

Slater, J.D. Calculator Workcards.
Set 1. M8. set of 46 cards w.Tchrs'.Booklet £10.50* Arnold-Wheaton (5.87) Mat 0 560 23600 X

Slavery,African,in Latin America and the Caribbean (Klein) D8.288. £19.50 Oxf.U.P.(N.Y.) (5.87) Pol 0 19 503837 1

Sleeper,The (Clark,Eric) D8.432. n.e. £7.25* Ulverscroft Large Print Bks. (5.87) Fic(M) 0 7089 1623 6

Sleeping Beauty Ed. Seymour,Peter. 8" x 8".12. Col.ill.J.Wallner. Lift the Pictures/Find the Words S. bds £4.95 Viking Kestrel (5.87) Chi 0 670 81708 2

Sloop of War (Kent,Alexander) D8.512. n.e. Charnwood Lib. £8.25* Ulverscroft Large Print Bks. (5.87) Fic(War) 0 7089 8405 3

Sluglett, Peter. Modern Iraq. D8. £29.95 Kegan Paul Internat. (5.87) Pol 0 7103 0238 X

Small Bachelor (Wodehouse) sC8.208. n.e. pbk £2.50 Penguin (5.87) Fic(G) 0 14 008506 8

Small Book of Extravagances (Luke) D8.144. Ill. pbk £2.95 Ravette (5.87) Hum 0 948456 78 7

Small Changes (Piercy) sC8.448. pbk £3.95 Penguin (5.87) Fic(G) 0 14 009954 9

Smith, C.Ray. Interior Design in Twentieth Century America: A History. D4.355. Ill.(some col.). pbk £22.50 Harper & Row (4.87) Arc 0 06 046322 8

Smith, Charles Pye-. Other Nile. C8.240. Ill.M. n.e. Travel Lib. pbk £3.95 Penguin (5.87) Trav 0 14 009564 0

Smith, Cynthia. Orthopaedic Nursing. IM8.336. £22.50 Heinemann Med. (3.87) Med 0 433 30490 1

Smith, David. Rise and Fall of Monetarism. C8.192. Pelican S. pbk £3.95 Penguin (5.87) Pol 0 14 0227...

Sne
Snook
(5.
Snoopy
Rave
Snoopy Jo
Ravett
Snow, Vern
Parliame
Snow White
Book. D
Chi
Snowdonia ((
David &
Soares, Patric
3r.e. pbk
Social Criticis
£9.95 Ha
Social Geogr
D8.368.
Social Organi
Graham)
sD8.290.
sD8.290.
Lang
Social Resear
it Count
Univ.Cali
Socialist Soci
Socialist
Sociobiology
Vaulting
£11.25 /
Sociology fo
Educatic
£5.95*
Sociology, I
(Persell
& Ro
Socolofsky
Benja
Kans
Soderbe
Tr.f
Softv

---

and the weekly list frequently includes titles bearing publication dates which are weeks or even months earlier, though no title is included in *The Bookseller* listing unless published in the current calendar year; late reports of publications of earlier years are, however, included in other Whitaker listings. (This explains why the 1987 totals differ in Tables 1 and 3. Table 1 is the record of titles published in 1987 *and notified to Whitaker in that year*. Table 3 records *all* titles notified to Whitaker during the year, including those published in earlier years.)

In a week in February and another in August of each year, *The Bookseller*, normally 100 or so pages long, blossoms into a bumper issue of over 800 pages. These are called the Spring Books Issue and the Autumn Books Issue – though you may sometimes hear them referred to by their old name of 'Export Numbers' – and they give details of books scheduled to appear in the following six months. They consist largely of publishers' announcements of forthcoming titles, and there is also an introductory section in which these same titles are briefly described – *not* reviewed – under subject headings. A full title/author index of all books advertised is included.

Whitaker's Books of the Month and Books to Come

ANNUAL SUBSCRIPTION £43 IN 1988

This cumulates in a single listing, in the usual Whitaker format, all the books recorded in the previous month's weekly listings in *The Bookseller*, together with those books which were ineligible for the weekly listings because of late notification. Also included are details of titles due for publication in the two months ahead. If your main bibliography is the hard copy version of *WBIP*, this is an essential back-up. Subscribers to *WBIP – on microfiche* and *Bookbank* have the same information included in their monthly issues.

Whitaker's Book List

PRICE £35 IN 1988

Published about March each year, this lists all the new titles and new editions published in the previous calendar year, together with those published in the preceding year but notified late. Whereas all other Whitaker listings are sooner or later superseded by updated information, *Whitaker's Book List* (formerly called *Whitaker's Cumulative Book List*) remains a unique single volume record of its year. While of interest to all booksellers, it is most useful to those dependent upon the hard copy version of *WBIP*.

As *WBIP* is six months out of date when published in September, you need at first to use copies of *Whitaker's Books of the Month and Books to Come* to cover those missing six months, and then the September–December issues to cover the rest of the calendar year, and the January–March issues as the new year moves on. By now, you are having to search for titles in thirteen different listings – plus, of course, the latest issues of *The Bookseller*. Once *Whitaker's Book List* is published, you can give all last year's *Books of the Month* to the dustman. Even so, before September comes round again, you'll be back to searching through up to ten listings.

Books 1976–88 Now OP – on microfiche

PRICE £93 + VAT IN 1988

Yet another Whitaker bibliography, published annually in June. The 1988 edition lists over 180,000 titles published during the period 1976–88 and which were out of print by May 1988. It comprises 34 fiches.

The value of this listing is that it enables you to end more of your searches with positive information – albeit that the title is unobtainable – rather than going on and on till weariness overtakes you.

Much of your searching through bibliographies will be for unstocked titles asked for by customers. Members of the public can be notoriously vague about bibliographical detail, and in your bookselling career you will often find yourself dealing with enquiries on the lines of "I wonder if you can get me that book on history – something like *Story of the World* – no, wait a minute, more like *History of the Planet* – something like that. By someone called Smith or Schmidt or Smedley. Begins with S anyway. Or M. Could be Goldsmith. Publisher? No, sorry, I can't help you with that one." Even with such confused detail, you have a good chance of being able to trace the title – eventually – from the bibliographies already mentioned, provided that it's still in print.

If, however, the title required is out of print, only *Bookbank* will be at all helpful – and only then if the title is *recently* OP. With the other bibliographies, you have no means of knowing whether your lack of success in tracing a title is due to the customer's misinformation, your lack of ingenuity in guessing which keyword to look up, or simply that the title is OP. This set of microfiches at least lets you eliminate or confirm the last possibility.

Publishers' catalogues

All publishers produce catalogues of their own current titles. The simplest of them are no more than stock lists, giving the sort of minimal detail you find in a Whitaker bibliography. Most, however, include content descriptions, at least of the newest titles. Publishers' catalogues generally arrive unsolicited by post or are left with you by the publisher's rep when he calls at your shop. Phone or write to the publisher to ask for any catalogues you would like but haven't got.

Catalogues come in a range of shapes and sizes – some on fiches – which make them difficult to file, and most are too flimsy to stand up, book fashion, on a shelf. The drawer of a filing cabinet or something similar, fitted with dividers which can be labelled with publishers' names, is often the best place to store them. Keep them in alphabetical order. Throw away old catalogues as soon as new ones are received.

You mainly use publishers' catalogues for your own stock selection. Occasionally, though, a customer seeking a particular book might be vague about the title but sure of the publisher, or experience may tell you that it's the sort of book a given publisher typically produces; in these cases, publishers' catalogues can help with specific title search.

Wholesalers' catalogues

Wholesalers' catalogues are designed as ordering tools rather than bibliographies, so their usefulness for title search is limited. However, they are usually issued either free of charge or at nominal cost, and they may well be updated more frequently than some of your expensively purchased bibliographies. Increasingly, major wholesalers are issuing monthly updated catalogues on microfiche free of charge.

Books in the Media

ANNUAL SUBSCRIPTION £50 IN 1988

(£42.50 to members of the Booksellers Association)

The weekly *Books in the Media*, published by Bookwatch, is in a class of its own. Unlike the Whitaker listings and the suppliers' catalogues, it is not concerned merely with what is or will be available but with what is or will probably be in demand because of current or planned media attention. It identifies books tying in with or being featured on radio or TV, in the cinema or the press, in current exhibitions or new video releases. Full author, title, publisher, price and ISBN information is given, and the books are listed, where appropriate, by date and medium – eg *The Times* on 31 October or BBC2 on 3 November.

Mailed to subscribers every Friday by first class post, it provides a quick and convenient guide to media coverage in the week from Monday to Sunday. It is an invaluable aid to tracing what customers want when they ask for "the book recently reviewed in *The Observer*" or "you know – the one mentioned on the box the other night." And if you're still stuck, there's a free *Helpline* service which deals with subscribers' queries over the phone at no extra charge.

SUBJECT BIBLIOGRAPHIES

While several of the Whitaker bibliographies already mentioned add a subject classification to the titles listed, only *Bookbank* allows you to *search* for titles by their classification. Most of the listings will tell you that *Alice in Wonderland*, for example, is a children's book. But only in *Bookbank* can you search for *children's books* as a category and so come upon *Alice in Wonderland* – among thousands of others – via the classification. Three Whitaker bibliographies go some way to making good this deficiency in the non-*Bookbank* listings.

Whitaker's Classified Monthly Book List

ANNUAL SUBSCRIPTION £30 IN 1988

This has the same coverage as *Whitaker's Books of the Month and Books to Come* arranged under 53 subject classifications.

Children's Books in Print

PRICE £35.50 IN 1988

Published annually in June, this lists about 27,000 children's titles under 98 subject categories, together with a directory of their 900 publishers and distributors. There is also a single sequence index of authors, titles and keywords.

Religious Books in Print

PRICE £24 IN 1988

Published annually in March, this lists about 22,000 religious titles under 18 principal categories with 127 subsidiaries, together with a directory of their 1,400 publishers and distributors. There is also a single sequence index of authors, titles and keywords.

OTHER BRITISH BIBLIOGRAPHIES

There are thousands of specialist bibliographies prepared by scholars and others attempting comprehensive listings of books on particular subjects or by particular authors. While these may interest specialist secondhand book dealers, they are of limited use to dealers in new books – even specialists – since most titles listed are inevitably long out of print.

Just being launched by Book Data Ltd at the time of writing is *Book Data* which collects new title information from subscribing publishers. Along with the usual basic bibliographical detail, it is able to supply a subject and readership classification for each new title on its database, together with a descriptive text and/or contents list.

The only other British bibliographies you should know of, though you will probably not require them, are those of the British Library.

British National Bibliography (BNB)

ANNUAL SUBSCRIPTION £315 IN 1988

(£245 + £13.88 VAT if annual volume on fiche)

Under the terms of the 1911 Copyright Act (as amended by the 1972 British Library Act) British publishers, at their own cost, have to deposit at the Copyright Receipt Office (CRO) in London one copy of each new book they publish. Under the Irish Copyright Act 1963, publishers in the Irish Republic are similarly required to deposit their books at the London CRO. All books received are catalogued and made permanently available to the public in the various reading rooms of the British Library (BL).

There are five other *legal deposit libraries* which have the right to claim free copies from publishers. These are: the Bodleian Library, Oxford; the University Library, Cambridge; the National Library of Scotland; the Library of Trinity College, Dublin; the National Library of Wales.

In addition to the statutory obligation to deposit their newly published books, there is also a voluntary scheme in which publishers supply to the BL details of titles they plan to publish over the next few months; this system of advance notification is called the Cataloguing-in-Publication scheme (CIP). A publisher who informs the BL of a forthcoming book is sent a block of cataloguing information prepared by the Library's specialist staff on the basis of the details supplied. The publisher prints this data on the *verso* (ie the back) of the title page of the book, so saving other librarians the need to work out cataloguing data when the book is taken into stock. When the book itself is received at the

BL on publication, the CIP data is confirmed or corrected.

BNB is the detailed record of books received at the CRO, and also of the advance information supplied under the CIP scheme. Notice the important difference from the Whitaker listings, which rely entirely on information supplied by publishers. In the end, *all* confirmed *BNB* entries are based upon an examination by trained bibliographers of the books themselves.

BNB is published weekly, cumulated every four months, the final cumulation – the annual volume – being the definitive record of the year's publications.

While books are indexed by author and title, and there is also a very detailed subject index, the main presentation is according to the Dewey Decimal Classification – as used in most UK libraries – which brings together books on the same subject, and brings books on related subjects near to each other. The Dewey arrangement allows you to track down books on specific topics, or to compile lists of such books, even when their titles are less than self-explanatory. This is *BNB*'s major advantage over the Whitaker listings.

Despite this, and despite its thoroughness and professionalism, *BNB* is of limited use to the average bookseller because, as an historical record of titles published, it does not tell you if a book continues to be in print, nor, if it is, its current price. Furthermore, because the definitive entries in *BNB* must await a bibliographer's examination of the books themselves, there is often a much longer delay between publication and listing in *BNB* than between publication and listing in *The Bookseller*, which uses only publisher-supplied information.

BNB is mainly used by librarians, at home and abroad, as a means of keeping abreast of what is being published in their own subject areas and making their stock purchases accordingly.

FURTHER SOURCES OF BIBLIOGRAPHICAL INFORMATION

Everything in *BNB*, *WBIP* – and a number of other databases too – is available online via BLAISE-LINE. BLAISE stands for British Library Automated Information Service. The only equipment needed to access these databases is a small microcomputer, a telephone, and appropriate connexions between the two. However, in addition to an annual subscription of £55, there is also an online hourly charge of £20 and a charge for the amount of data accessed. (All prices subject to VAT and as at 1988). The telephone calls have to be paid for too. As with *BNB* itself, the service is more suitable for librarians than booksellers.

If the flexibility of computerised bibliographical search appeals to you, *Bookbank* – despite its higher initial cost – is likely to be the better investment because you can use it all day and night without running up your phone bill or incurring online charges. And though its database is less extensive than BLAISE-LINE, it is probably more suited to your needs as a bookseller.

For the occasional problem which defies all your best efforts, it's worth knowing that Book Trust (see page 58) has a Book Information Service, backed up by a large and comprehensive collection of bibliographical indexes. Short enquiries are accepted by telephone.

FOREIGN BIBLIOGRAPHIES

There are bibliographies for other countries produced on similar lines to the British ones discussed above. Among the main ones covering English-language titles are the American *Books in Print* – also available in an enhanced form as *Books in Print Plus* on CD-ROM (both published by Bowker), *Canadian Books in Print* (University of Toronto Press), *Australian Books in Print* (Thorpe), *New Zealand Books in Print* (Thorpe) and *Indian Books in Print* (Indian Bibliographic Bureau).

Bibliographies of English-language titles from more than one country include *Cumulative Book Index* (Wilson), *Books in English* (the British Library) – a microfiche bibliography produced from records created by the British Library Bibliographic Services and the United States Library of Congress – and *International Books in Print* (Saur) which lists English-language titles published outside the UK and the USA.

Similar bibliographies are produced for many non-English-speaking countries, often covering all titles in the language irrespective of their country of publication. Among them are the French *Les Livres Disponibles* (Le Cercle de la Librarie), the Italian *Catalogo dei Libri in Commercio* (Editrice Bibliografica), the Spanish *Libros Españoles en Venta* (Agencia Española ISBN) and the German *Verzeichnis lieferbarer* Bücher (Saur).

Many of these bibliographies may be purchased from their publishers' UK agents or distributors. Details are included in the Bibliography beginning on page 243.

If you are searching for overseas bibliographies beyond those mentioned above, it is always worth contacting the appropriate embassy or consulate for information.

MINIMUM BASIC REFERENCE MATERIAL

The serious bookseller must, as a minimum, have one or other of the following sets of material.

EITHER a) *Whitaker's Books in Print*; and
b) *Whitaker's Books of the Month and Books to Come*; and
c) *Whitaker's Book List*; and
d) *The Bookseller*; and
e) *Publishers' catalogues*

OR a) *Whitaker's Books in Print – on microfiche*; and
b) *The Bookseller*; and
c) *Publishers' catalogues*

OR a) *Bookbank*; and
b) *The Bookseller*; and
c) Publishers' catalogues.

For the non-computerised bookseller, the middle option – *WBIP – on microfiche* etc – is probably the best compromise between cost and convenience.

INTERNATIONAL STANDARD BOOK NUMBERS

A major help in the tracing, identification and ordering of books is the International Standard Book Number (ISBN) system. An ISBN is a reference number which uniquely and permanently identifies each title published, wherever in the world it is published and however confusingly similar its title, author's name or publisher's name may be to those of another published book. There is, by the way, no copyright in titles, so it is quite possible to have two entirely different books with the same title. It is, however, quite *im*possible, within the ISBN rules, to have two titles with the same ISBN.

An ISBN consists of ten digits, divided into four parts, the last part being a single digit, the other parts varying in length, but always resulting in an ISBN with a total of ten digits.

The first part of the ISBN is the *group identifier* – that is, it identifies a national, geographical, language or other convenient group. British books, for example, all begin with the group identifier 0 or 1 (as do the books of other English-speaking countries). The second part of the ISBN is the *publisher prefix* identifying the publisher, and the third part is the *title number*. Publishers with a large output of titles have short prefixes, thus leaving more digits available within the fixed length of the ISBN for the title numbers. Publishers with a small output of titles have longer prefixes as they can make do with fewer digits for their limited number of titles. The final single digit of the ISBN is a check digit – any of the arabic numerals 0–9 or the roman numeral X – which allows a computer to confirm the correctness of the preceding digits.

The scheme is administered in the UK by the Standard Book Numbering Agency. The Agency allocates prefixes to publishers who then assign an ISBN to each of their titles.

Here is an example of an ISBN: 0 949999 06 7. This, like all ISBNs in the UK, begins and ends with a single digit, the opening 0 being one of the two group identifiers used for all UK books, and the closing 9 being the check digit of this particular ISBN. The 949999 is the publisher prefix, and in this case identifies the publisher as the Standard Book Numbering Agency, and the 06 identifies the particular title in that publisher's output. The book ISBN 0 949999 06 7 is in fact *International Standard Book Numbering* (6th revised edition, reprinted with minor corrections) published in 1988 by the Standard Book Numbering Agency. This is a book which explains how the ISBN system works, and the reader seeking further information is referred to it.

ISBNs should always be written with either a space or a hyphen between each of the four parts. Thus the ISBN of *International Standard Book Numbering* may be written either as ISBN 0 949999 06 7 or ISBN 0-949999-06-7. Misguidedly tidy-minded people sometimes list ISBNs arbitrarily split into digit groups of, say, four-three-three so that they all line up neatly with one another when tabulated on a typewriter, for example. While arbitrary grouping of the digits of an ISBN need not destroy its unambiguity, it always makes it more difficult for the eye to decode. With the correct grouping of digits, the publisher prefix always stands out clearly.

You will generally find a book's ISBN printed on the title page verso or at the foot of the title page itself. It also usually appears at the bottom right of the book's back cover in three different forms: ordinary print, an Optical Character Recognition font (OCR-A), and a bar-code. The OCR-A and bar-code forms are machine-readable and are for use with electronic systems of stock and sales monitoring.

In order that the book trade's products should fit into the European Article Number (EAN) bar-code marking system used for a range of products, the machine-readable forms of an ISBN are incorporated into a 13-digit EAN. This is achieved by prefixing the ISBN with the number 978 – to identify the product as a book – and recalculating the final check digit accordingly. Note that this means that the ISBN embedded within the EAN is not identical to the basic ISBN itself, and it is the basic ISBN with *its* check digit which is used in the book trade.

USING ISBNs

ISBNs are vitally important to any bookseller who uses a computerised ordering or stock control system, or who has dealings with publishers or wholesalers who use such systems. That more or less covers everybody.

Before a computer entry can be made, titles usually have to be translated into ISBNs, and if booksellers do not supply the ISBN when placing an order, then someone at the other end will do it for them, increasing the chances of error and delay. The use of the ISBN also unambiguously identifies which one of different editions of the same title is required: a hardback edition has a different ISBN from a paperback edition of the same title, and there are also different ISBNs, for example, for the same title with maps and without maps, for a hand-bound limited edition and for the ordinary trade edition, and so on. In other words, each title in the book trade sense (see page 17) has its own unique ISBN.

The ISBN of any UK title may be found from any of the bibliographies listed earlier. The author/title/publisher/price of a book of which you known only the ISBN may be directly traced from *International Standard Book Numbers Listing – on microfiche* (£160 plus VAT in 1988) which includes all titles on the Whitaker master file, including OP and forthcoming titles, arranged in ISBN sequence. Over a million titles are listed, the OPs clearly marked, and the details given are: ISBN, author, title, size, number of pages, illustrations, series, edition, binding, price, publisher, date of publication.

An indirect method of tracing the author/title/publisher/price of a book of which you know only the ISBN is to identify the publisher prefix from the list given in *WBIP*, and then to check the catalogue of that publisher or to ask the rep or contact the publisher himself for the other details you require. *Publishers in the United Kingdom and their Addresses* (see page 116) may also be used in this way.

Chapter 2

The Book Trade

Intending bookshop owners need an overview of the book trade as a whole. You can't see where you might fit in without first having a picture of what it is you're trying to fit yourself into.

LEARNING ABOUT BOOKSELLING

The four ways of learning about the trade are from books, trade journals, personal experience and training courses.

BOOKS

Apart from the present guide, not a great deal of up-to-date information for beginners is published in book form.

The Federation of Radical Booksellers (FRB) publish *Starting a Bookshop* which is a good introduction to some of the basics of the trade, and also touches on more general business matters like book-keeping, legal structure of the business, employer's responsibilities and so on. The text is coloured by the FRB's ideological commitment to bookshop co-operatives which pursue "non-hierarchical, non-sexist, non-racist working practices" and are "not expected to distribute any profits for personal gain beyond a fair living wage for shop workers." A book dealing with the more conventional trade is *Teach Yourself Bookselling* (Hodder & Stoughton) edited by John Cheshire, and due for publication late 1988. The Level 2 manuals which form part of the Booksellers Association's course leading to the Certificate in Bookselling Skills (see page 89) are also of interest.

Business and economic surveys

There are a number of detailed studies of the book trade presenting interesting facts and figures, though the figures do tend to vary from one report to the next. These studies throw light on the trade in a generalising manner, but are not to be thought of as guides to day-to-day practicalities for the new bookseller. They are, however, well worth reading for the detailed picture they give of the book trade as a whole. Unfortunately, they are not cheap. Two titles you should certainly read if you can are the Publishers Association's annual *Book Trade Year Book* (£40 in 1988) and Euromonitor's biennial *Book Report* (£160 in 1988). Other studies include ICC's *Business Ratio Reports* and *Key Note Reports* (one on publishing, one on bookselling in each series), Euromonitor's *The World Book Industry* and *Booksellers and Stationers in the 1980s*, and Eric de Bellaigue's *The Business of Books* – now out of print – published by Hutchinson. You may be able to consult some of these books in a specialist business library; your local public reference librarian should be able to advise you.

Two studies of particular interest are the *Charter Group Economic Survey*, which we shall be looking at in some detail in Chapter 6, and *Book Retailing in the 1990s*.

Book Retailing in the 1990s: the Arthur Young report

Book Retailing in the 1990s is a report by Arthur Young Management Consultants, commissioned by the Booksellers Association (BA) in 1987. Priced at £25 for BA members, and £40 for non-members, it is usually referred to in the trade as *the Arthur Young report* or just *Arthur Young*. While its primary purpose is to predict the decade ahead and to suggest to booksellers strategies for survival and success, it first surveys the state of the trade in the 1980s, drawing upon various published figures, assessing their validity and deducing their implications. It thus presents a picture of bookselling today, a forecast of bookselling tomorrow, and a set of recommendations for traders, large and small, hoping to straddle the two. Intending booksellers wishing to pursue their studies should put the Arthur Young report at the top of their reading list.

Unless otherwise attributed, general trade statistics in the present chapter are based upon the Arthur Young report.

TRADE JOURNALS

Trade journals, studied over a period of time, give an insight into the trade, its routines and current preoccupations.

The main trade journal is *The Bookseller*, published weekly. Its news coverage is very good. Its letter page provides a lively forum for anyone who has anything to say. Its feature articles cover in some detail most developments of interest to the bookseller. Regular items include bestseller lists, book news and reviews from a bookshop rather than a literary point of view. There is also a good deal of advertising by publishers and others, and this can be as important a source of up-to-date information as the editorial sections of the journal.

Despite its name, *The Bookseller*, established in 1858, gives a good deal of coverage to publishing as well as bookselling. Its self-professed role, in the words of its masthead, is to be *The Organ of the Book Trade*, an old-world pomposity which explains why you may occasionally see it familiarly referred to as *the Organ* – a nickname used sometimes affectionately, sometimes suggestively, always slightly tongue-in-cheek.

The history of another trade paper goes back only to 1979. *Publishing News (PN)*, like *The Bookseller*, covers both publishing and bookselling, but is rather more lightweight. Along with the basic diet of news, bestseller lists and articles, it features full colour displays of point-of-sale material – dumpbins, crowners, counter packs, posters and so on – available from publishers to give in-shop support to their latest titles. With an annual subscription of £40, *PN* is cheaper than *The Bookseller* at £57 (1988 rates), but you need the latter anyway for its Publications of the Week listing (see page 25), so if you can only afford one of the two, it has to be *The Bookseller*. But if you can afford both, you'll probably enjoy *PN*'s rather more newsy and gossipy approach.

A third journal, *Bookselling News*, goes free to BA members five times a year. It keeps the membership informed of the services and activities of the Association, and carries articles – often reports of specially undertaken research – on aspects of bookselling, bookshop management and trade matters in general.

PERSONAL EXPERIENCE

There is no better place to learn about bookselling than a bookshop. You will find it invaluable to have worked in someone else's bookshop before taking on one of your own. Even a week or two can give you a sense of the day-to-day realities of the trade, impossible to achieve in any other way.

A small independent bookshop, most like the sort of shop you have in mind for yourself, is the best place to see how things are done. It would be nice if you could get a paid job in such a shop, but offering your services free in exchange for being allowed to see what goes on behind the scenes may give you the best opportunity of poking your nose into all the things you would like to.

Use the BA's *Directory of Members* (see page 95) to find the names and addresses you need if you wish to make a direct approach to individual booksellers. If you seek their advice, the BA may be able to recommend possible shops where you might spend some time either working or shadowing the working owner as he or she goes about the daily tasks. Contact the BA's Membership Manager.

TRAINING COURSES

Details of training courses run by the BA are given later (page 88). Although most are aimed at people already in the trade, there is a good deal to interest the intending bookshop proprietor. And since you will almost certainly find it easier to spare the time *before* your shop is open, it would be a good idea to get a copy of the current programme as soon as possible to see which courses you think might be worth attending.

STRUCTURE OF THE BOOK TRADE

In a world of accelerating technological change, each new marvel treads on the heels of the last, and something which at first seems complex and remote, not at all the concern of the shopper in the street or the bookseller in the shop, very quickly becomes at least superficially understandable and affects us all. Nor is it technology alone which turns the world ever faster. Everything is up for challenge, and new philosophies, attitudes and values – or old ones found suddenly to have renewed merit and vigour – are emerging everywhere. The book trade is undergoing the same rapid changes as the rest of the world.

We saw in the last chapter that much bibliographical information, formerly available only in book form, is now available on microfiche. Print technology was unchallenged for five hundred years. *WBIP – on microfiche*, first published scarcely ten years ago, already looks comfortably old-fashioned. Tomorrow will belong to the CD-ROM. As for the day after tomorrow, all that seems certain is that it will be different again.

These are not idle reflections. New bookshop owners, putting at risk substantial sums of money, must appreciate that they will not be pleasantly paddling along calm, untroubled waters towards a distant retirement. There are rocks and rapids ahead, and just staying afloat will need more than a Sunday sailor's skills.

BOOKSELLING IN THE RETAIL ECONOMY

Despite the very large number of new titles published each year and the impressive sales notched up by the titles that make it to the bestseller lists, total *consumer* expenditure on books – ie not counting the money spent by institutions like schools, libraries and so on – is pretty low. It amounted in 1986 to £717 million. According to Euromonitor's *Book Report*, consumers spend *three* times as much on newspapers and magazines, *nine* times as much on cigarettes, and *twelve* times as much on beer. Book expenditure of £717 million compares to a total consumer expenditure of £232 *billion*. Reach for your calculator to see what that means in less mind-numbing figures. One way of putting it is this: of every £3 spent by consumers, less than a penny went on books. A marginally less depressing way of putting it is to say that the UK population – roughly 56 million people – spent about £13 per person on books in the course of 1986.

That last figure is worth remembering, even though, as all averages, it conceals wide variations, and anyway is based upon the historical figures – themselves estimated – of a single year. Those caveats admitted, £13 per person per year provides at least a crude starting point for estimating the potential of a particular location. A bookshop with a catchment area of 2,000 souls, for example, could well be looking at a total market potential of no more than £26,000 a year – far too little for commercial viability. Of course, the 2,000 may all be bibliophile millionaires. Then again, they may not be. More about such calculations in Chapter 8.

BOOK BUYERS

More people read books than buy them. The public library service lends books free of charge, at the point of use, to virtually anyone who wants to borrow them. The Registrar of Public Lending Right (PLR) – that's the state-funded scheme which rewards authors according to the number of times their books are borrowed from public libraries – mentioned in his 1988 Notification to PLR Authors that there were some 639 million loans in 1986/87. If that number of books were bought rather than borrowed, booksellers' tills would be ringing up many times the amount that they do.

Few people are book buyers of necessity. While some people need to buy them for their studies or their work, book buying for most of the population is an optional extra, an activity competing for funds with all life's other delights: holidays, theatre going, dining out, collecting records and so on – to say nothing of newspapers, cigarettes and beer. About 30 per cent of the population buy books, not all them from bookshops, and women are slightly more likely to be book buyers than men.

The Arthur Young report identifies the characteristics *of a household* which make it more likely or less likely to include book buyers; and since local areas tend to be composed of similar households, the identification suggests where book buyers in general are to be found. As with per capita expenditure, these indicators have meaning only when dealing with populations in the mass. They say nothing whatsoever about any particular household you may point to. Their value to the intending bookshop owner is that they can help you to a better assessment of regions or towns which you are considering as possible locations for your shop.

It is important to stress that no statistical indicator should be blindly relied upon; its significance must be weighed intelligently along with all the other factors. In the end you cannot avoid exercising your own judgement.

We see below, for example, that households in Greater London and the South East are more likely to include book buyers than households in other regions. But it is worth noting that there is a preponderance of bookshops in London and the South East – the region accounts for nearly a quarter of the BA membership (see Table 4) – and that the people in the region therefore have a greater opportunity to be book buyers than those elsewhere. It is a matter for debate whether relatively low book-buying in certain other regions is attributable to the lack of bookshops or whether the lack of bookshops is attributable to the dearth of customers. The old chicken-and-egg problem. Are we to conclude that certain regions are disaster areas for bookselling or that those are the very places which offer unexploited opportunities? Over to you.

Likeliest buyers

The most favourable characteristics – in descending order – of households likely to include book buyers are these: the head of the household is (1) a professional, a manager or a teacher; (2) aged 45–59; (3) aged 30–44; (4) an owner occupier; (5) living in Greater London or the South East; (6) aged under 30; (7) in a clerical or sales job.

Least likely buyers

The least favourable characteristics – listed with the more negative indicators first – are these: the head of the household is (1) unemployed; (2) over 60; (3) a council tenant; (4) a manual worker;

TABLE 4 Source: BA membership records mid-1988

BA BRANCH MEMBERSHIP *Corporate membership 3260*

(a) alphabetical order		*(b) numerical order*	
176	East Midlands	747	London
226	Eastern	332	North Western
151	Hampshire	255	Scottish
113	Irish	252	Western & South Wales
747	London	226	Eastern
198	Midland	205	Yorkshire
70	North Eastern	198	Midland
93	Northern Ireland	176	East Midlands
332	North Western	170	South Western
115	Oxford	151	Hampshire
255	Scottish	142	Sussex
170	South Western	115	Oxford
142	Sussex	113	Irish
15	*Unattached*	93	Northern Ireland
252	Western & South Wales	70	North Eastern
205	Yorkshire	15	*Unattached*

(5) living in Scotland, Wales or Northern Ireland; (6) living in rented accommodation; (7) the owner of a colour TV.

Almost buyers

Arthur Young identified a third section of the population as *almost buyers*, and suggested that the bookselling market could best be enlarged by trying to sell to this group, rather than trying to sell more books to already committed buyers or trying to convert the non-buyers. In the Arthur Young analysis, *almost buyers* are predominantly in the 30-44 age group and live outside Greater London and the South East. There are an estimated 5.2 million people in the *almost buyer* category.

PUBLISHERS

Next to the multiplicity of book titles, it is the multiplicity of book publishers which lies at the root of many bookselling problems. In a fairy-tale world in which all books were published by just one publisher, booksellers would order everything they wanted from a single source, receive a single statement the following month, and pay with a single cheque. Bliss.

The reality is otherwise. In any given month, you may find yourself ordering from scores of different sources. Your different suppliers may follow eccentrically different paperwork procedures, but in one form or another, scores of statements will in due course arrive for payment, each needing to be checked individually and possibly paid for by a separate cheque (but see page 93). One of the large bookselling chains estimates that just processing this paperwork costs them £250,000 a year. It won't be anything like that in your small independent shop, of course, but there will be a real cost to you in the number of hours you have to spend at your desk shuffling bits of paper around.

Numbers

There are some 13,000 different publishers noted in *WBIP*. Whitaker identifies about 2,000 of the most active of them, and publishes this smaller list annually as *Publishers in the United Kingdom and their Addresses* (see page 116). Most of your dealings with publishers are likely to be with the leading houses among the active few, but that is still a pretty large number. And the small number of orders you place with minor publishers, though possibly only a fraction of your turnover, will generate a disproportionate amount of paperwork.

Trends

Enormous upheavals have been taking place in the publishing world in recent years. Mergers, take-overs, management buy-outs – all the activities of big business in general are to be seen also in publishing. The main trend has been for small independent publishers to be swallowed up by larger publishers, and for larger publishers to be swallowed up by conglomerates for whom book publishing is only one interest among many. It's like one gigantic game of Monopoly, except that inside the little green and red buildings there are human beings trying to get on with the basic business of publishing – at its heart, a co-operative midwifery between editor and writer – while glamorous business deals are negotiated over their heads. Publishing has become much more commercial.

More mergers mean fewer publishing houses for new writers to hawk their wares around. Fortunately, trends always provoke reactions. While the big business end of publishing moves to larger and larger amalgamations, there is no shortage of new small publishers setting up on their own – many of them refugees from the big publishing houses.

For booksellers, the net position is probably unchanged. Some of the amalgamations will hopefully lead to a rationalising of order processing and distribution, and this may lighten the booksellers' load. But with new publishers appearing all the time, booksellers are likely to be dealing with as many different suppliers as before.

WHY SO MANY BOOKS?

If major chunks of the publishing industry are becoming ever more commercially-minded, one might well wonder why so many titles, with their depressing effect upon trade profitability, continue to be produced. There are two likely explanations.

First, if you have a publishing machine in place – premises, editors, designers, marketing people, distribution network and so on – it costs a large amount of money just to maintain it. By comparison, the cost of churning an extra title out of the machine is only marginal.

Second, while many titles are near or actual commercial flops, the odd bestseller, or one that becomes a steady seller over the years, makes the whole business worthwhile. With every title unique, it is never possible to be certain which will succeed and which will not. So it becomes a matter of playing the percentages. Publish X number of titles, and you can expect Y per cent of them to succeed. Reprint the successes and dump the failures. Only the writers of the failures find the exercise painful, and there are plenty more writers where they came from. If that sounds a bit cruel, it's because it is.

Packagers

Packagers, in the publishing context, do everything that traditional publishers do except market and distribute. They concern themselves solely with the origination of titles – taking a book all the way from bright idea to finished product – which they then sell to traditional publishing houses, who publish the books under their own imprints, and market and distribute them in the usual way.

Packaged books are often elaborately illustrated, expensively produced, and frequently published in several different countries at more or less the same time. Multi-national publication allows the packager to spread costs over very much larger print runs than would be feasible if the book were published only in the UK; and it is only the large print runs that make possible the publication of expensively produced books for sale to the public at relatively modest prices.

From a bookseller's point of view, there is nothing special about a packaged book. It is just another title on a publisher's list. Whether it was originated entirely in-house by the publisher or was bought in from a packager is without significance for the bookseller.

WHOLESALERS

The central frustration of the book trade is the mismatch of numbers: a huge number of low-value products from a large number of suppliers ultimately sold to a small number of customers who buy them in ones.

If only you were selling toothpaste or bags of crisps or packets of screws you could expect satisfied customers to keep coming back for more of the same; and you could therefore afford to purchase the products in quantity yourself. Not so with books. However delighted the customer may be – *will* be – with his purchase of *The BA Guide to Starting and Running a Bookshop*, he is most unlikely ever to return to buy a second copy.

Booksellers have to be wary of overstocking particular titles. If you have ten copies of a title, for example, you will in the ordinary way need ten different customers wanting it before you sell out. If you sell only seven copies and are stuck with three that nobody wants, you'll be doing little more than covering your costs on the whole deal: certainly no profit to speak of.

Prudent booksellers therefore stock as few copies of any given title as they can get away with. For the small bookseller, this means stocking mainly singles – one copy per title.

Single copy orders, however, are the bane of publishers' lives. They are so costly to process that, for some books and some publishers, they're barely worth the trouble. Many publishers therefore frame their terms of supply so as to discourage small orders in general and single copy orders in particular. We can see the logic of this from the publishers' point of view but it's one more disaster for booksellers, since small orders for any given publisher may be all they can afford or want.

At which point, enter the wholesalers, galloping to the rescue.

By stocking a range of titles from a range of publishers, wholesalers go some way to overcoming the trade's small order problem. They themselves buy in quantity from individual publishers and are then able to meet the consolidated quantity orders for the titles of several publishers from their own bookselling customers. Instead of, say, a dozen small orders to a dozen different publishers, the bookseller places one large order with a single wholesaler, and such a transaction is worthwhile to publisher, wholesaler and bookseller alike.

Trends

The trends observable in publishing are taking place in wholesaling too. But with fewer wholesalers than publishers – no more indeed than a handful of major companies – realignments in this sector of the trade easily lead to significant shifts of power.

Although wholesalers are middlemen between publishers and booksellers, if one drew a single line down the trade, wholesalers would lie on the bookselling rather than the publishing side. Amalgamations can produce concentrations of purchasing power which allow the wholesaler to bargain strongly for better terms from the publisher. This seems to be part of a long-term shift of power away from the publishing side of the trade, which has held it for so long, towards the bookselling side – a shift which manifests itself also, as we see later in this chapter, in the rise of large bookselling chains with *their* concentrations of purchasing power. And this ultimately – though not yet – may produce advantages even for the small independent trader.

None of the trends has an unstoppable momentum. Some major booksellers remain unconvinced of the merits of buying through wholesalers rather than direct from publishers, and this may limit the growth of the wholesalers, which in turn will limit the advantages that would accrue to booksellers in general from a flourishing wholesale sector.

Stock lists

It is no more possible for a wholesaler to stock everything in print than it is for a bookseller to do so. Some wholesalers specialise in paperbacks, some in hardbacks, some deal in both. Some stock the entire lists of particular publishers, some stock selections only from various publishers. Some deal in general books, some only in particular subjects.

The BA's *Directory of Book Publishers and Wholesalers* (see page 95), lists about ninety wholesalers, together with details of stock range carried and terms of supply. Here are some details of the stock ranges of a few of the major national wholesalers in 1988.

Bertram Books has selected titles from 200 publishers: 8,000 hardback titles and 1,000 paperback titles. Heathcote Books has 38,000 paperbacks titles and 2,000 hardback titles from 100 publishers. Gardners has 23,000 paperback titles and 7,000 hardback titles – about 20 complete lists and selections from some 200 others. Hammick's has 15,000 paperback titles and 10,000 hardback titles, representing some 350 different imprints. J. Barnicoat has 26,000 paperback titles – about 40 complete lists and selections from a few others.

The raw figures of a wholesaler's stock tell only part of the story. Wholesalers are interested in rapid turnover. They choose their stock on the basis of what they judge to be the fast-selling titles: these are the very ones that you want in your shop too. To the extent that you choose your stock from wholesalers' catalogues, you are in a sense being guided by the wholesalers' expertise – no bad thing, especially in your early days in the trade.

Service

Wholesaling most comes into its own in the matter of service. A perennial complaint of booksellers is that so many publishers take an age to process orders and to get their books out to the shops. The best of the wholesalers, on the other hand, have a splendid record of speedy service. Typically, books ordered by phone from a wholesaler this morning will be in the shop tomorrow or the day after. Publishers have been known to take weeks.

From time to time, the BA undertakes a detailed delivery survey, and individual suppliers' performances are listed in what has become known as the *Delivery League Table*. The most recent survey (1985) found that the time lapse from the placing of an order to the receipt of the books in the bookshop – the *lead time* – was 2.8 working days for the average wholesaler and 8.5 working days for the average publisher. In terms of calendar days, the lead time worked out at 4 days for the average wholesaler and 13 days for the average publisher. Interestingly, the figures show little regional variation in mainland Britain.

The poor delivery performance of a number of major publishers has been a characteristic of the trade for as long as most people can remember, and exasperated booksellers often raise their eyes heavenwards and wonder why it should be so: don't they *want* to sell their books? As with the proliferation of new titles, what looks to be commercially curious must have an explanation.

A publisher offering a speedy service receives frequent small orders – precisely what he doesn't want. Booksellers, knowing they can replenish stock quickly, order just enough to see them through the next few days. If, however, the publisher is known to be a sluggard, booksellers – if they want the publisher's books at all – place larger orders at longer intervals to make sure they don't risk running out of stock. So the good publisher is 'rewarded' by many small orders – which are the least profitable to deal with – while the bad publisher gets a few large orders – which are the most profitable to deal with. Hardly surprising, then, that bad publishers are so little inclined to reform their ways.

But how do wholesalers afford to give such good service? Mainly by specifying a minimum order value, which is very easy for the bookseller to reach – even if it's as much as £50 or £75 – because of the wide range of fast-selling titles on offer. So the wholesaler who provides a speedy service can look forward to frequent *large* orders. That's what makes the whole thing work.

BOOKSELLERS

There are bookshops and there are shops that sell books; the two are not the same. A shop – or department within a shop – which specialises in the sale of books is quite different from one which sells books as one commodity among many. If you lump all retail outlets together, there may be as many as 60,000 which deal in the sale of books. But if you count only those which *specialise* in the sale of books, there are probably not more than 2,000 or so.

Specialist bookshops are 'real' bookshops. Their owners or managers choose their stock title by title, in line with the character they want their shops to have, and their considered assessment of what their customers will wish to buy. Such booksellers know their stock, can talk about it knowledgeably, can advise customers on the characteristics of different books, have a good idea of what is available in their field of interest even if they have decided not to stock it, hold adequate bibliographical reference material so that they can help customers seeking unstocked titles, and are willing to obtain unstocked titles to customers' special orders.

By contrast, those shops which sell books as just another commodity treat them as not essentially different from cans of beans or boxes of paper-clips. They're bought in batches, put on display, and replaced by further batches when they sell out. The help offered to customers seeking any particular title is limited to nodding towards the shelves and saying that if it isn't there they haven't got it.

There are some shops or departments which look at first glance like 'real' booksellers but which, because of poorly trained or inexperienced staff, are little different from outlets with no pretensions to being other than variety retailers. Such shops or departments are most frequently found where staff are switched from product to product, with little regard for their personal interest or expertise; so Miss X may be on electrical goods one week and helping out in the book department the next.

There are other shops again which sell books relating to their own non-book speciality – camera shops with books on photography, health food shops with books on cookery, and so on. And there are some sellers of books who have no shops at all – most book clubs, for example, or publishers selling their own titles by mail order.

TABLE 5 Source: *Book Retailing in the 1990s*, 1987

PERCENTAGE MARKET SHARE BY VALUE
OF DIFFERENT TYPES OF BOOK RETAILERS

	1985 *ESTIMATED %*	*1996* *FORECAST %*	*CHANGE %*
Multiples (5+ outlets)	17	23	+ 6
Large independents (>£200,000 p.a.)	5	4	− 1
Small independents (< £200,000 p.a.)	8	5	− 3
Specialists subtotal	30	32	+ 2
W.H. Smith (excluding book stalls)	20	17	− 3
CTNs (including Menzies)	16	15	− 1
Book clubs	10	8	− 2
Department stores	2	2	0
Variety stores (Woolworth, Boots etc)	7	9	+ 2
Marks & Spencer	1	1	0
Supermarkets	2	3	+ 1
Others	12	14	+ 2

Market share

Table 5 shows Arthur Young's estimate of the market share of these different sectors of the retail book market, together with a forecast of how it might change in the next few years. Roughly speaking, the specialists have about a third of the market, W.H. Smith, John Menzies and newsagents another third, and all the others put together the remaining third. (Newsagents, by the way, are usually referred to in the retailing trades as CTNs, standing for Confectioners, Tobacconists, Newsagents.)

SPECIALIST BOOKSHOPS

The present guide is mainly concerned with 'real' bookshops. There is unfortunately no completely satisfactory epithet for such shops – *real, serious, pedigree, stockholding* and *specialist* may all be heard from time to time.

Real only does for occasional use as it seems too weak to convey the required sense without self-conscious quotation marks, and is also perhaps gratuitously insulting to other shops which may quite properly be fulfilling a different function, meeting their own customers' needs in their own way. *Serious* is open to similar objections. *Pedigree*, much used in the Net Book Agreement case of 1962 (see page 63), while appropriate for long-established shops, like Hatchards in Piccadilly or Blackwell's in Oxford, sounds rather strange when applied to a newly opened small independent. *Stockholding*, though sanctioned by usage, is less than apt since all sorts of bookshops, 'real' or not, may be stockholders. The distinguishing feature of a 'real' bookshop is not so much its stock*holding* as its basis of stock *selection* – title by title rather than batch by batch.

So that just leaves *specialist*, which is apt and understandable, but unfortunately ambiguous. Is a specialist bookshop a shop which specialises in books, or a bookshop which specialises in particular categories of books? To overcome the ambiguity, we will in this guide use the term *speciality bookshop* to refer to a bookshop which specialises in particular categories of books. The term *specialist bookshop* will be reserved for the 'real' bookshop as described above.

Stock

A specialist bookshop, then, may be either a *general bookshop*, stocking a broad spread of titles likely to appeal to a cross-section of the general public, or a *speciality bookshop*, stocking a limited subject range in depth. Many shops include a speciality section within their general range, seeking to get the best of both worlds. It is general stock that pulls book-buying passers-by off the street and into the shop, while speciality stock pulls enthusiasts in from further afield. People will go out of their way to find a shop that caters for their particular interests, but they have little incentive to go further than their nearest well-stocked bookshop for their more general requirements.

NON-BOOKS

Specialist booksellers do not necessarily deal exclusively in books. Greetings cards, stationery, records and cassettes are among the most frequently stocked non-book lines (see Table 12 on page 195). Interestingly, few dealers in new books also deal in secondhand books: less than 10 per cent of BA members do so. The two types of bookselling have far less in common than the casual observer might suppose (see also page 55).

Non-book lines rarely account for more than 20 per cent of a specialist bookshop's turnover. Any more than this, and the shop may be in danger of losing its specialist image – though much depends upon how and where the goods are presented in the shop. Consider the case of a shop with a street-level sales area and another floor above. If the shop window and all the ground floor are given over to books, and all the upper floor to stationery, people will think of the shop as a bookshop with a stationery department. Put the stationery in the window and on the ground floor with all of the books upstairs, and people will think of it as a stationer's with a book department. The effect of these different arrangements upon book sales and the type of customer attracted into the shop could be substantial.

Chains

Recent years have seen the emergence of a new kind of expansionary aggressiveness among the specialist bookshop chains – the multiples like Hatchards, Pentos, Waterstone's, Sherratt & Hughes, Hammick's and so on. The big chains are now thought to share between them about 17 per cent of the market in new books, and likely to have about 23 per cent in ten years' time.

There have always been chains of bookshops, but until the current phase, they occupied a fairly stable position within a fairly stable market. Booksellers, large or small, could confidently expect that the pattern of trade in their own towns would be pretty much the same tomorrow as it was yesterday. That is no longer the case. The big chains are opening new branches as fast as they can, wherever they identify a marketing opportunity.

Bookselling, once popularly regarded as a genteel occupation for persons of refinement and sensibility, nowadays sometimes looks more like all-in wrestling. A small independent general bookshop which happens to be in a location coveted by one of the big chains will, if it's lucky, be bought out; if it's unlucky, it may have to watch as customers desert in droves to the wonderful new bookshop just opened across the way. The big chains have the money, the management expertise, the marketing skills, the courage and the *drive* to take and develop large prime sites in major centres of population.

Although the chains see the major battle as between one chain and another rather than between themselves and the small independents, there's no doubt that the small independents get trampled on while the giants slug it out among themselves for market share.

Some book trade watchers think that there are currently too many giants and not enough market, and that one way or another the two must come into balance. Everyone in the trade would be delighted if the balance were achieved by an enlargement of the market – that is, if a percentage of non-book-buyers were converted to the book-buying habit. But most people think that the balance will be achieved by take-overs, mergers, or simple, old-fashioned commercial failures, and that in time the number of major specialist bookshop chains will be reduced to just two or three. Meanwhile, small intending booksellers should know that there are fierce wars raging in the high street, and they must therefore consider very carefully both the type and location of their own ventures before committing themselves to the trade.

Independents

The independents – traditional high street bookshops, usually owner-managed – are estimated to have about 13 per cent of the market. Only a handful of independents can be considered large, with an annual turnover in new books of above £200,000. A slightly larger handful can be considered small, with a turnover between £80,000 and £200,000. Most of them must be considered very small, with a turnover below £80,000.

This is the usual point of entry for most new bookshop owners. It's not a place to make a fortune fast.

NON-SPECIALIST BOOKSHOPS

About 36 per cent of the £717 million spent by the public on books each year is thought to be rung up on the tills of shops like W.H. Smith, John Menzies and so on. Chains like these have a major commitment to bookselling though they also deal extensively in non-book products. They are clearly of immense importance to the book trade, selling far more books than the specialist bookshop chains. And W.H. Smith in particular has for a long time played a major role in initiating and supporting developments in trade practice which benefit the trade as a whole. But because non-specialist bookshops are so differently perceived by the general public, most booksellers feel that they do not present the same sort of competitive challenge to the small independent bookseller as the specialist bookshop chains. And that's just as well, because it's very difficult to get away from them. In mid-1988, for example, there were 374 branches of W.H. Smith in membership of the BA – and even 48 of Boots the Chemists and 76 of the Automobile Association.

OTHER BOOK RETAILERS

The remaining third of the market is served by various other suppliers, some operating out of shop premises, some not.

Book clubs

The book clubs, with about 10 per cent of the market, operate at present almost entirely by mail. Club members are offered special book club editions at prices substantially lower than those of the trade editions – ie those published for sale through specialist bookshops – and in return must commit themselves to buying not less than a specified minimum number of books a year, usually four.

Other mail order booksellers

There is a certain amount of mail order selling, normally of ordinary trade editions, by speciality booksellers operating without bookshop premises. And there are a number of bookshops – something over 20 per cent of BA members (see Table 11 on page 189) – which offer a mail order service to their customers, though the volume of business done in this way is not easy to ascertain.

DIRECT SELLING

Mail order is used also by publishers selling books direct to the general public. Booksellers concede the justification of this in the case of books of limited appeal which are unlikely to sell in quantity from the shelves of general bookshops, but they feel badly done by when they take a stock risk on a title only to find the publisher competing with them for retail sales. Such competition is the more hurtful when the publisher sells the book direct to the public on terms which the bookseller cannot match – or, indeed, is not permitted to match (see the next chapter on the Net Book Agreement) – by offering a discounted price or some other incentive.

Direct selling is one of the trade's contentious issues. Booksellers feel that publishers' advertising should in the first instance direct customers to their local bookseller, and only direct-sell as a last resort, using some such formula as '. . . or in case of difficulty direct from the publisher at . . .'.

CTNs

Small newsagents frequently have a rack or two of mass-market paperbacks – the classic example of books being retailed as just another commodity.

Supermarkets, variety stores, etc

Supermarkets, variety stores (like Woolworths) and department stores account for most of the rest of the sales of new books. Some department stores have *specialist* book departments – and these, of course, are in an entirely different class from those referred to here.

Institutional suppliers

So far we have been considering only the selling of books direct to members of the public. However, an important part of bookselling – though a declining one in recent years – is the selling of books to schools and libraries. For some independent booksellers, this *institutional business* may amount to 15 per cent or more of the shop's total annual turnover. It is an area of bookselling, however, much under threat as local authorities are increasingly making their purchases direct from publishers. More about this later in the book (page 87). All that need be noted here is that there are some booksellers who specialise in institutional supply, often on a national scale, and who do not themselves have shop premises at all.

SECONDHAND BOOK TRADE

The secondhand book trade is a distant cousin of the new book trade but very different from it. While the new book trade buys its stock from publishers and wholesalers, the secondhand trade buys its stock from auctions, individual members of the public and other dealers. At one end of the market are the antiquarian booksellers, among whose varied customers may be found those who collect fine old books the way other people collect fine antiques or ivories or classic postage stamps. At the other end of the market are the street stalls piled high with old paperbacks and the sad and dusty collections of the popular reading of half a century ago. The two ends of the market shade into each other by imperceptible degrees.

Unlike the publisher-fixed prices of most new books (see the next chapter), the prices of secondhand books are determined, deal by deal, in the marketplace. The price of a secondhand book is what you can get for it. Only by actively taking part in the trade, whether as dealer or customer – and the distinction between the two is often rather blurred – will you develop a sense of values and prices.

A good introduction to the world of secondhand books is John Chidley's *Discovering Book Collecting* (Shire Publications); and a good and readable reference book is John Carter's *ABC for Book Collectors* (Granada Publishing).

A number of periodicals, annuals and reference books of interest to antiquarian booksellers are published by The Clique Ltd. The monthly *Book and Magazine Collector*, consisting mainly of lists of books wanted and for sale, is published by the Diamond Publishing Group, and is available on annual subscription (£19 in 1988) or from newsagents.

The Antiquarian Booksellers Association is the major association for this section of the book trade. Applicants for membership are required to have been trading as antiquarian booksellers for a minimum of five years.

BOOK PUBLICITY

Books get a good deal of media attention. Serious papers carry regular reviews; radio and television put out book programmes; authors are interviewed; lengthy book extracts are published in the press; book adaptations frequently appear in the cinema and on radio and television; and features, plays and serials which start life in other media produce spin-offs in book form. Books are often found on the news pages too, as the subjects of litigation or as players in a public controversy.

There are also a number of non-trade journals which concern themselves exclusively with books – among them *The Times Literary Supplement, The London Review of Books* and *British Book News*. The latter is published by the British Council, a government body which, among other things, does much to promote British books abroad.

One way or another, books get an enormous amount of largely free publicity. If the trade actually had to pay for all this promotional space and time at the going rate, its advertising bill would exceed its sales by a substantial margin. From time to time, blessings should be counted.

EVENTS

In addition to this continuing media coverage, not a little of which – let's admit it – is engineered by publishers' publicity departments, there are also a number of set-piece events of value to the trade.

Book fairs

Book fairs are primarily trade events, though some also welcome the public. Among the best known are the Frankfurt Book Fair, mainly patronised by publishers trading rights (see page 106), and the Bologna Children's Book Fair. The UK's major fair is the London International Book Fair and this, among other things, gives booksellers the chance to see a range of publishers' titles all under one roof. The BA's Trade Exhibition (see page 81) provides a similar opportunity and, as the only fair specifically directed at booksellers, it is the one of greatest interest to them.

There are other book fairs at home and abroad, some specialising in particular categories of books. Keep an eye on the trade press for details of forthcoming fairs.

Book prizes

The major book prizes have increasingly become important media events, surrounded by the kind of ballyhoo formerly reserved for Hollywood Oscar ceremonies. They are exploitable, and exploited, at many levels. Short-listed authors, who might otherwise scarcely rate a mention on the book page, find their work reviewed and discussed on radio and television programmes broadcast into millions of homes. Bookmakers quote odds on the candidates so that you can have a flutter and enjoy yourself without actually having to read a word. The final award ceremonies, broadcast on television and radio, generate the same kind of breathless excitement that characterises the wait for the returning officer's declaration at a crucial by-election. It's all good harmless fun. The sponsors get the publicity they want, the successful authors get a lot of money, both from the prizes and from the increased sales that winning books invariably achieve, their publishers are content for the same reasons, the media have put on a good show and the public have enjoyed themselves. Happiest of all are the booksellers: they make sales whoever win the prizes.

The biggest prizes are currently sponsored by Whitbread – administered by the BA – at £27,500, NCR (National Cash Registers) at £25,000, the *Sunday Express* at £20,000 and Booker at £15,000 – though the Booker is probably still the best known. A detailed list of literary prizes and awards is published in the annual *Writers' and Artists' Yearbook* (Black) and in *Guide to Literary Prizes, Grants and Awards* published by Book Trust (see below).

TRADE AND OTHER ASSOCIATIONS

Various associations concern themselves with promoting and protecting the interests of particular sections of the book world and the book trade. Their names are usually self-explanatory: Society of Authors, Library Association, Book Publishers' Representatives' Association, Independent Publishers Guild and so on. By and large, the ordinary bookseller has little, if anything, to do with them. Up-to-date addresses for many such associations are included among the Useful Addresses in the BA's annual publications *Directory of Members* and *Directory of Book Publishers and Wholesalers*. A number are similarly listed in Whitaker's *Publishers in the UK and their Addresses*. A longer and annotated list of societies, associations and clubs may be found in the *Writers' and Artists' Yearbook*.

The two major trade associations which directly concern the dealer in new books are the Booksellers Association and the Publishers Association. A third organisation which plays a major role in the book world is Book Trust. The Booksellers Association is considered in detail in Chapter 4.

BOOK TRUST

Book Trust is an educational charity whose function is to encourage reading and the use and enjoyment of books. It has a number of touring exhibitions which are available for display anywhere in the UK by various bodies, including bookshops.

The Children's Book Foundation, a separate division of Book Trust, aims to make reading and books more accessible to children of all cultures and ages – introducing books at the earliest possible stage and sustaining the interest through adolescence. Its children's reference library is a collection of virtually every children's book published in Britain in the previous two years, together with much reference material about children's books and reading. The collection – an invaluable aid to book selection for new children's booksellers – is catalogued by author, series, subject and illustrator, and may be freely browsed through by visitors to Book House, Book Trust's London home.

Book Trust also administers various literary awards, including the Booker Prize, publishes various guides to books and authors, and produces authoritative reference lists to aid selection of the best titles available in specific areas. Of particular interest to the bookseller is Book Trust's Book Information Service, which answers enquiries about authors, titles, publishers, dates of publication, and so on.

Both in its direct services and in its behind-the-scenes prompting and co-ordinating of the efforts of other organisations, Book Trust does much that is valued by all concerned with books – the schools, the general public and the trade.

Anyone may become a Friend of Book Trust for an annual subscription of £25 (in 1988). Friends receive Book Trust's quarterly journal *Booknews*, which is otherwise available on subscription at £5 a year.

PUBLISHERS ASSOCIATION

The Publishers Association (PA) has a membership of some 500 publishing firms. These account for about 75 per cent of UK publishing turnover, and include most of the major publishing houses.

The PA's principal roles are to represent and promote the needs of publishers, to work to expand the markets for books, and to provide management services to its members.

The PA has five divisions: *Home Trade and Services Council (HTSC)*, responsible for general trade matters and for co-ordinating the work of specialist committees concerned with distribution, employment and so on; *Book Marketing Council (BMC)* which promotes book sales in the UK; *Book Development Council (BDC)* which promotes the sale of British books abroad; *Educational Publishers Council (EPC)* which looks after the interests of school publishers, and campaigns for the improved provision of books in schools; *University, College and Professional Publishers Council (UCPPC)* which looks after the interests of academic and professional publishers.

As far as booksellers are concerned, the PA's major role is as guardian of the Net Book Agreement and as the licensing authority which grants exemptions to it. Which takes us on to the next chapter.

Chapter 3

Book Prices

Booksellers have no problem in deciding at what price to sell most new British books they take into stock. They have no problem because they have no responsibility in the matter. The price below which booksellers must not sell – which in practice means the price at which they *do* sell – is decided by the publisher, and the publisher's decision is enforceable at law. That simple fact determines much of the character of contemporary bookselling.

A retail price specified by a publisher who may legally enforce it is said to be a *net price* or a *net published price*. A book published at a net price is said to be a *net book*.

THE NET BOOK AGREEMENT

The legal document from which the retail price maintenance of books derives is the Net Book Agreement 1957 (NBA), the text of which is printed in Appendix A. Do read it carefully in order to make sense of what follows.

Note first of all that the NBA is an agreement made *by publishers* with each other. It is not a booksellers' agreement. The reason why booksellers are bound by the NBA is that publishers may legally specify in their own conditions of sale that their bookselling customers shall observe the *Standard Conditions of Sale* as set out in the NBA. The consequence of this is that any given net book costs customers exactly the same whether they live in Land's End or John o'Groats, and whether they buy it from the smallest independent bookseller or the largest branch of the biggest bookshop chain.

A minority of books are outside the scope of the NBA and some important sales are exempted from it by licence, but the general effect of the NBA upon the trade in new books is crucial. Bookselling is as it is today because of the Net Book Agreement; if, for whatever reason, the Net Book Agreement were to go, bookselling would change decisively – and most people in the trade are convinced that the change would be for the worse.

WHAT THE NBA AGREES

Each of the signatories to the NBA – all of them publishers, you remember – promises all of the other signatories that if he publishes a book at a net price then he will enforce that net price. The PA is appointed by the Agreement to be the NBA watchdog.

At first glance, the NBA seems hardly necessary. What business is it of Publisher A if Publisher B countenances the underselling of his own net books? The traditional view of the trade is this: If there is to be an orderly market in new books, the public must have confidence in net prices – all net prices. The customer in the bookshop cannot be expected to distinguish between the marketing practices of different publishers. If some net prices were undercut, all the customer would notice was that some books were being offered below their published prices and others were not; could it be that in another shop or in another week, the other books would be marked down too? As soon as any net price is called into question, *all* net prices are called into question. Hence the trade's commitment to a common policy universally enforced.

The maintenance of public confidence in net prices requires also that any relaxation of the rules should follow a strict code of practice which itself must be a matter of common policy. A number of such relaxations form part of the NBA and we shall be looking at them later in the chapter.

NET BOOKS AND NON-NET BOOKS

Most books sold to the general public are net books; most books designed to be used as school textbooks are non-net books and therefore not subject to the NBA. There is nothing intrinsically different between a net book and a non-net book; it is entirely a matter for the publisher whether any particular book shall be designated net or non-net. A book is a net book if the publisher says it is, and there's an end of the matter.

A net book may be signalled as such by having its price followed by the word *net* printed on its cover or jacket. The invoice from the publisher or wholesaler should include similar information, as should the publisher's catalogue. A book not signalled as net in any of these ways may be assumed to be non-net.

Publishers are free not only to designate their titles net or non-net on publication, they are similarly free to *de-net* any of their titles at any time – ie to remove a book, formerly net, from the scope of the NBA, or to declare a book, formerly non-net, as henceforth net. Indeed, in all respects, publishers' freedom of action is entirely unfettered by the NBA, apart from the undertaking to fellow publishers already noted. There is nothing even to stop publishers from underselling their own titles, while insisting upon the observance of net prices by their bookselling customers. Such behaviour would breach the spirit but not the letter of the Agreement. Fortunately it is rare.

Why do publishers bother with net and non-net at all?

Most publishers are largely or completely dependent upon the display and sale of their books in bookshops. Without bookshops, the prospect for publishers would be bleak. Bookshops, however, must make a reasonable profit to survive. Without maintained prices, bookshops, which today compete with each other on *service*, would inevitably compete with each other on *price*. Bookselling is not startlingly profitable even now, and if the reduced margins implied by price competition came about, some shops would undoubtedly be driven out of business. With fewer bookshops there would be fewer book sales, and in the end many publishers would suffer as much as the booksellers.

It is to maintain a healthy distribution network of booksellers that publishers net virtually all books which they intend to be displayed and sold through bookshops. Only by building into net prices an acceptable retail profit margin can publishers hope to tempt booksellers into taking a stock risk on their titles.

With some titles, however, the stock risk is negligible because the bookseller only orders from the publisher after receiving a firm order from the customer. While this may be true from time to time of any title, it is routinely true of sets of school textbooks – and these are the titles that are most usually non-net.

Booksellers' view of the NBA

Even though the NBA vests in publishers the right to dictate retail selling prices, thus denying booksellers control over a crucial element in their own businesses, there are few booksellers who are not overwhelmingly in favour of its continuation. What *does* upset many booksellers is publishers' consistent failure to build adequate retail margins into net prices, and it is this failure that keeps many a small independent bookseller permanently teetering on the edge of disaster.

Despite this, and despite heretical voices – powerful but few – which condemn the Agreement, the general trade view prevails that without the NBA, bookselling would go into a severe decline. It is from outside the trade that the NBA is most under threat.

THE NBA CHALLENGED

There was a time when the prices of almost all manufactured goods were fixed by the manufacturers, acting in concert, who made it a condition of trade supply that retailers adhered to those prices. Then came the Restrictive Trade Practices Act 1956 which effectively outlawed price fixing in this way unless it could be shown to be in the public interest. With varying degrees of enthusiasm most manufacturers relinquished control of retail prices to individual retailers. But in the book trade, both manufacturers and retailers – publishers and booksellers – were determined to continue with their well-established net price system.

The case before the Restrictive Practices Court

Conscious of the hostile environment created by the 1956 Act to anything that smacked of a restriction upon trade, the Publishers Association scrapped the form of the NBA then current, and replaced it by a very carefully constructed document, designed to serve the old purpose without offending the new law: this was the Net Book Agreement 1957. No one doubted that sooner or later the Registrar of Restrictive Trading Agreements would challenge the NBA, so once the new Agreement was in place, the book trade considered its strategy, held councils of war, and awaited the attack.

It came in July 1959. The Registrar informed the Publishers Association that he intended shortly to serve Notice of Reference in respect of the Net Book Agreement, and on 23 October 1959 that Notice was duly served. In plain English, the Registrar was taking the PA to court, the essence of the charge being that the NBA was contrary to the public interest.

From 1959 until the hearing in 1962, an enormous amount of work was done by both the PA and the BA in preparing the trade's case. Although the NBA is a publishers' agreement, and it was the PA membership therefore who were the respondents in the case, the two trade associations worked in the closest collaboration throughout to ensure the vigorous defence of the NBA by the trade as a whole.

The hearing opened on 25 June 1962. It lasted for five weeks, during which the court met on twenty-four days. Some of the leading publishers and booksellers of the day gave evidence, describing, often in fine detail, the workings of the book trade and of their own particular businesses, and the adverse effects they feared if the NBA were abrogated. On 30 October 1962, Mr Justice Buckley delivered the Judgement of the Court: the Net Book Agreement was *not* contrary to the public interest.

The transcript of the case ran to twenty-five volumes and well over a million words. An abridgement edited by R.E. Barker and G.R. Davies in a mere nine hundred pages or so was published by Macmillan in 1966 as *Books are Different* – an aphorism used by Mr Arthur Bagnall QC in his opening speech for the Publishers Association, quoted at the end in the Judgement, and used by the book trade ever since as both shield and spear in every battle. The book, now out of print, makes fascinating reading for anyone interested in bookselling in the twentieth century.

In 1967 further thought was given to challenging the NBA under the Resale Prices Act 1964, but the case did not proceed to a full hearing as it was agreed on all sides that the earlier Judgement effectively exempted books from the newer legislation. And so the NBA is still in force, and books are one of only two products for which resale price maintenance is legally permitted; the other one is branded pharmaceuticals.

Will the NBA survive?

The NBA has always seemed a fragile creature. Pessimists have been predicting its imminent demise almost from birth. Yet thirty years on, the 1957 Agreement is still in place. And it is worth recalling that the current NBA is merely the latest incarnation of an Agreement which first saw the light of day at the turn of the century. So it can't be all that fragile.

Nevertheless, it needs only a decision of the courts or a simple piece of parliamentary legislation to consign the NBA to history. Nor are these the only threats. It is not just in Britain that restrictions on competition run counter to the spirit of the age; challenges to the NBA are as likely to come from the EEC Commission in Brussels as from the government in Westminster.

Furthermore, seemingly unrelated happenings could undermine the NBA. For example, if the currently zero VAT rate on books were, by a stroke of the Chancellor's pen, to be changed to a positive rate – and this could happen literally overnight – book prices would have to rise by the VAT percentage. Such evidence as there is suggests that consumer spending on books is very price-sensitive, and an overnight price rise of, say, 15 per cent, would leave book buyers shellshocked, and sales, at least for an interim period, deeply depressed. To counter this, some of the major booksellers might, without ceremony, slash their prices to bring the customers back in. It would be a salvage operation to save as much as possible from the disaster, and some things – the NBA among them – might have to be abandoned. This is not an inevitable scenario, but it is a possible one.

Indeed, if any of the big bookselling chains decided unilaterally to ditch the NBA – whether prompted to it by external events or not – it seems unlikely that the Agreement could survive. How long could publishers refuse supplies to a major customer? And since, as we have already seen, confidence in the universality of net prices is the heart of the matter, a defeat for the NBA in one sector of the market could rapidly lead to its collapse everywhere.

So will the NBA confound the pessimists for another thirty years? Or are we near the end? Your guess is a good as anybody's. But if you're thinking of coming into the trade to run your own bookshop, you must consider seriously not only whether you could succeed in the trade as it is today, but also whether you could survive in the trade as it might be tomorrow. The following look at the differing views of supporters and opponents of the NBA may help you in your deliberations.

THE CASE FOR THE NBA

Although when the pro-NBA case is argued in public, the book trade takes its stand upon the public interest – a view upheld, as we have seen, by the Restrictive Practices Court – the ultimate explanation of the trade's commitment to the NBA is that it also believes it to be in its *own* interest. No bookseller or publisher would support the NBA for a moment if they thought its abolition would enable the trade to double its profits. It is because the book trade fears that profits would be reduced – indeed, that many existing bookshops and publishing houses would be forced out of business altogether – that it fought so strongly in 1962 to defend the NBA and still maintains its commitment to it.

The public interest and the trade interest are different sides of the same coin. If a bookshop ceases trading because of inadequate profits, all members of the public who use that shop will be deprived of its services, and to that extent their lives will be the poorer. As in all supplier–consumer relationships, there is a shared interest in trade continuity: if you don't pay the farmer enough to keep him in business today, tomorrow you may go hungry.

The core of the case in support of the NBA is that without it there would be fewer specialist bookshops, a narrower range of titles would be stocked, fewer books would be published, and those that *were* published would in general be more expensive. In outline the pro-NBA argument goes like this:

> Good bookshops must stock a range of titles, both popular books and those of minority interest. But as no bookshop can possibly stock everything in print, obtaining books to special order is a vital part of specialist booksellers' service to the public; it is, however, a service that is frequently uneconomic. The one thing that permits booksellers to offer an uneconomic service is the knowledge that they are making an adequate profit from their bread-and-butter stock – the bestsellers of the moment, popular paperbacks and the hardy perennials like craft books, gardening books, glossy cookery books and so on. It is only because they have fast-moving titles like these that they can afford to stock a number of less popular books as a service to minority tastes, and only because of the overall profitability of their businesses that they can offer a special order service. The bestsellers and the fast sellers and the steady sellers subsidise the poor sellers, the slow sellers, and those titles that a bookseller may be asked for only once in a lifetime.
>
> Books are different from other products, and the sort of retailers' price competition which invigorates other markets would only diminish the book trade; indeed it would risk destroying large sections of it.
>
> If booksellers were permitted to offer their most popular books at cut prices, they would increase their sales and profits only until competing booksellers offered these same popular books at even lower prices. Only the biggest booksellers with enough commercial clout to extract higher discounts from publishers could survive for long. And even they would find themselves challenged when the supermarkets, primarily interested in selling groceries and household articles, started offering these same popular books at little more than cost price, hoping to make a profit on high turnover, or possibly content to make no profit at all if the mere offer of the books at low prices enticed customers into the supermarkets to buy more groceries and household articles.
>
> Very soon, the major booksellers and the supermarkets would be creaming off all the popular book sales, and small specialist booksellers would be left with only the books of minority interest and the special order service. No longer able to subsidise these aspects of their businesses from the profits of the popular sellers, specialist booksellers would have to raise their prices very steeply on such books and services as they continued to offer. Higher prices would lead to fewer customers, and in the end such businesses would risk collapse.
>
> With the pattern repeated over the country, many of the smaller specialist booksellers would go out of business. Publishers would then have fewer bookshops through which to sell their books, and would therefore find themselves selling fewer books. The sales prospects of some titles would decline to the point where they were not worth publishing; other titles would have to be increased in price to compensate for the unavoidably lower print runs. Fewer books would be published, and some publishers would cease trading altogether.

The book trade would polarise. At the popular end of the market, book sales would rise and books would become – at least for a time, while the competitive wars were waging – cheaper. Less popular books and books of minority interest would become more expensive or cease to be available. Minority-interest books which continued in print would be more difficult to come by, at any price, because of the reduced number of bookshops holding stocks of such titles or offering the special order service.

In the end, the public would have fewer books to choose from, fewer bookshops to choose them in, and higher prices to pay for anything slightly out of the ordinary. QED.

THE CASE AGAINST THE NBA

Opponents of the NBA argue that it keeps book prices high by suppressing competition and feather-bedding the inefficient. The anti-NBA argument goes something like this:

It must be in the public interest to enable someone to buy a book at, say, £9 which might otherwise have cost £10. It is all very well talking about an adequate stock range and a special order service, but booksellers at present enjoy the same high maintained prices whatever their stock range or quality of service. The NBA doesn't protect the specialist bookseller; it just provides easy pickings for the non-specialist bookseller.

The absence of price competition means not only that a shop offering a take-it-or-leave-it service charges exactly the same as one offering the full range of traditional bookshop facilities, it also means that inefficient traders have nothing to fear from more efficient competitors, as any inefficiency is comfortably subsidised by a high controlled price. It might be possible for efficient booksellers to offer, say, a 10 per cent price reduction to the public with no diminution of service. Surely it is in the interest only of the inefficient booksellers that they are prevented from doing so by the NBA.

And what if prices *did* polarise on the demise of the NBA? If the most popular books become cheaper and the least popular books become dearer, doesn't that precisely reflect the public interest in the most literal sense? Why should a hundred buyers of *Slimmer's Cookbook* pay more for their reading merely that one buyer of *The Wheel in Medieval Art* might pay less? Let prices find a level in a free market which accurately responds to the commercial realities. If that means that abstruse and scholarly works will cost more – so be it.

Other trades in the UK survive without maintained prices. What's so special about books? It's no answer just to close your eyes and chant the book trade mantra – *books are different, books are different*. Of course books are different from other products, just as other products are different from each other. Every trade has characteristics that set it apart, but what all trades have in common – including the book trade – is that they are commercial ventures which are undertaken because they make money, and which would cease to be undertaken if they stopped making money. In this respect, books are the same as brandy-snaps or billiard tables.

The sooner the book trade rolls up its collective sleeves and gets down to the business of aggressive selling in a competitive world instead of languishing behind the protective screen of the NBA, the better for the trade and the better for the public. If a fraction of the energy squandered on the defence, maintenance and enforcement of the NBA were instead to be devoted to the business of actually going out and selling books, the trade would be far healthier than it is.

We too often confuse the welfare of the individual bookseller with the welfare of the trade. Of course it will be tough on those booksellers who can't find an answer to the competitive challenge, but the trade itself will be stronger and more profitable when its weaker members retire from the field.

NBA LICENCES

The arguments for and against the NBA are academic. The Agreement exists: it is legal, enforceable, and the key document in the regulation of the trade in new books. But as you can see, if you look again at the *Standard Conditions of Sale* in Appendix A, there are a number of relaxations to the strict application of its central principle.

The central principle

This is the now familiar rule, contained in Clauses (i) and (v) of the *Standard Conditions*, that no net book shall be sold to the public for less than its net price.

This prevents booksellers from using the sort of promotions favoured by most other retailers. You can't, for example, offer 10 per cent off net prices to get your business off to a good start on opening day. You can't offer a free hanky to purchasers of the latest weepie.

Clause (v)(b) particularly affects library suppliers, whose customers frequently require them to *service* books before delivery – add protective covers, stamp the library name on the books, and so on. So that there shall be no hidden price reduction in the book supply, these additional services must be charged at not less than cost. But is the cost of a plastic cover the amount that the bookseller paid for it, or that amount plus the labour cost of putting the cover on, or all that plus the purchase and maintenance costs of any equipment used – or what? When in doubt, ask the BA for advice. But in the end it's what the PA says that counts: the NBA is *their* agreement, and *their* interpretation is final.

The relaxations

Clauses (ii), (iii) and (iv) of the *Standard Conditions* define when and to whom net books may exceptionally be sold below their net prices. Briefly, the relaxations cover the sale of old or secondhand stock, and sales specifically authorised by the PA. Only in the case of secondhand stock can the bookseller just get on with it; in all other cases, set procedures must be followed or licences obtained from the PA.

OLD STOCK

If you have had a net book in stock for over twelve months, and have not during that time bought further copies of the title, Clause (ii) of the *Standard Conditions* allows you to offer the book for sale at any price you choose below the net price, *provided that* you first give the publisher the option to buy it back at cost price or at your intended selling price, whichever is the lower.

SECONDHAND BOOKS

Secondhand books, published at a net price, remain subject to the NBA for six months from the date of publication. Thereafter all secondhand books are non-net books, even if new copies continue to be in print at a net price. Effectively this means that the secondhand book trade is outside the scope of the NBA.

NATIONAL BOOK SALE (NBS)

The National Book Sale acts a a safety valve for the NBA, permitting booksellers to unload dead stock at bargain prices. Normally held in January of each year, the Sale is administered by the PA and organised jointly by the BA and the PA. To take part in the Sale, booksellers must apply to the PA for a licence at a fee (in 1988) of £15 plus VAT.

Subsidies are available for local NBS press advertising: 50 per cent of the first £200 spent, plus 25 per cent of the next £300 – a total maximum subsidy of £175 on advertising of £500 or more (1988 rates).

During the Sale, participating booksellers can sell at a discount – which must be not less than 33⅓ per cent off the net price – any net books they have had in stock for over twelve months, *provided that* the publisher has not excluded his titles from the Sale (in which case see *Old stock* above).

The Sale is also an opportunity for publishers to sell off some of their overstocks at bargain prices without permanently de-netting the titles concerned. Any such publishers' overstocks will be offered to booksellers at 50 per cent off the Sale price – the latter being fixed by the publisher at not more than than 50 per cent of the net price. Take an example: a book with a net price of £10 may be put into the Sale at £5 and offered to participating booksellers at £2.50.

Once the Sale is over, all unsold net books which have been in the Sale revert to their net prices, fully subject to the price maintenance rules of the NBA. So the National Book Sale really is an (almost) unrepeatable bargain time for book buyers, and it does much to instil some life into the otherwise rather dull post-Christmas period.

The conditions of the National Book Sale are given in Appendix B.

LIBRARY LICENCE

Any library which allows members of the public access to its collection, and advertises this fact to them – it doesn't have to be a public library in the usual sense – may apply to the PA for listing as a licensed library authorised to buy net books at a discount of up to 10 per cent.

The Library Licence (see Appendix C) is granted to the library, not the bookseller, though it must name the bookseller(s) which the library intends to use. Thus possession of a Library Licence does not allow any bookseller to supply to the library at a discount, but only the bookseller(s) named on the licence. So if you are intending to sell to libraries, make sure they get your name on their licences.

PRIMARY AND SECONDARY SCHOOL BOOKS LICENCE

At the time of writing, a new licence was in preparation. It will work broadly like the Library Licence and will permit the bookseller to supply net books at a discount of up to 10 per cent to licensed primary and secondary schools.

BOOK AGENT'S LICENCE

A book agent is someone running a bookstall in a church or school or some other place where there are bookselling opportunities that an ordinary bookseller is unable to exploit. A Book Agent's Licence (see Appendix D) permits the agent to purchase supplies of net books from a local bookseller at a discount not exceeding half that received by the bookseller from the publisher or wholesaler. The agent undertakes not to sell the books at less than their net published prices.

As with the Library Licence, it is the agent, not the bookseller, who applies for the licence, naming the proposed supplying bookseller(s).

There is a special Book Agent's Licence for Service Unit Libraries, which allows the bookseller to give up to 7½ per cent discount on net books.

QUANTITY BOOK BUYING SCHEME

The Quantity Book Buying Scheme is designed to allow booksellers to supply net books at a discount to an organisation buying in bulk – which can means as few as twelve copies – *provided that* the books are to be distributed as gifts or presentations in connexion with the purchaser's business, or are to be used for philanthropic or propaganda purposes. The books must not be offered for sale by the bookseller's customer. A typical qualifying transaction would be the purchase by a parent–teacher association, with its own funds, of a quantity of books for presentation to the school library.

Licences issued under the Scheme are for one transaction only. It is the bookseller this time who must apply for the licence, specifying the books to be supplied and the purchaser's intended use of those books.

The allowable discounts are precisely laid down: 10 per cent for an order for twelve copies or more of a single title if the total value comes to at least £25; 10 per cent for an assorted order of £750 or more; lesser discounts for smaller assorted orders, down to 5 per cent for orders in the range £250–£349. Assorted orders below £250 don't qualify.

The text of the Quantity Book Buying Scheme is given in Appendix E.

SALES OUTSIDE THE SCOPE OF THE NET BOOK AGREEMENT

The only new book sales which fall outside the scope of the NBA are those of non-net books. But there are two categories of books which look at first sight to contradict this statement: remainders and book club books.

Remainders

When sales of a particular title decline to the point where it ceases to be economical for the publisher to keep it in print, he has to decide how remaining stocks are to be disposed of. The simplest way would be to destroy them, but that would produce no income; and since any income is better than no income, it is preferable for a publisher to accept, say, 10p a copy for a book he has hitherto been selling for £10 a copy, than to get nothing at all for the remaining stock by merely throwing it away. Tail-ends of print runs that publishers sell off as a job lot for the best price they can get are known as *remainders*, and the publishers are said to have *remaindered* the titles concerned. Some of these tail-ends can be pretty long; in the case of a title that has flopped badly it may be almost the entire print run.

Remainders are all non-net – irrespective of whether the title was net or non-net before it was remaindered – and booksellers may sell them for whatever they like.

There are a number of firms which specialise in buying up publishers' remainders in bulk, which they then sell on in smaller quantities to retail bookshops. They are in effect the wholesalers of the remainder trade. Names and addresses of remainder merchants are listed in the BA's *Directory of Book Publishers and Wholesalers*.

Prices of remaindered titles are always low, and the retailer can offer his customers a selection of 'bargain books' at as much as 50 per cent or more off their original published prices. These books can be real bargains, sometimes selling to the retail customer for less than they cost the publisher to produce – and still making the bookseller a profit.

But a word of warning: titles are remaindered because they have stopped selling in sufficient numbers. If it was the original high net price that was deterring customers, the massive price reduction of the remaindered copies may lead to their rapid sale. But if the book failed as a net book because no one was interested in it anyway, it may be that the price reduction, however great, will not sell a single extra copy. A bargain is only a bargain if somebody wants it. Beware of taking remainders indiscriminately into your shop; choose them by reference to the sort of titles you know your customers habitually buy, not by reference to the degree of the price cut.

Book club books

Book club editions are often barely distinguishable from publishers' own trade editions. This is hardly surprising as the book club edition often comes from the same print run as the publisher's edition, and is merely badged on the cover and the title page to identify it as something different. But this is enough for the purposes of the NBA to make the book club edition an entirely different product from the trade edition. Indeed, in certain circumstances (see clause 17 in Appendix F), book clubs are permitted to use the trade edition without modification and sell it as a book club title.

So – though many people think this something of a legal fiction – book clubs do not sell net books at cut prices. The trade editions may be net, but the book club editions are not. Just as a bookshop may have a hardback edition of a given title at £12.95 net and a paperback edition of the same title at £3.95 net, so there can also be a book club edition at, say, £4.50. These three editions can all sell at their own different prices, and the NBA remain unsullied.

The existence of flourishing book clubs selling a very wide range of popular titles below bookshop prices would seem to be a major challenge to the specialist bookshop. Yet in practice it may not always be so. Book club offers are available only to club members, and membership always entails a commitment to buy a certain minimum number of books over a specified period. This means that intending purchasers of one particular book are still obliged to buy the trade edition at the net price in a bookshop, even if it is available more cheaply as a book club edition – unless, of course, they are willing to take on the book club commitment of further purchases.

It is easy to see why publishers like book clubs: instead of the usual business of selling ones and twos to bookshops round the country, the publisher makes a substantial sale to a single trade customer. But what do booksellers think of the clubs? By and large, they have come to accept them, and some believe that publication of a title in a book club edition actually increases bookshop sales of the trade edition. The paradox may be accounted for by the highly professional advertising undertaken by the book clubs – advertising which promotes not merely the services the clubs offer but also the specific titles on their lists. This promotion of titles arouses public interest, some of which leads to book club membership and some of which leads to the local bookshop.

It is worth noting that booksellers who feel a book club edition *would* affect their sales can get advance warning of it. The PA advertises in *The Bookseller* a list of book club editions expected to be on offer four or more months ahead. While there is nothing booksellers can do to prevent publication, they can – if they think it prudent – run down their stocks of the titles and order no more of them. Or if they expect club advertising to *increase* interest in the titles, they can lay in extra stocks.

To ensure what it calls 'the orderly working of the book trade', the PA has a set of *Regulations for Conduct of Book Clubs* (see Appendix F) – the four-month warning mentioned above forms part of them. Clubs which undertake to abide by the Regulations are added to a register maintained by the PA; and PA members are recommended to allow only registered clubs to publish book club editions of their titles.

In addition to the Regulations, which seek to protect the interests of the book trade as a whole, there also exists a *Concordat between Book Clubs* – of which the PA is the custodian – which is designed to encourage fair competition between the clubs themselves.

PRICES OF INDIVIDUAL TITLES

Nothing in the NBA specifies the actual price, in pounds and pence, at which a net book is to be sold. That is the responsibility of the publisher and of the publisher alone. As a bookseller, you have only one option if you think a net book is too highly priced for the market: don't stock it.

AVERAGE PRICES

The Bookseller publishes tables of book prices in February and August of each year, but these merely show the average of published prices of new titles and new editions and take no account of the numbers of copies actually sold.

Books in the Media (see page 29) publishes the average prices of current bestsellers, and you can work out similar averages for yourself using the bestseller lists that are published weekly in the *The Bookseller* and *Publishing News*. Such averages still fail to reflect detailed sales volumes but probably come quite close to the typical prices at which books are currently selling. Among the bestsellers in mid-1988, for example, popular paperbacks averaged about £3.80 and hardbacks about £13.

PUBLIC PERCEPTION OF BOOK PRICES

It is unfortunately the case that the general public – both those who buy books and those who don't – perceive books as expensive. People who don't give a second thought to spending £20 or more per head for a couple of hours in a restaurant may be seen to recoil in horror at the sight of a £10 sticker on a book which would last a lifetime. The unreasonableness of the attitude is so overwhelming that it cries out for correction. The single most important message which the book trade needs to convey to the public is that *books are remarkably good value for money*. But the contrary view is so deeply held that it would require the skills of the most gifted advertising agency over a lengthy period even to begin to change it. Those skills don't come cheap. The rewards of success, however, would be substantial for everyone in the trade.

But this is to digress into thoughts of *generic advertising* – ie advertising undertaken on behalf of the trade as a whole, designed to encourage book buying in general, rather than the buying of any particular book from any particular bookseller. It's one of those topics permanently on the book trade's agenda, which – so far – has never got further than pious resolution. We've seen generic advertising in other trades, and we all still remember the slogans: *Go to work on an egg, Say it with flowers, Drinka pinta milka day.* Books can't be *that* different. But if it's to be done, it must be done *massively*. Individual or sectional efforts, however well-meaning, are unlikely to get anywhere.

Meanwhile, back in the bookshop . . .

Even though you can do nothing about it, you should have some understanding of the general principles of book pricing from the publisher's point of view, if only to enable you to explain to occasionally resentful customers why books cost what they do and why there is sometimes such a large price difference between seemingly similar books.

People complaining about the high price of a book typically go through the motion of weighing it in their hands, as if they bought books, like potatoes, by the pound; then they look to see how many pages it has, and comment on whether it has a hard cover or not. It would be an exaggeration to say that these characteristics have no bearing upon a book's price, but it wouldn't be much of an exaggeration.

HOW THE PUBLISHER PRICES A BOOK

In deciding the net selling price, the publisher takes account of many factors – author's royalties, possible sale of rights, distribution costs, trade discounts, expected life of title and so on. But the single factor which most usually concerns the publisher in his early calculations is the print run. The *print run* is the number of copies the publisher gets printed, based upon a hopefully inspired guess of the number of copies likely to sell over a reasonable period.

Notice that none of these price-influencing factors in any way affects the size or appearance of the individual copy of the book in the bookshop.

Production costs

Publishers' production costs are a mixture of origination costs and running costs. *Origination costs* cover all the expenses the publisher incurs to get the book ready for printing; *running costs* are the costs of printing and binding, both the labour charges and the cost of the materials used.

Suppose a publisher spends £5,000 on the origination of a

book – a sum which covers advance royalties, editorial salaries, artists' and designers' fees, typesetting costs, general overheads, and so on – and suppose that the printers/binders quote £3,000 for producing the first 1,000 copies, and £2,000 for each further 1,000 copies printed at the same time (the latter known as *run-on costs*). You can see from Table 6 how the publisher's unit cost is decisively affected by the number of copies printed, and the effect is most marked at the short print run end. In the example given, it costs the publisher £8 a copy to print 1,000 copies, but only £4 a copy to print 3,000 copies.

Two titles compared

Suppose that two different publishers produce two different books, one of them a rose growing handbook, and the other a statistical survey of the flea population of Outer Scratchiphobia. As manufactured objects the books look very similar – same size, same number of pages, same weight, same quality of paper, and so on – and no one can tell from the inspection of the books in the bookshop that the rose book publisher has printed 50,000 copies while the flea book publisher has printed only 2,000.

If the Table 6 figures applied to both publishers, as well they might, the unit production cost of the rose book would be £2.12, while that of the flea book would be £5. Some publishers use a rule-of-thumb multiplier – typically about 5½ – to convert unit cost to cover price. On this basis, the rose publisher would consider a net price in the region of 5½ × £2.12 = £11.66, while the flea publisher would go for 5½ × £5 = £27.50. The point is that the publisher has to build into the net price not only his production costs and target profit, but also the bookseller's discount of about 35 per cent, the author's royalty of about 10 per cent and an allowance of, say, 15 per cent for advertising, marketing, distribution and so on.

In the event, let's say that the rose publisher decides on a selling price of £10.95, while the flea publisher opts for £25. Both publishers need to sell about half the print run to avoid losing money. The lower priced book only moves into profit when 24,200 copies have been sold; the higher priced book moves into profit after the sale of only 1,000 copies.

It must be admitted that the above account distorts the detail of the problem for the sake of simplicity. Often enough, the whole calculation goes through the mincer again when the people in the publisher's sales department categorically assert that the market just wouldn't bear the proposed price. But if the acceptable price for the market is too far below the economic price for the publisher,

TABLE 6

BOOK PRODUCTION COSTS FOR DIFFERENT PRINT RUNS

Number of copies printed	*Origination cost: £*	*Running cost: £*	*Total cost: £*	*Unit cost*
1,000	5,000	3,000	8,000	£8.00
2,000	5,000	5,000	10,000	£5.00
3,000	5,000	7,000	12,000	£4.00
4,000	5,000	9,000	14,000	£3,50
5,000	5,000	11,000	16,000	£3.20
10,000	5,000	21,000	26,000	£2.60
20,000	5,000	41,000	46,000	£2.30
30,000	5,000	61,000	66,000	£2.20
40,000	5,000	81,000	86,000	£2.15
50,000	5,000	101,000	106,000	£2.12
100,000	5,000	201,000	206,000	£2.06

the book doesn't – or shouldn't (but publishers are funny people) – get published anyway. For those that do get published, the major determinant of most net prices is still the print run.

So when you see the flea fancier in your shop, incredulously weighing the book in his hand, checking the number of pages, and demanding to know why it costs more than twice as much as the rose book which in all but content it so much resembles, you can offer him a reasoned explanation. He probably won't believe you.

Chapter 4

The Booksellers Association

The Booksellers Association of Great Britain and Ireland is usually referred to more briefly as the Booksellers Association or more briefly still as the BA. Virtually all specialist booksellers are in membership, and many non-specialists too. The BA had approximately 3,300 corporate members in mid-1988, the number not having altered greatly in recent years. About 180 withdraw each year, and a similar number join. Note that it is the book*shop* rather than the book*seller* that is in membership. The 374 W.H. Smith shops, for example, account for over 10 per cent of the membership. The BA also has a number of *individual* members (about 170 in mid-1988); these are bookshop employees with at least three years' experience and a Certificate in Bookselling Skills (see page 89) or previous qualification.

A booklet called *Working for Booksellers* describes the Association's services and activities, and may be obtained free of charge from the BA.

ROLE OF THE BOOKSELLERS ASSOCIATION

The BA seeks to promote and protect the interests of its members both collectively and individually.

At the collective level, the BA speaks for the bookselling trade in dealings with publishers, book trade associations at home and abroad, other trade organisations, the government, the press and the public. Its primary object is the maintenance of bookselling as a profitable activity.

At the individual level, it provides services to help members operate more efficiently, more professionally, more economically and in the end more profitably – which comes back to the primary object again.

Inevitably, individual members tend to be more keenly aware of the services that produce measurable effects on a day-to-day basis in their own shops – Book Tokens, the Christmas Catalogue, the provision of in-shop promotional material, etc – than on those collective matters which are arguably the major work of the Association and which affect the very environment in which booksellers work. Putting the bookseller's case when, for example, new laws or regulations are being hatched in Westminster or Brussels on such matters as Sunday trading, obscenity, VAT, price maintenance on books, copyright, data protection, and so on – in such forums and on such matters, BA officers and executive staff devote much of their energies. Ironically, success in such work is often invisible. If, as a result of the BA's efforts, new burdens are not put upon the trade, nothing changes, nothing happens. And booksellers go about their daily affairs, perhaps not entirely unaware of what has been achieved but perhaps not quite as aware as they might be.

JOINING THE BA

A bookseller is under no obligation to join the BA. You can trade in new books whether you are a member or not, though it is difficult to conceive of a specialist bookseller who could seriously consider *not* applying for membership of the key trade association, and forgoing the various advantages it offers.

QUALIFYING FOR MEMBERSHIP

Applications for membership are considered by the Finance and General Purposes Committee, which meets ten times a year – every month except August and December – and advises the Council (see below) on admissions. Application forms are available from the Membership Manager.

To qualify for membership, applicants must already be committed to trading as booksellers, and this commitment must be more than a mere declaration of intent. You need not already have opened your shop but you must at least have secured bookshop premises.

Only after your application has been approved and you have paid your first annual subscription can you apply to take part in the Book Tokens scheme (see page 92) and the Booksellers Clearing House (see page 93). These things take time, exactly how long depending in part on when your application is received at the BA in relation to the date of the next Committee meeting. So get your application in as soon as you fulfil the minimum requirements. Otherwise you risk finding yourself ready to start trading but unable, for example, to deal in Book Tokens.

Bookshop premises

Your bookshop must be rated for business purposes by the local authority; a business run from a private house will not be considered. The shop floor area must be not less than 100 sq ft, and there must be a window display not less than 4 ft wide. Only intending wholesalers, library suppliers, school suppliers, book departments in department stores and booksellers operating exclusively by mail are exempt from these space and display requirements. Your shop must be open to the general public throughout the year during normal business hours.

As part of the vetting procedure, a local BA representative may call to inspect the premises and then submit a confidential report to the Committee.

Stock

The value of your stock of new books at published prices must not be less than £3,000. You will be asked for details of other stock – secondhand books, non-book items and so on – but it is the value of the new book stock alone which counts.

Undertakings

You have to undertake to observe the *Standard Conditions of Sale of Net Books* (see Appendix A) and to maintain adequate trade reference material and bibliographies.

Fees

Your completed application form must be accompanied by a fee of £21.75, returnable if the application fails. If it succeeds, you then have to pay your first annual subscription: this is calculated at 0.0575 per cent of your expected annual new book turnover, with a minimum of £50 a year if the figure is less than £86,950, and a maximum of £400 if it is more than £696,000. VAT must be added to all the fees quoted, which were those in force in 1988.

THE BA'S CONSTITUTION

The ruling body of the Association is the Council, and its chief officer is the President. Officers and other members are elected to the Council at the Association's annual conference – except the branch representatives, whose earlier election by ballot is reported to the Conference. The President, Officers and Council are assisted in their work by a permanent secretariat of salaried executive staff.

COUNCIL

The President, who may hold office for two successive years, is Chairman of the Council and ex officio member of all its committees. The other Officers of the Association who serve on the Council are the Vice President (who normally succeeds to the Presidency), Honorary Treasurer, Immediate Past President (for one year only) and the Director, who is the permanent head of the secretariat. The rest of the Council consists of six general members (each serving for three years), fifteen branch representatives, the Chairman of the Charter Group (see page 83), and up to two members co-opted by the Council at its discretion.

Only the Director and the co-opted members are unelected.

SECRETARIAT

The executive staff is headed by the Director, the only member of the secretariat who is also an Officer of the Association and a member of Council. Other senior staff are the Assistant Director, Accounts Manager, Marketing Executive, Meetings Executive, Membership Manager, Publications/Exhibition Co-ordinator, Trade Practice Executive and Training Officer.

CONFERENCE

The Conference is the Annual General Meeting of the BA. Its constitutional function is to allow a report of the Association's work over the past year, together with financial statements, to be presented to the membership; to elect Officers and general members of the Council; to confirm appointments by the Council of representatives to joint committees and outside bodies; and to consider motions submitted by the Council, branches or members.

Held in the spring at a different venue each year, the Conference typically runs from Wednesday evening to Sunday morning and includes much else besides the main constitutional business.

The Trade Exhibition and other events

Among the major events of the Conference is the Trade Exhibition, normally held on the Saturday, where publishers and service providers to the trade – wholesalers, shopfitters, manufacturers of computer and security systems, and so on – display their wares and promote their services. Additionally, there are business meetings and presentations on different topics, meet-the-author receptions and a number of social functions culminating in a dinner and dance on the Saturday evening. Perhaps most valuable of all for practising booksellers, who necessarily spend so much time in their own shops, is the chance to meet colleagues, exchange ideas, and make new trade contacts.

Members may attend the Conference on payment of a registration fee (£55 plus VAT in 1988). The Saturday dinner and dance is an extra (£25.50 plus VAT per person in 1988). And of course there is the further expense of hotel accommodation over the four days. However, those wishing to attend just the AGM and/or Trade Exhibition may do so free of charge provided they are employed in businesses in membership of the BA.

BRANCHES

The geographical spread of the BA membership may be seen from Table 4 on page 43 which shows the number of members in each of the regional branches. The large London branch, by the way, has a catchment area extending as far as Kent, Surrey and Hertfordshire.

Branches hold their own meetings – some business, some social – at varying intervals. Some branches run training programmes, others hold seminars on subjects of trade interest, most from time to time bring in outside speakers – authors, publishers and others who provide booksellers with a new perspective on familiar matters.

On joining the BA you automatically become a member of the branch in whose region your shop is situated. Do try to get to branch meetings. It is all too easy to convince yourself that such time as you have to spare on trade matters should be directed inwards to your own affairs rather than occasionally directed outwards to talk to colleagues grappling with similar problems. The advantages that accrue from making contact with others in the trade are unquantifiable but real.

GROUPS

Within the BA there are a number of special-interest groups which hold their own meetings and elect their own officers and executive committees. These groups bring together booksellers with interests not shared by the membership at large, though the groups sometimes confront problems in an acute form which either actually or potentially concern the trade as a whole, and their deliberations are often therefore of wider interest to the BA membership.

Except for the Charter Group, which accepts new members only

TABLE 7 Source: BA membership records mid-1988

BA GROUP MEMBERSHIP *Corporate membership 3260*

(a) alphabetical order		*(b) numerical order*	
446	Charter	446	Charter
162	Children's	238	Religious
98	College & University	162	Children's
45	Export	105	Library Suppliers
105	Library Suppliers	104	School Suppliers
238	Religious	98	College & University
104	School Suppliers	45	Export
25	Wholesalers	25	Wholesalers

after an assessment of their suitability, the groups are open to any BA member wishing to join and paying the group annual subscription. In 1988, this was £15 for each of the groups except the Charter Group, which is funded by a levy of £7 per head of staff employed in the member bookshop and an application fee of £25. All figures quoted are subject to VAT.

Group membership numbers at mid-1988 are shown in the Table above.

CHARTER GROUP

The Charter Group is dedicated to excellence is bookselling. Members must conform to certain minimum standards in such matters as staff training, book display, maintenance of trade reference material, stockholding, service to the customer and so on. They are required to make an annual, confidential, return of their trading results – together with details of rent, rates, staff wages and all other overhead or variable costs – and these provide the raw material for the annual *Charter Group Economic Survey* which is a valuable statistical resource for all existing and intending bookshop owners and managers. We shall be considering the Survey in some detail in Chapter 6.

Enhanced discounts

Some publishers offer better terms to Charter Group members than to other booksellers. The differential may amount to 2½ per cent or more – a welcome boost to the typically tight finances of a bookshop – and it is probably this more than anything that makes booksellers, large and small, anxious to be admitted into membership.

FIGURE 2

CHARTER GROUP LOGO

The Booksellers Association of
Great Britain and Ireland
CHARTER
BOOKSELLER
★ ★ ★ ★ ★

Critics

The Charter Group, however, is not without its critics. There are some who argue that the public is scarcely aware of the existence of this professional elite. Ask typical book buyers if they are impressed with the standards of the Charter Booksellers, and you're likely to get a shopful of blank looks. The Group has its own logo (see Figure 2) and many feel there is an unexploited opportunity for the membership to promote themselves to the public as Something Special.

Others are unhappy that some of the Group's criteria for membership may depress rather than raise standards of professionalism. Clearly, for example, a good bookshop needs a good stock. But how do you define a good stock without getting into endless debate? The Charter Group, for the purpose of membership qualification, chooses a monetary value as its definition. In 1987/88 Charter bookshops were required to have a minimum new book stock of not less than £30,000 at retail prices. One of the most important of a bookseller's skills, however, lies in the control of stock levels. A large stock of books that the customers don't actually want to buy can hardly be considered better than a smaller one which sells like hot cakes. A bookseller who achieves a turnover of £100,000 a year for a stock investment of £25,000 is using financial resources to better effect than another who achieves only £90,000 a year from a stock investment of £30,000. The former plainly has the better stockturn (see page 103), but it is the latter who at present qualifies for Charter membership.

The critics of the critics, however, point out that the bookseller with the poorer stockturn may well be offering a splendid stock range and an excellent service – and aren't *these* what good bookselling is all about? The high-stockturn bookseller, by contrast, may be no more than a conveyor belt, shifting current bestsellers from publisher to public, with little in the way of customer service at all.

So has the Charter Group got it right or not? Are absolute stock values a better indicator of bookshop quality than stockturn? Or is the reverse true? Or is there an objective way of judging bookshop quality in non-monetary terms? In due course, you will form your own opinions on these and other contentious issues in the trade, and may even be instrumental in moving the argument decisively in one direction or the other.

CHILDREN'S BOOKSELLING GROUP

In addition to the speciality children's bookshops, many bookshops find room for a sizable children's section within the general stock. Children's booksellers tend to be passionately concerned that children should be introduced to the joys of reading, browsing and buying at as early an age as possible. A vigorous book trade tomorrow depends upon the establishment of a love of books among children today.

The Children's Bookselling Group liaises closely with other bodies like the Children's Book Foundation (see page 58) to promote the welfare of this vital section of the trade.

COLLEGE AND UNIVERSITY BOOKSELLERS GROUP (CUBS)

This group looks after the interests of members serving a market which is both easy to define and easy to locate. Selling to the market, unfortunately, can sometimes be a bit of a problem, especially in times when education budgets are cut back. Other headaches include direct selling by publishers (see page 54) and the concentration of business at the start of the academic year in the autumn. These and other relevant matters are addressed by CUBS, which you should certainly consider joining if you intend to sell to this market on any scale. CUBS holds its own annual working conference in addition to meetings and seminars throughout the year.

EXPORT BOOKSELLERS GROUP

It is easy enough to pack the odd book for mailing overseas, but booksellers who specialise in exporting in quantity share the problems of exporters in all trades – daunting paperwork, complex carriage procedures, currency fluctuations, credit control – quite apart from the matter of finding customers. The Export Booksellers Group encourages members to share ideas and look for solutions to common problems. It maintains close contact with the British Council (see page 56), which alerts the Group to specific opportunities abroad.

LIBRARY BOOKSELLERS GROUP

There are two sorts of library booksellers: (1) bookshops which in addition to their main over-the-counter business with the general public also supply books to their local libraries; and (2) booksellers – normally referred to as *library suppliers* – who operate nationally and who do nothing other than supply to libraries, an activity which traditionally includes not just obtaining the books but also servicing them before delivery (see page 68).

There is bound to be some conflict of interest between the two types of library booksellers, but over the years they have managed to co-exist fairly happily: the national suppliers often being used by the libraries for bulk orders placed well ahead, and the local bookshop being used for urgently needed items or books that the librarian wants to examine in the shop before purchase. Some library authorities order a percentage of their requirements from local booksellers as a matter of policy, seeing this as a way of helping to ensure the survival of an important amenity for the local community: a good bookshop.

The real threat to library booksellers of all kinds comes from publishers' direct selling to the library authorities, and, prospectively, from the expansion of the activities of the DPOs – see *The DPO problem* below.

RELIGIOUS BOOKSELLERS GROUP

The crucial role of the NBA was examined in detail in the last chapter. Here it need only be noted that religious booksellers find themselves surprisingly in the front line of the battle against the cut-price sellers. The situation arises because some outlets for religious books are more committed to spreading the Word than to running viable businesses. Furthermore, many use voluntary helpers and operate out of non-commercial premises and so do not have a normal bookseller's overheads. Quite a few are either indifferent to, or ignorant of, the NBA and its significance to the trade; and the fact that so many religious books are indeed non-net

– the Authorised Version of the bible, for example – also contributes to the confusion. The upshot of it all is that the livelihood of religious booksellers trying to run specialist bookshops on a commercial basis is seriously under threat.

The key role in this is played by the publishers and wholesalers. It is because some of them are willing to supply direct to non-trading bodies, or to turn a blind eye when the NBA is flouted, that the survival of the traditional religious bookseller is jeopardised. The Religious Booksellers Group seeks to protect its members' interests by trying to thrash these problems out with individual publishers, wholesalers, the PA, the Christian Booksellers Association and others.

SCHOOL SUPPLIERS GROUP

School supply consists of sets of text books for class use and single copies of ordinary trade books for school libraries. Like the Library Booksellers Group, the School Suppliers Group comprises both local bookshops, who do a certain amount of school supply along with their main over-the-counter business, and specialist school suppliers who operate nationally from warehouse premises. And once again, the main conflict is not between the different types of bookseller but between the booksellers on the one hand and publishers who bypass them on the other.

The DPO problem

The key problem is not publishers' direct supply to individual schools, but their supply to a number of Direct Purchasing Organisations (DPOs). The DPOs are consortia of local education authorities which buy school books at a discount direct from the publishers and distribute them at discounted prices to the schools they service. This means that the bookseller doesn't get a look-in. It also means that the ultimate purchasers – the schools – are not paying the full retail prices for their books. And insofar as those books are net books – as some of them are, particularly those destined for school libraries – this seems to fly straight in the face of the NBA, though it has been ruled that technically it does not.

DPOs feel they're doing well by their local rate-payers, while booksellers complain that their livelihood is being poached by non-trading organisations. Meanwhile, some DPOs have started thinking 'If school books, why not library books?', and both the School Suppliers Group and the Library Booksellers Group look to have a long-running problem on their hands.

The PA's proposed Primary and Secondary School Books Licence (see page 70) is intended to help school suppliers compete with the DPOs on more equal terms by permitting, on specified conditions, the sale of net books to licensed schools at discounts of up to 10 per cent. Whether more equal is equal enough remains to be seen. There has to be a limit to the amount of gross profit a bookseller can give away in order to win or maintain business.

WHOLESALERS GROUP

As you would expect, this is a group for wholesalers only and therefore not of direct interest to readers of the present guide, whose concern is only that wholesalers should flourish and maintain their high standards.

BA SERVICES

It has already been noted that the BA has a dual role: to represent the membership collectively and to help members individually. At bottom, the distinction is illusory because anything that benefits the membership as a whole necessarily benefits each individual member. But the personal impact of those activities which promote the trade's collective welfare is less obvious, though not less important, than those directly and immediately affecting the individual bookseller. If you are new to bookselling you are understandably more concerned with your own immediate welfare than with the welfare of the trade. Your first objective must be to get your business up and running successfully, and the rest of this chapter looks at the range of services the BA makes available to you as an individual bookseller.

TRAINING

The BA runs a number of training courses. Most are one-day courses, some last up to a week. Fees in 1987/88 ranged from £45 to £385 plus VAT. Courses are held at different locations round the country – Birmingham, Bristol, Glasgow, London and Manchester. The one-day courses particularly are often repeated on different dates at different locations. Among the subjects offered in the 1987/88 programme were Buying Skills, Marketing for the Bookseller, Display, Merchandising, Customer Relations, Security, Time Management, Bookselling Practice, Introduction to Management, and Financial Control for Managers.

The BA's Training Department can also advise on in-house training and the availability of training grants for bookshop staff.

Certificate in Bookselling Skills (CIBS)

The Certificate in Bookselling Skills is awarded by the BA to booksellers who have successfully completed a course consisting of a number of manuals which students work on at their own pace and, largely, in their own time. The course is intended for bookshop employees rather than owners, and it covers a number of general retailing skills in addition to specifically bookselling ones. It divides into two Levels, both of which must be taken by students seeking the CIBS qualification.

Students are supervised and helped in their work by a member of staff in their own bookshop who acts as trainer. Additionally, each student has an external tutor who provides help and advice, and who marks the written assignments which form part of the course work. The complete course costs £170 plus VAT (in 1988), and consists of a Study Guide, Audio Tape, Trainer's Guide, Induction Guide, Level 1 Manual, two Level 2 Manuals and a Glossary of book trade terminology. Those not seeking the formal qualification can buy the training manuals separately (1988 prices: £60 for Level 1, £110 for Level 2).

The study units which make up the CIBS manuals are graded in detail and difficulty. *Induction* topics are job description, terms and conditions of employment, company information and emergency procedures. *Level 1* includes dealing with customers, money procedures, premises, stock and bibliography. *Level 2* covers bookselling and retailing skills, stock knowledge, book evaluation, marketing, shop layout and display, book trade practice, basic finance and staff supervision.

Further details of CIBS are available from the BA's Training Department.

MARKETING

The BA's Marketing Department aims to develop a more professional attitude to marketing among the BA membership. It liaises with other bodies such as the PA's Book Marketing Council and Book Trust to ensure that campaigns, research etc are as effective as possible from the bookseller's point of view. It provides advice and support to help booksellers compete more effectively for their share of consumer expenditure in the high street.

Promotional and marketing aids

The BA produces a number of aids to promote books and bookshop services. In addition to those described below, there are high density bags in two sizes, bearing the slogan *Welcome to Your Bookshop*, and polystands – stands to hold a single title displayed either face out or open. The bags are supplied in multiples of 2,000 (minimum order 4,000); the polystands may be bought singly (minimum order 5). The major promotional aid from the BA is undoubtedly the Christmas Catalogue.

Books for Giving: the Christmas Catalogue

Published by the BA in October of each year, *Books for Giving* is a colourful catalogue of 200 or so books from a variety of publishers, the titles being chosen by a panel of experienced book buyers drawn from the BA membership.

Something between three and four million copies of the Catalogue are printed, and booksellers can buy them for £45 a thousand (1988 price). At no extra cost, the BA will overprint the Catalogue with your shop's name and address and any other advertising you wish – possibly further titles of purely local interest, details of your shop's various services and so on. All this for a fraction of the cost and none of the effort it would take to produce a comparable catalogue for yourself.

You can exploit *Books for Giving* in a variety of ways: give it away in your shop, pop it into the bag with customers' purchases, do a door-to-door distribution in your catchment area – have it delivered, for example, with the local free paper or, if you have mail order customers, direct mail it to your list.

To encourage wide distribution, Book Tokens Ltd (see page 92) refunds (in 1988) the lesser of 50 per cent or £100 of a bookseller's costs for door-to-door distribution. This is an excellent way of reaching people who might never have been into your shop before, and so helps to boost sales not only over the current Christmas period but over the indefinite future during which customers secured now may stay with you for life.

The merits of the Christmas Catalogue are the professionalism of its production and marketing – the BA Marketing Executive undertakes a major promotional effort in the media for a month in the run-up to Christmas – and its concentration upon a limited number of key titles of broad appeal. There are wholesalers who make a point of holding all Catalogue titles in stock so if you use the Catalogue you don't risk landing yourself with horrendous ordering problems. Even if you decide not to stock all Catalogue titles yourself, you will know how to get them quickly and painlessly if customers require them.

BUYER'S GUIDES

The Buyer's Guides, published in the spring, summer and autumn, are intended to help booksellers evaluate the season's crop of new books. They list recommended titles, selected by the same booksellers who compile the Christmas Catalogue. Separate lists cover paperbacks, general books and children's books. Titles are listed alphabetically by publisher, and within the publisher listing alphabetically by author. Brief notes are appended, but the main evaluation is shown by symbols – eg an asterisk means the book is expected to be a bestseller, S means it's worth stocking, *DH* means it's a dark horse. Of course, no one can relieve you of making your own decisions in your own shop, but these Buyer's Guides do draw your attention to titles worth your consideration. The price of the Guides is under review at the time of writing.

SERVICES PROMOTION KIT

The Services Promotion Kit (£4 plus VAT in 1988) consists of two A2 posters in green and black, plus self-adhesive strips in red and white detailing various bookshop services. Choose the strips which name the services you wish to promote and add them to the poster – *We sell and exchange Book Tokens, We accept credit cards, We can provide books for exhibitions & special events, We will order books not in stock for you.* There are fourteen different bookshop services to choose from.

CROWNER KIT

Each Crowner Kit comprises ten different, professionally designed, crowners – show cards – printed in green, black and yellow on tough card, laminated to survive repeated used. The messages, with simple illustrations, include *Book of the month, Signed copies, Just published, Local author* etc. BA Crowner Kits cost £4.50 plus VAT; individual crowners may be ordered at 45p each plus VAT, provided a minimum of five are ordered at a time (1988 prices).

PROMOTIONAL CALENDAR

The Promotional Calendar is designed to help forward planning. It highlights trade events like Children's Book Week or the Whitbread Awards, and non-trade events like the Chelsea Flower Show or the Wimbledon fortnight, all of which may be used as pegs upon which to hang particular book promotions in your own shop. The price of the Calendar is under review at the time of writing.

BOOK TOKENS

Book Tokens are big business. Sales in the financial year 1987/88 exceeded £11 million. The scheme is run by Book Tokens Ltd, a company wholly owned by the BA, and only BA members are eligible to take part in it. A Book Token sold in any bookshop may be exchanged for books up to the Token's face value at any other bookshop in the scheme. In the Irish Republic, Book Tokens denominated in Irish punts are sold and exchanged, though sterling Tokens are also dealt in. In the United Kingdom, only sterling Tokens are sold and exchanged. There is no time limit on a Token's validity.

The basics of the scheme are simple. The customer chooses a Book Token card (at a VAT-inclusive price of 15p in 1988) from a range of about 40 designs, and the bookseller sticks Token stamps on the card to whatever value the customer requires, rubber-stamping the card with the shop's name. Token stamps are available in denominations of 50p, £1, £2, £5, £10 and £20. So the cost of the complete Book Token to the customer is the value of the stamp(s) plus 15p.

The cards themselves cost the bookseller the same 15p charged to the customer, so no profit there. The profit comes from the stamps themselves and the additional book sales they generate. You retain 12½ per cent of the value of the stamps you sell, and remit the remaining 87½ per cent to Book Tokens Ltd. When you take Tokens in exchange for books, the Company pays you 87½ per cent of the value of the stamps on the card. Accounting for Book Token transactions takes place once a quarter when the value of stamps sold is set against the value of stamps exchanged. If you sell more than you exchange, you owe the Company money, and if you exchange more than you sell, the Company owes you money.

The pros and cons of Book Tokens

Many people wishing to give a book as a present either cannot find a suitable book or are uncertain what sort of book would be most welcome. The Book Token is an ideal way of dealing with the problem, and it is no surprise that about 45 per cent of Book Token sales take place over the Christmas period.

Of course, it is always preferable to sell a book, but it is better to sell a Token than to sell nothing. And while you would always prefer to sell a book for cash, it is better to sell it in exchange for a Token than not to sell it at all.

The apparent disadvantage of Book Tokens is that the profit has to be shared between two booksellers. When you sell a book off your shelves for cash, a typical 35 per cent of the net price is your gross profit (see page 101). But if you accept a Book Token in exchange for a book, you end up with a gross profit of only 22½ per cent – the other 12½ per cent going to the seller of the Token – and if you are the seller of the Token, then yours is the seemingly paltry 12½ per cent.

But these figures are much better than they seem. First, Token sales are rarely alternatives to cash sales, but additional to them. If you declined the Token business you wouldn't take extra cash, you'd take nothing at all. Second, provided you can supply Book Tokens Ltd with suitable credit references, you pay nothing for your stamps until you have sold them; you have no capital tied up in stock and therefore no stock risk. The 12½ per cent of Token sales that represents your profit is in fact an *infinite* return on your nil investment. Third, because you only account to the Company quarterly, the proceeds of stamp sales go to enhance your cash flow for up to three months – all of it interest-free. Fourth, customers exchanging Tokens frequently select books above the Token value and pay the difference in cash. Fifth, Book Token holders are captive book buyers: they can't go next door and buy a box of chocolates instead. What's more, some of them may not have been into your shop before – or possibly into any bookshop before – so you're offered a chance to win a customer who might come back in the future and buy books off your shelves for cash.

Notice, by the way, that the Book Token seller's 12½ per cent and the Book Token exchanger's 87½ per cent add up to 100 per cent. There's no rake-off for anyone else – no administrative costs, no membership fees, no annual subscriptions. Furthermore, there is a comprehensive range of point-of-sale promotional aids available free of charge from the Company, and these can help boost your Token sales without losing you any book sales. The scheme is not only self-financing – largely because about 2½ per cent of Tokens sold are never presented for exchange – but it also produces a healthy surplus which the Company invests and uses to support the book world through such organisations as the BA itself, Book Trust and the Book Trade Benevolent Society. The latter is a charity which assists booksellers and publishers in financial need who at some time have worked in the trade for at least a year.

BOOKSELLERS CLEARING HOUSE (BCH)

The Booksellers Clearing House enables booksellers to pay most of their monthly bills to publishers and others by a single cheque. BCH is administered by Book Tokens Ltd, and BA members using the service receive a printed list every month of publishers and other suppliers who have agreed to have their bills settled via the Clearing House.

All you have to do is is to write beside any given supplier's name the amount you wish to pay, and send the completed list, together with suppliers' statements and a single cheque, payable to BCH, to cover the grand total. BCH collates the statements and payments of all the booksellers' returns, and forwards a single cheque to each of the suppliers for the grand total due to them.

Though not all accounts can be settled in this way, most of the major ones can be. BCH makes no charge for the service, the scheme being financed from the interest earned on booksellers' money in the short interval between its receipt at BCH and its distribution to suppliers.

BCH saves both time and money. No matter how many accounts you settle, you need put only one cheque into one envelope bearing a single postage stamp. Even with only two accounts to settle, you still save something.

The one snag with BCH is that it closes for booksellers' payments on the 21st of the month. That means that you pay a few days earlier than you might otherwise do, to the slight detriment of your cash position, though only in the case of a very large single bill is it likely to be worth excluding it from your BCH account and paying it direct to the supplier at the later date.

Early Bird Draw

As an incentive to use the service, all error-free BCH returns received by the 20th of the month go into a monthly draw, and the first names out of the hat win £50, £20 and £10 respectively. It all helps.

BOOKSELLERS ASSOCIATION SERVICE HOUSE (BASH)

Booksellers Association Service House Ltd, a company wholly owned by the BA, is responsible for the BA's trading activities – mainly the sale of books, stationery and promotional aids.

PUBLICATIONS

In addition to its journal *Bookselling News* (see page 39), the BA publishes a number of books, booklets and leaflets of trade interest, and stocks and sells selected titles published by the PA and others. Ask for a complete list of currently available titles and their prices. There are three annual titles of particular interest: two directories, described below, and the *Charter Group Economic Survey*, discussed in Chapter 6.

Directory of Members

PRICE £15 IN 1988

(Corporate BA members are entitled to one complimentary copy)

This lists in alphabetical order of towns all BA corporate members, giving such details as shop name, address, telephone number, SAN (see page 97), manager's name, BA branch and group membership, subject specialisation, special services provided, nature of non-book stock if any. The entries are also indexed under shop names.

Other information in the Directory includes a list of BA officers and senior staff; directors of wholly-owned BA companies; a list of useful trade addresses; names, addresses etc of the head offices of bookselling chains. There is also a preface which provides interesting statistical information on branch membership, group membership, subject specialisation, non-book stock and services provided.

While the *Directory of Members* is plainly of use to publishers and other trade suppliers – providing a convenient listing of their actual or potential customers – its value to prospective bookshop owners should not be overlooked. Here in a single volume you effectively have a profile of the trade as a whole – services offered, subject specialities, etc – and also individual town profiles which, prima facie, can suggest where new bookshop ventures may or may not be worth considering. Add to this the detail of particular shops which you might like to visit and whose owners you may perhaps care to approach, and you have a useful research tool.

Directory of Book Publishers and Wholesalers

PRICE £27.50 IN 1988

(£20 to BA members)

In addition to basic name and address information, the Directory includes in each entry such information as the publisher's ISBN prefix, VAT registration number, personnel of special interest to booksellers, types of books published, imprints, trade terms and procedures to be followed with imperfect copies and returns.

An *imprint*, by the way, is the 'brand' name under which different titles are published. It may just be the publisher's name, though more usually it refers to a name that distinguishes a particular set of titles in a given publisher's output – eg Corgi Books is an imprint of Transworld Publishers Ltd. Quite a number of imprints are simply the names of former independent publishing houses which have been swallowed up by larger ones. An *imperfect copy* is a book with an individual production defect – eg transposed or blank pages – while a *return* is any book that a bookseller wishes to send back to the supplier for whatever reason – eg received damaged, wrong title supplied, dead stock, etc.

Undoubtedly, the most interesting data in the Directory for most booksellers are suppliers' trade terms. Most entries include the supplier's basic trade terms and also any special terms which relate to order size or value or to the individual bookseller – as already noted, for example, some publishers offer Charter Booksellers enhanced terms. Although a few suppliers remain unhelpfully coy about publishing their terms, most now do so. Bear in mind, however, that suppliers' terms are in no way regulated by the NBA or anything else; in the end, terms are a matter for negotiation between the supplier and yourself. Don't hesitate to try to negotiate better terms if you are placing a substantial and continuing amount of business with any particular publisher or wholesaler. Sound out the rep about this (see page 197) or pick up the phone and talk to the sales manager – you'll find his or her name in the Directory.

While the bulk of the Directory is the alphabetical list of publishers – about 4,000 of them – the separate list of some 90 or so wholesalers is at least as important to most booksellers. The wholesaler section gives similar information to the publisher section, and additionally indicates the number of hardback and paperback titles stocked, publishers represented and whether complete lists or selected titles only, non-book products stocked, minimum order requirements and regions of the country served. Wholesalers are also indexed by county.

Two further listings in the Directory are useful trade addresses, and a name-and-address list of about 25 dealers in remainders (see page 71).

STATIONERY

The BA produces a number of standard trade stationery items, most of it for communicating with publishers. The advantages of standard stationery are that its headings prompt you for everything that needs to be included, and on successive forms you can be sure that similar data is similarly located, which is useful when you are checking through a batch of forms for a particular item under a particular heading; the forms look professional; publishers, large and small, instantly recognise them and are more likely to assume you to be a bona fide bookseller even if they've never heard of you before – this can sometimes make the difference between having your orders processed without question or having them delayed for vetting.

The one disadvantage of standard stationery is price. A thousand standard A5 order forms, for example, cost £62.11 plus VAT in 1988, whereas ordinary office duplicate books, with a similar number of blank sets, can be bought from a local stationer for a quarter of the price or less. Of course, you'll need to rubber stamp your name and address on the blank sets, but you'll be getting a rubber stamp anyway for a variety of purposes so though this is an extra chore it is not an extra expense. What it comes to is this: it probably won't be worth having your own individually designed forms printed – much better to use the BA's standard stationery. But if you think you can make do with all-purpose duplicate books, you'll save money. Send for current details of BA stationery prices to help you make up your mind.

Standard order forms

See Figure 4 on page 118. Standard order forms are available in either A4 or A5 and are overprinted with your shop's name, address and Standard Address Number (see below). They come in three-part sets on self-duplicating paper; you retain one copy as your record and send the other two to the publisher, who can use one of them as a delivery note with your order and keep the other as a record.

STANDARD ADDRESS NUMBER (SAN)

Bookshops are allocated a Standard Address Number on joining the BA. The SAN identifies a single bookselling outlet, just as an ISBN identifies a single title/edition. A SAN consists of seven digits, the final one a check digit, just as with ISBNs.

The intention is that publishers who assign account numbers to their customers should use the SAN instead of inventing a number of their own. This helps avoid confusion between different shops or between different branches of the same group. And because the Address Number is *Standard*, the bookseller can – and should – print it on all stationery. The SAN thus reduces the possibility of error both in the despatch of goods and the preparation of accounts.

Single copy order slips

These are designed for special customer orders. They come as four-part sets, so that in addition to providing copies for the publisher and yourself, there is copy which may be given to the customer when the order is placed.

Giro order forms

The Girobank Small Order Scheme was devised by the BA in collaboration with National Girobank. It uses the Girobank system of credit transfers from one account holder to another and so avoids the need for cheques. Using the special Giro order form, the bookseller orders from the publisher but sends no money. The publisher completes the form with the amount due, sends the transfer to National Girobank, where the bookseller's account is debited and the publisher's account credited.

From the publisher's point of view it's just like a cash-with-order system, even though the bookseller does not in fact send cash with the order and may not even know in advance how much is due.

The system is designed to save the to-ing and fro-ing of pro formas and payments, and in return publishers are encouraged to give booksellers full discount terms, however small the particular order.

To work the scheme, you must use the special Giro order forms, which include full instructions, and both you and the publisher must of course have Girobank accounts. Entries in the *Directory of Book Publishers and Wholesalers* identify participating publishers.

Standard returns forms

Before returning books for credit or replacement, booksellers normally need the supplier's permission – and *always* need it if the reason for the return is something other than the fault of the supplier or carrier. The standard returns form is a convenient way of seeking permission to return, the supplier authorising the return by signing the appropriate box on the form.

Check the *Directory of Book Publishers and Wholesalers* for individual suppliers' routines with imperfect copies and returns. Some publishers, for example, accept a torn-out title page from an imperfect book and do not require the return of the whole book.

Errors labels

These address labels, prominently marked ERRORS, are for use when a return does not need the supplier's prior permission. Whatever the rights and wrongs of the situation, however, it's normally advisable to obtain the supplier's authorisation before returning anything, otherwise what is at best a costly and time-wasting exercise easily descends into irritating confusion.

Query forms

Pre-printed with a number of standard queries – order chasers, short deliveries, credit chasers, etc – these forms standardise typical queries and save you the need to compose individual letters.

Stock control cards

See Figure 5 on page 153. Unlike the stationery items above, stock control cards are only for the internal use of your business. They may be used in a variety of ways – either one card per book, in the book, or one card per title held on a master file, or one card per face-out display. See Chapter 7 for a detailed consideration of stock control.

OTHER SCHEMES AND SERVICES

There are a variety of other schemes and services either offered directly by the BA, administered by the BA, or set up and maintained at least in part with the BA's collaboration though administered by other bodies. The major ones are detailed below.

BOOK TRADE IMPROVEMENT LTD

Book Trade Improvement Ltd is a wholly owned subsidiary of Book Tokens Ltd. It is able to make loans – up to £15,000 (in 1988) – to help BA members improve existing bookshops, create new retail outlets or finance changes of bookshop ownership. Interest is charged at only two per cent above base rate. The repayment of capital doesn't begin until three years after the date of the loan, thus allowing the improvement to be effective before the debt starts to be paid off.

BUSINESS INSURANCE

A tailor-made insurance policy for booksellers, underwritten at Lloyds, is available to BA members from Byas Mosley & Co. Ltd. *The Bookcover Insurance Plan* offers very good cover in a simple and straightforward manner. See what it has to offer and at what price before taking out insurance elsewhere.

MEDICAL CARE INSURANCE

BA members qualify for a discount of up to 15 per cent off the normal annual premiums charged by British United Provident Association (BUPA).

PENSIONS

A special Booksellers Pension Scheme for employees of corporate members of the BA is administered by Hinton Hall Life and Pensions Consultants Ltd. The Company is also able to offer self-employed BA members pension plans on favourable terms.

POST OFFICE SERVICES

Full current details of the two services below are available from Post Office Marketing Department.

Post-A-Book

This special mail service, jointly devised by the Post Office, the PA and the BA, aims to encourage the giving of books as presents for mailing. After choosing a book, the customer buys from the bookseller a special pre-paid mailing pack, which includes a book-mark gift card for completion, and the bookseller then arranges for the book to be mailed later that day. The post-inclusive cost of the special book packs range from 86p to £2.13, depending on size, and Booksellers pay an annual fee of £20 to be in the Scheme (1988 rates).

Booksell

Booksellers mailing more than 1,000 book parcels a year qualify for a concessionary rate negotiated annually by the BA and the Post Office.

OPEN UNIVERSITY SET BOOK STOCKISTS SCHEME

Booksellers who undertake to stock titles which are either required or recommended reading for students of the Open University (OU) are included in a register of booksellers which the OU sends to students, tutors and others – a total of about 80,000 people. There are three stockist categories: (1) local stockists of only the dozen or so titles for the Foundation Courses; (2) local stockists of all recommended course titles – about 250; and (3) regional stockists who not only hold all titles for sale to the public but also undertake to supply urgent orders to fellow booksellers in their region.

The fee to register with the BA as an official OU stockist is £18 plus VAT (in 1988).

Chapter 5

Buying Books for Resale

Like all trades, bookselling is a matter of buying at one price and selling at another. The difference between the two is the so-called *profit margin* or *gross profit*, though it may not include any real profit at all. From it you first have to pay all the bills of the business – rent, rates, staff wages, phone, electricity, bank charges, etc. Then you have to take a salary for yourself to pay you for the time and effort you put into running the shop – after all, if you weren't doing the work, you'd have to pay somebody else to do it. And if there's anything left over, *that's* the real profit – the *net profit*. According to published statistics, over half the small bookshops in the country end the year with a net *loss* (see Figure 3 overleaf) – though the reality may not be quite so bad as the bald figures suggest. More about this in the next chapter.

EXERCISING CONTROL

The individual bookseller has almost no control over the relationship between cost price and selling price. As we have seen, most selling prices are net – the publisher sets the price. And though a net price is theoretically only a *minimum* resale price, in practice it *is* the resale price because a book with the publisher's price printed on the cover is plainly unsaleable at anything above that price. The same would be true even if it were only a recommended price.

Cost price is only slightly more under the bookseller's control. A substantial customer of any particular supplier should be able to negotiate improved terms, but most small booksellers have little option but to deal on suppliers' basic terms. The gradual shift of power from publisher to bookseller, observable in recent years, has

FIGURE 3 Source: *Charter Group Economic Survey 1985/86*

BOOKSHOPS MAKING A NET LOSS 1981–86

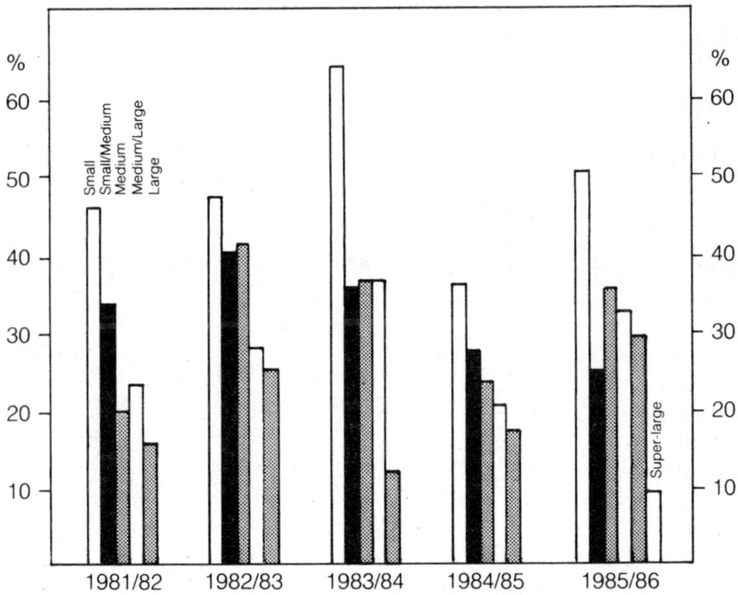

Note: % of Respondents classified by size of book sales.

so far been achieved by, and produced benefits for, only the major booksellers. The small independents have too little commercial muscle to wring better terms from suppliers, a situation unlikely to improve in the near future unless they are prepared to relinquish some of their independence and form co-operative buying groups with a purchasing power that the publishers would have to reckon with. The idea of co-operative buying has been floated from time to time in the trade, but nothing ever gets going. Sometimes it seems that the independents are too independent for their own good. For the present, the piper calls the tune, and you either pay up or do without.

One area where the small bookseller *can* exercise control is in stock management – making sure that stock is selected for its saleability, that orders are made up to qualify for best terms, that no title is bought in unnecessary quantity, and that stock which fails to sell fast enough is – within the NBA rules – cleared out of the shop. By these means you seek to maximise the profits produced by the capital you invest in stock.

STOCKTURN

The measure of your efficient use of stock investment capital is known as *stockturn*: the number of times the equivalent of your total stock is sold each year. Suppose you were to calculate the retail value of your stock on the first of each month, and found that over the year it averages £40,000. If your total annual sales amount to £120,000, then your stockturn is 3 – that is, £120,000 divided by £40,000. If you could raise your stockturn to 4, you would maintain your annual turnover of £120,000 with an average stock investment, at retail prices, of only £30,000. Raise your stockturn to 5, and the comparable stock investment figure would be £24,000.

Only booksellers with computerised stock control can easily calculate stock values each month. For the non-computerised it's enough of a chore to do it once a year for the preparation of the annual accounts. So, conventionally, stockturn is calculated as the year's sales divided by stock value at the year's start. In practice, of course, stock value fluctuates throughout the year. In many shops it is at its lowest at the annual stocktaking, the date of which is often chosen for this very reason, since the lower the stock, the less there is to count. As a result, the calculated stockturn figure will tend to err on the high side. And the error will be compounded if the shop does a lot of institutional business or special orders, both of which increase turnover without increasing stock.

Despite these possible distortions, stockturn is a useful measure of performance. You can see some typical bookshop stockturn figures in Table 8 on page 132. Most successful booksellers feel that 4 is a reasonable figure to aim at, though Arthur Young suggests that 4.5 or 5 should be the minimum target. Newcomers to the trade should not be surprised if they achieve rather less: a new shop's opening stock represents little more than a hopeful guess at what customers will want to buy, and it will almost certainly include a number of titles which they won't.

There is nothing theoretical or academic about a stockturn figure. It is a matter of hard cash. In the above example, the difference between a stockturn of 3 and a stockturn of 5 amounted to £16,000 at retail prices – which could represent £10,400 of stock investment at trade prices. That means that if you achieve the higher stockturn, you can have £10,400 in your building society collecting interest, instead of on your shelves collecting dust. Alternatively, it means your borrowings reduce by £10,400 with a corresponding reduction in your interest payments. Whether it is a matter of saving more or borrowing less, the effect on your income can be significant. Of course, more marginal improvements produce more marginal benefits, but any stockturn improvement shifts the odds of business success in your favour.

And title evaluation is where the whole process begins.

EVALUATING TITLES FOR STOCK

The character of your bookshop is ultimately determined by the titles you stock, and much of the skill in bookselling lies in choosing that stock well. However devoted you may be to books in general or to a particular subject speciality, success in bookselling implies stocking the books the customers want to buy. Evaluating a title for stock is less a matter of assessing its intrinsic merit than in predicting the disposition of your customers to buy it. Like the business it is part of, title evaluation in bookselling is a commercial and not a literary activity.

Perhaps that overstates the case, but not by much. There is room for you to select titles which you personally admire and then to steer your customers gently in their direction. Success in this is gratifying but not easily achieved; failure is costly. The influencing of public taste is the job of critics, reviewers, teachers, advertising copy writers and the media. The bookseller's role is to make available what the public wants to buy, and you necessarily select the bulk of your stock on that basis or you wind up broke.

GUIDES TO STOCK SELECTION

Once trading, your stock control system identifies the winners and losers, and you restock the titles that sell and destock the titles that don't. Taking a new title into stock is more of a shot in the dark, though there is plenty of guidance available if you care to use it. The degree of demand for a book in the short term usually relates to the amount of publisher promotion and media attention it receives.

The Bookseller and *Publishing News* routinely review forthcoming titles, evaluating them from a bookselling point of view, and drawing attention to media tie-ins with new or existing titles. The BA's Buyer's Guides also look ahead and provide experienced booksellers' judgements of titles worth considering. *Books in the*

Media is particularly useful for its coverage of media attention.

Some of the major wholesalers also provide buyers' guides, and indeed their entire stock lists reflect their assessment of the titles most likely to be in demand. The stock lists are particularly useful in the early days of your bookselling career as they include the *continuing* sellers, while most other published advice is concerned only with new and forthcoming titles.

BACKING YOUR OWN JUDGEMENT

Most titles are not the subject of publisher hype or media interest. Such publicity as they receive – and many receive none at all worthy of the name – is directed at booksellers rather than the public. The publisher's rep may show you a book or even just a book jacket, or you may notice the book advertised in the trade press or possibly merely mentioned in the editorial section of the Spring Books or Autumn Books issue of *The Bookseller*. Some books may never get mentioned anywhere except in their publishers' catalogues and the trade bibliographies.

Among this mass of unsung material you may find titles of merit which you believe will sell in your shop. Since your customers will not have been softened up by advertising or media coverage, you must be confident that something in the physical presence of the books – title, jacket, the favourable impression given on cursory inspection – will appeal to the customers in your shop. Again, intrinsic merit is not enough. A book with a pretty face is to be preferred to a more homely production with a heart of gold. A pretty face *and* a heart of gold is what we're all looking for.

COMPETING TITLES

In most popular non-fiction subject areas, there are usually a number of competing titles. Unless a given book is likely to be asked for by name – because of the publicity it has received – you should be guided in your choice first by considerations of value for money and stock range, and second by discounts and other supply terms. With limited resources, it is difficult to justify stocking two books on the same subject, dealt with in a similar way, and costing about the same; choose the better value for money or the one you can buy on the better terms. Two or more competing books are normally worth stocking only when they offer plainly different advantages – for example, one is a cheap paperback, the other a more expensive hardback, or, if both cost the same, one has a superficial text but is well illustrated while the other, though unillustrated, is textually detailed.

LEGAL CONSIDERATIONS

Booksellers are responsible in law for the content of the books they sell. Books which the state might consider obscene or seditious or liable to stir up racial hatred or which do anything else that Parliament or the courts have ruled shall not be done can land the bookseller in the dock alongside the author, the printer and the publisher. The bookseller may similarly be cited as defendant in a libel action in the civil courts if a plaintiff feels wronged by a book's content. No one, of course, expects booksellers to have read and weighed the significance of every word in every book they sell; usually it is enough to withdraw from sale a book which is alleged to have offended or is found to have done so. But booksellers should be quite clear about their liability, and should seek legal advice from the BA on the wisdom of offering for sale any book which they feel might put them at risk.

Copyright

Copyright is the right to make copies of an original work. In the case of books, the copyright normally belongs to the author, who, in Britain, acquires it without formality or registration merely by the act of composing the original text. The © copyright declaration which you find on the verso of a book's title page is there only to ensure that copyright is enforceable outside Britain under the terms of the Universal Copyright Convention.

Copyright is a property with a separate legal existence from that of the text or of the author, and it may be traded like any other property. In a typical publishing contract, an author – without relinquishing the copyright – grants a publisher the right to produce copies of the work in consideration of a royalty on each copy sold.

TERRITORIAL RIGHTS

The publisher, acting on his own and his author's behalf, may sell to a foreign publisher the right to publish the book in that other publisher's country. As far as English-language titles are concerned, this is mainly a matter of British publishers selling US rights to American publishers, and American publishers selling British rights to British publishers. Traditionally, US rights include the right to sell to American dependencies, and British rights include the right to sell to Commonwealth countries. (Canadian rights are anomalous, usually included in the US rights for US-originated titles, and in the British rights for British-originated titles.) These territorial rights are exclusive; so, for example, the US edition of a title also published in Britain may not be sold in Britain or any Commonwealth country.

A complication, currently unresolved, concerns the EEC. Continental Europe has traditionally been an *open market* – ie both the publisher with the US rights and the one with the British rights are free to sell their editions into continental Europe. However, the Common Market philosophy that anything freely traded in one part of the EEC should be freely traded in all parts of the EEC threatens to allow US editions into the UK via the back-door of Europe, so undermining the position of the British rights holder. At present, any such importation into Britain breaches the rights of the British publisher, who may seek legal redress.

The importance of all this for the bookseller is that you could be in trouble if you import books without first checking on the copyright position. The danger is most acute if you import from wholesalers who may not be fully aware of the copyright restrictions applying to particular titles.

It is worth noting that you would also be in breach of copyright if you exported a British book to a customer in a country where a local edition of the book enjoyed the exclusive right of local publication.

RETURNS

One of the consequences of the Net Book Agreement is that booksellers cannot get rid of dead stock as easily as other retailers. A jeweller who has vainly tried to sell a £99 necklace for the past month simply changes the ticket to £89 and adds the word 'bargain'. If that doesn't do the trick, he tries it as a £79 'fantastic bargain', then a £69 'absolutely unrepeatable offer', and so on till the wretched thing finds a buyer. Not for the bookseller anything so vulgar.

The National Book Sale offers you the chance to clear out dead stock, but by the time the annual event comes around you may have had the book for anything up to two years. And even to take advantage of Clause (ii) of the *Standard Conditions of Sale*, you must have stocked the non-seller for at least a year. These are excessive lengths of time to keep your money unproductively locked away.

Given the current regulations and practices of the trade, booksellers are rarely able to avoid the risk of being stuck for months on end with books they cannot sell at the net price and may not sell at a lower price. All they can do is ask the supplier nicely to take the books back for credit, though they cannot insist upon it unless the right to return formed part of the terms of supply.

When booksellers and publishers talk of *returns* – and they do so frequently – they are referring to this shifting back to suppliers of retailers' unsold stock. It generates a depressing amount of paperwork, authorisation, packing, carriage costs and just plain irritation. Yet it is probably unfair to think of it as the unacceptable face of the NBA, since returns are apparently an even more significant feature of bookselling in the United States where there is nothing like the NBA at all; over there, publishers have been known to talk wryly of their books being 'gone today and here tomorrow'.

Whatever the cause, returns are an important part of the bookselling equation, to which you will, in due course, have to give as much attention as to the purchase of stock in the first place. And it is not to be morbidly pessimistic to say that an awareness of a supplier's likely response to a future request to return should influence your calculations at the time of purchase.

TRADE TERMS

The trade terms offered to booksellers vary from one supplier to another and often from one type of order to another sent to the same supplier. The key components of trade terms are ownership, discount and credit. These respectively determine the extent of your risk, what you have to pay and when you have to pay it.

OWNERSHIP

The moment when ownership passes from supplier to bookseller has an importance which, fortunately, is rarely tested. The outcome of insurance claims, bankruptcy proceedings (yours or the supplier's), tax disputes and other unpleasantnesses can all turn upon who owns what when. A few suppliers put a so-called *Romalpa clause* in their contracts, the effect of which is that ownership passes to the bookseller only on full payment. Although this clause may come into play in the event of your shop's going into receivership, it doesn't have much bearing upon the day-to-day supplier–bookseller relationship or upon the bookseller's right to return unsold stock for credit or refund.

The regrettably routine matter of returns is governed by the more general terms of the transaction, sometimes only implicitly or informally stated – as when the rep says something like "Believe me, you'll sell these hundred copies before you know what's hit you. If you don't, I'll see you don't get stuck with them. OK?" Even when more precise terminology is used, its exact significance is not always clear. The difficulty is that none of the expressions commonly heard have universally agreed meanings. If in doubt, ask the supplier to spell out precisely what he means by whatever expression he uses: who owns the stock? when does the bookseller incur a liability to pay for it? can it be returned? is there a deadline for return? who pays the return carriage costs? are returns for cash or credit? The descriptions below indicate how the terms are most usually understood, but they are not to be relied upon as precise definitions.

Firm

Unless there has been some explicit agreement to the contrary between bookseller and supplier, all trade orders are understood to be firm – ie the bookseller becomes the owner of the books, pays for them in the usual way, and cannot later require the supplier to take them back if they remain unsold. The bookseller's stock risk, therefore, is total. If you turn out to have bought unsaleable stock, bad luck! You can ask the supplier to repurchase the books from you but you cannot require him to do so. Most book trade supplies are firm.

Sale or return (SOR)

Some CTNs and other non-specialist shops are supplied by wholesalers or publishers on a *racking* basis – ie the shop makes available a rack or set of shelves, and the supplier puts in a selection of stock, checking it regularly, moving out unsold books and putting in new ones. The operation is often referred to as *merchandising*, and is normally done on a sale or return basis.

Books supplied on sale or return are invoiced to the trader, become his property and are paid for in the ordinary way. But the trader has the right to return them for credit or refund before the end of a specified period.

In a typical merchandising operation, because the supplier regularly clears out the unsold books and puts in new ones, the trader in effect never invests in stock but only pays for what he sells. However, when specialist booksellers are supplied on sale or return, they are required to pay at the end of their normal credit period and are typically expected to retain the stock until towards the end of the specified period when the option to return lapses.

See safe

See safe in practice comes to virtually the same as *sale or return* as described above, except perhaps that see safe returns are for credit only and never for refund. The bookseller acquires the ownership of the stock from the start and pays for it in the ordinary way. However, the supplier underwrites the bookseller's risk by promising to take back – within a specified period – anything the bookseller wishes to return. The return carriage is normally at the bookseller's expense. A book supplied *on approval* – so that, for example, the bookseller can show it to a customer – is in effect supplied see safe.

The reason for the existence of two such confusingly similar terms as *sale or return* and *see safe* probably lies in their connotation rather than their meaning. *Sale or return* seems to be used when the supplier, from the start, expects there to be returns, and builds that expectation into his marketing strategy. *See safe* is used when the supplier *doesn't* expect returns but wants to reassure his bookselling customer that there's nothing to worry about.

On consignment

The ownership of books supplied on consignment is retained by the supplier. The bookseller pays only when a sale is made or at the end of a specified period. The total stock risk, therefore, is borne by the supplier. You will not be surprised to learn that on consignment terms are rarely offered.

DISCOUNT

The trade price of books is invariably expressed as a discount off the retail price, whether that retail price is net or non-net.

Publishers' discounts

The BA has for years urged publishers to give a minimum 35 per cent discount on all orders, carriage paid and with no surcharges; but such terms are still the exception rather than the rule, though 35 per cent is commonly the basic maximum discount offered on net books. Non-net books are typically offered at a discount of 17½ per cent.

Small orders are subject to the greatest variety of terms as publishers try to cope with what is likely to be the most uneconomic part of their business. A distinction is commonly made between orders for a single copy of a title and orders for two or more copies of a title. A publisher giving 35 per cent for two or more may give only 25 per cent for a single copy.

Much of a small bookshop's stock may consist of one copy per title – an inevitable compromise between limited funds and/or space on the one hand and the broadest choice for the customer on the other. Furthermore, since bookshop customers typically buy in singles, stocking two or more is really a matter of holding reserve stock: for as long as the first copy remains unsold, the second copy does nothing but lock your money up. It needs only one copy of a title to say to the customer "Buy me!"; a second copy sitting obscured behind the first does nothing to reinforce the message. These are generalisations, of course, and the question of what to stock, and in what quantity, will be examined in more detail in Chapter 7 on stock control. For the moment, take it that most of your stock – particularly in the early days – is likely to be in singles, and that if you're routinely getting no more than a 25 per cent discount you're going to be in trouble.

Publishers who do vary their terms between single copy orders and orders for two or more often maintain the distinction whatever the size of the total order placed. They attach less importance to order value than to the number of *order lines* – an order line being an order for a single title of any quantity. Thus an order for one copy of each of a hundred titles may attract less favourable terms than an order for two copies of the same title. The publisher argues that the hundred line order, whatever its value, creates much more work than a single line order: invoicing a hundred titles and looking out one copy of each from the warehouse (this is known as *picking*) is a lot more work than invoicing and picking two copies of the same title, or even two hundred copies of the same title.

Some publishers penalise the *single line single copy* order – that is, an order for just one copy of just one book – compared with single copy orders for two or more books. But there are no standard publishers' terms which you can expect to be offered. Publishers are an individualistic lot, and they all make their own rules; indeed, they would be breaking the law if they colluded so as to standardise their terms.

Here are some other variations you may meet, many of them having a decisive effect on your profit or lack of it. Some publishers make a delivery charge; some don't. Some impose a small order surcharge, which may be either modest to cover the cost of handling a small order, or punitive to discourage small orders altogether. Some offer more favourable terms for cash-with-order; some don't. Some offer different terms for different categories of books on their lists – not merely distinguishing net and non-net, but, for example, giving 35 per cent on general books, 25 per cent on technical books, 17½ per cent on non-net educational books, and so on. The category into which a book falls is at the whim of the publisher; to be certain, you need to check the publisher's catalogue. Some give more favourable terms to orders placed in a certain way – teleorders or journey orders, for example (see below). Some give specially favourable terms to members of the BA Charter Group.

School textbooks are virtually always non-net and attract the lowest discounts. In one way this seems not unreasonable, as booksellers rarely take any stock risk on them, obtaining them only to special order and in batches of 20 or 30 copies a time. But local education authorities regrettably often insist on a discount off the recommended price, and if you find yourself having to give your customer a 10 per cent discount when your supplier is giving you only 17½ per cent, you really have to ask yourself whether the exercise is worthwhile. Don't confuse busyness with business.

The standard reference book which sets out publishers' trade terms is the BA's *Directory of Book Publishers and Wholesalers*. In its weekly Trade Notes section *The Bookseller* has a Distribution, Terms and Addresses column which gives corrected and updated information as supplied by publishers from time to time. Publishers' advertising characteristically makes no reference to trade terms at all, unless unhelpfully to observe something like 'Normal trade terms apply'. If you don't know what the terms are, ask the publisher.

If you don't know the terms before placing your order, you're running your business blind. Particularly with special customer orders, it is not unknown for the bookseller to be billed by the publisher for more than the net price to be paid by the bookseller's customer. This can happen when a publisher, after allowing a derisory discount for a small order, then loads the invoice with a surcharge because it *is* a small order, and adds a delivery charge which may or may not relate to actual delivery costs. Don't be caught unawares. Better still, don't be caught at all. Even Charter Group members who commit themselves to ordering unstocked books for customers qualify the commitment with the phrase 'whenever economically feasible'.

Wholesalers' discounts

Once again the main source of information about terms is the *Directory of Book Publishers and Wholesalers*; and again as with publishers, discounts vary from supplier to supplier. They typically centre on 33⅓ per cent or 35 per cent, carriage paid, with surcharges and lesser discounts applying to small orders.

To qualify for the standard discount the bookseller normally has to place a minimum order, which may be defined by value or number of books or both: an order minimum of £70 or 50 books is fairly typical. But with major wholesalers offering thousands of titles from scores of publishers, no specialist bookseller should have any difficulty in getting the best terms on every order.

CREDIT

Although there is a certain amount of cash-with-order business done, most sales within the trade are on credit, accounts being normally due for settlement not later than the last day of the month following the month of invoice and supply. This means that booksellers are conventionally allowed credit for between four and eight weeks, depending upon the way the invoice dates fall in relation to the calendar month.

Different suppliers have different credit control systems, some more lax than others. A new bookseller, however, will generally have to supply two trade references and a banker's reference before being granted credit facilities. The usual trade references required are from two suppliers with whom you already have a credit account, and who can bear witness to the promptness of your settlement of their bills. As a newcomer to the trade, your problem is how to get these first two references. Try offering references from outside the book trade, or references attesting to your personal integrity from your accountant or solicitor.

A supplier not willing to supply to you on credit will usually respond to an order with a pro forma invoice requesting pre-payment. If you know a given publisher requires cash with order but you are uncertain of the exact trade price of the title(s) you require, it saves time – and often secures better terms – if you send your order accompanied by a cheque marked with an upper limit but left open for the publisher to write in the precise amount.

Wherever possible, however, you should buy on credit, and the longer the credit period you can obtain, the more securely based your business is likely to be.

Relationship between credit and stockturn

It was the Arthur Young report which focused booksellers' attention upon the importance of trying to harmonise credit and stockturn. A stockturn of 3, for example, means that on average a book is sitting on your shelves for 4 months before it gets sold; and that in turn means that if your supplier allows you a credit period of only a month, your money is tied up in stock for 3 of those 4 months. Even a small bookseller may have a stock, at trade prices, of about £20,000; just consider how much interest you have to pay to borrow that amount, or – if you are investing your own savings – how much interest you lose by having your money in stock rather than on deposit in an interest-bearing account.

As a small trader, you can do as little about credit periods as you can about discounts. But if the time comes when you are in a position to negotiate improved terms, remember that extended credit can sometimes be as valuable as an enhanced discount.

The time-honoured – but shabby – way of getting extended credit is to delay the payment of bills. Big booksellers have been known to get away with it when dealing with small publishers. But small booksellers simply get put *on stop* – ie the supplier won't supply any more books until you pay up. Since a trading bookseller needs a continuous supply of fresh stock, delaying payment is no answer to your problems.

One bright spot for the new bookseller is that some publishers and wholesalers will give you extended credit on your opening stock. In 1988 at least one major national wholesaler offered 60-days credit to new bookshops. It is before you start trading that you make a bigger stock purchase in one go than you're likely to do again for a long time. So you begin by presenting an attractive prospect to suppliers, who may be moved to offer you better than basic terms. But the honeymoon ends once you start trading and place only topping-up orders.

PUBLISHERS *v* WHOLESALERS

For the small independent bookseller, buying from a wholesaler is generally to be preferred to buying from a publisher. It isn't always possible; but only rarely when it *is* possible, is it undesirable.

Basic discounts and credit periods are broadly similar from both publishers and wholesalers. But it is normally easier to bulk up an order that qualifies for best terms when you're ordering from a wholesaler – who stocks the titles of a range of publishers – than when you're placing an order direct with a single publisher.

Nor is it just a matter of terms. The fewer suppliers you deal with, the less your paperwork, book-keeping and order processing costs. But probably the clinching argument in favour of wholesalers is the excellence of their service. Publishers can be cavalier about service because they have a monopoly of their own titles. If the public actually wants a specific title, the order, directly or indirectly, always gets back to the publisher, no matter what the standard of service. Wholesalers, by contrast, are in competition with each other, and to some extent with the publishers too. A popular paperback may be available from scores of suppliers. Whichever source the bookseller uses, the publisher benefits; but the individual wholesaler only benefits if he is the one who makes the sale.

And this keeps wholesalers on their toes, to the advantage of the bookselling trade.

SERVICE

The service wholesalers offer is not just the rapid fulfilment of orders – crucially important though that is – but may also include the provision of updated catalogues, ordering material, sales aids, stock control slips (see page 157), stock recommendations, bestseller lists, buyers' notes, media news and so on. Some publishers too provide some of these things, but publishers' promotion of their own titles is perhaps less convincing than a wholesaler's promotion of titles freely selected. Wholesalers, first by the selection of their own stock, second by their highlighting of particular titles within the stock, are in effect providing the bookseller with a shortlisting and evaluation service. You won't agree with their judgement every time, nor will your customers, but it is at least a helpful starting point.

IMPROVED TERMS

However much wholesalers want your custom, they are constrained in the terms they offer by the terms they themselves receive from the publishers. If, therefore, you are placing large and continuing orders for the books of a single publisher, you may be able to negotiate a better discount from the publisher than from a wholesaler. On the other hand, better terms obtained from a wholesaler usually apply across the complete range of your purchases from him; and this means, for example, that an extra 2 per cent from a wholesaler may be worth more than an extra 3 per cent from a given publisher.

Work it out. If a wholesaler offers you an extra 2 per cent when you reach £60,000 of business with him annually, you're £1,200 better off. If you move £30,000 of that business to the publisher, who offers you an extra 3 per cent, you're £900 better off on half of your purchases but no better off at all on the other half. In such a case, the wholesaler is still offering the better deal.

Bear in mind also the point already made that discount is only one ingredient in the trade terms mix. A longer credit period or a more liberal returns policy are also worth negotiating. And since the supplier with whom you place the largest amount of business is the one most likely to be impressed by the force of your argument for better terms, there is much to be said for channelling the bulk of your orders to your chosen wholesaler.

What it all comes to is this: most small independent booksellers should buy as much of their stock as they can from wholesalers.

Find not more than two or three who between them can supply the bulk of your stock titles. This is likely to maximise discounts and minimise order processing. For regular substantial orders for a particular publisher's books, a direct approach to the publisher to negotiate special terms is always worth a try – but don't be seduced just by the big numbers: calculate the total effect on your gross profits of different ordering strategies. And don't underestimate the advantages of dealing with fewer rather than more suppliers.

For titles not stocked by your wholesalers, you'll usually have to deal direct with the publishers whether you like it or not, though some wholesalers are prepared to process special orders for major customers, albeit at lower discounts.

PUBLISHERS' ADDRESSES

Finding publishers' addresses and phone numbers is not always easy. There are, after all, thousands of them, from the largest international companies down to one-person enterprises. Some have been publishing for years; some started yesterday. The BA's *Directory of Book Publishers and Wholesalers* and Whitaker's *Publishers in the United Kingdom and their Addresses* (£4 in 1988) will give you most of the addresses you need. The latter directory is an alphabetical list of publishers, giving addresses, telephone numbers, telegraphic addresses and telex numbers. It also gives publisher prefixes under the ISBN system, and provides a checklist of these prefixes in a single numerical sequence from which publishers may be identified. *WBIP* gives similar information, and also gives the publisher's address in the main author/title entries in the case of minor or occasional publishers. Regular publishers and their addresses are listed separately in *WBIP*. Book Trust's Book Information Service may be able to help if none of this published material provides the answer.

CHOOSING A WHOLESALER

Check the BA directory to see what is available, and keep your eye on *The Bookseller* for news and advertising of any new suppliers starting in business or moving into your area. There are some excellent wholesale services operating nationally, but a more local service, perhaps with cash-and-carry facilities, may also be of use to you. Shop around. Get details of a number of different suppliers. Consider and compare the different mix of service/terms/stock/facilities. Dealing with two or three wholesalers will probably give you the best range of services without complicating your ordering procedures too much. It is, at any rate, always a good idea to familiarise yourself with alternative sources of supply so that you know where you can turn to in an emergency.

Some book wholesalers also supply non-book products – stationery items, newspapers, toys, fancy goods, etc – and this may influence your choice if you are planning to stock non-book products in your shop. Details of wholesalers' non-book stocks are included in the BA directory.

HOW TO ORDER BOOKS

There are various ways of ordering books, each with its own cost and convenience implications.

If you accept special orders from your customers, you can find yourself having to order from any one of thousands of publishers. Even your own stock orders may lead to your dealing with scores of publishers, however much business you try to channel through wholesalers. With so many different suppliers, some of whom you will deal with not more than once or twice a year – or even once or twice a lifetime – it is often not practicable to go through any lengthy preliminary negotiation to set up a commercial relationship. Check the publisher's terms in the *Directory of Book Publishers and Wholesalers*: some publishers, for example, specify cash-with-order for small orders and/or non-account customers, others accept Visa or Access for small orders.

Orders arriving out of the blue from booksellers not previously dealt with are commonplace in most publishers' offices, and will normally be accepted without fuss provided they seem to come from bona fide booksellers. A publisher who has doubts can easily check the BA's *Directory of Members* or even the PA's *Directory of Booksellers* which is designed to serve as a guide to PA members of those booksellers considered to have genuine bookselling businesses. To be registered as such a bookseller, you should apply to the PA; registration costs £10 plus VAT (in 1988). However, the appearance of your name in the directories of either association is neither a condition of supply nor a guarantee of it. Individual publishers make their own decisions. In practice, no specialist bookseller should have any real difficulty in getting supplies, though the newcomer may experience the odd delay while credentials are checked.

POST

Written orders to publishers are usually made on your own stationery; those to wholesalers are usually on the wholesaler's stationery.

FIGURE 4

BA STANDARD ORDER FORM *Actual size A5 or A4*

ORDER PLEASE RETURN YELLOW COPY ORDER WITH BOOKS AND/OR REPORTS

TO	FROM	Always QUOTE ORDER No.
		605953
	STANDARD ADDRESS No.	DATE POSTED
CONSIGNMENT ADDRESS (IF DIFFERENT)	SPECIAL INSTRUCTIONS	

CUSTOMER'S REF.	QUANTITY	ISBN	TITLE, SERIES, AUTHOR	H/Bk P/Bk OR PRICE	PUBLISHER'S USE

Small orders taking advantage of the Girobank Small Order Scheme must use special stationery (see page 98).

Look at the BA's standard order form in Figure 4 to see the information a written order should include: your name, address and SAN, the supplier's name, an order number and date, the quantity, ISBN, title and author of each title required. To err on the side of caution, you could also specify whether the book is hardback or paperback or what its retail price is: strictly speaking, this information is unnecessary – as indeed are title and author – since the ISBN alone uniquely identifies the required book, but for suppliers still operating manual rather than computerised systems, the redundant information helps to minimise errors. Human beings more easily take in title/author/price information than the seemingly arbitrary string of digits that make up an ISBN.

You will, of course, always keep a carbon copy of the order, and you may therefore wish to include on the form information purely for your own internal use: a customer reference number that allows you to match the book when it arrives to the particular customer who ordered it, and possibly the supplier's full address – but see *Orders clearing houses* below.

Suppliers are generally not keen to mail books direct to your customers, so the *Consignment address (if different)* box should be used sparingly. Although in theory it should save time and money, it rarely does either. Suppliers normally charge postage for direct supply to your customers even if the same orders would be supplied to you post free. Furthermore, while you have the central role in the transaction, you lose all contact with what's going on: you don't know when or if the supplier has sent the book, or when or if the customer has received it. Only if something goes wrong and the customer complains do you get involved again, and then only as the helpless intermediary conveying messages between trade supplier and retail customer – responsibility without power. Keep clear of it.

The *Consignment address* box is worth using only if you have a warehouse at a different address from your retail shop; though if that is the case, it would be better to put your warehouse address in the *From* box, and so avoid the inevitable mistaken deliveries to your shop.

Orders clearing houses

One consequence for booksellers of the large number of separate orders they may need to place with separate publishers is a potentially large postal bill. Consider what even fifty orders a week would cost in postage over a full year – to which you would need to add the cost in envelopes plus the cost in time or money of addressing them and preparing them for mailing. Fortunately, there are well-established clearing houses for orders, just as there are for payments, and these help keep costs down.

A clearing house system works like this: the bookseller fills in the order forms in the usual way, but instead of mailing each direct to an individual publisher, puts them all into one envelope addressed to the clearing house. There, the orders of all booksellers using the service are sorted according to the publishers they are intended for and forwarded to them by first class post. A bonus of the clearing house system is that the bookseller is spared the need to check and copy out each publisher's address; provided the publisher's name is on the order form, the clearing house automatically routes it to the correct address.

Two commercial organisations offering a clearing house service are Booksellers Order Distribution (BOD) and IBIS Information

Services Ltd. BOD invoices booksellers monthly at the rate of 12.5p per order. IBIS requires booksellers to buy a book of vouchers in advance, each voucher covering up to five orders; the rate per order works out roughly at 12.4p each. Both services are therefore substantially cheaper than direct individual orders to publishers in the first class post, though for non-urgent orders, which you might send in the second class post, there is not a lot in it. All figures relate to 1988; clearing house costs are subject to VAT.

Use of a clearing house increases the transit time of an order by a single day, though a few publishers make their own daily collections from the clearing houses, thus overcoming even this small delay.

TELEPHONE

For really urgent orders, a telephone call may be the best method. Many booksellers also use the phone routinely out of shop hours for orders to wholesalers with 24-hour answering services. The method frees you from the deadline imposed by ever earlier final collections by the local post office, and absolutely guarantees that your order will be there for processing first thing the next working morning. The information needed is as for written orders.

On the approach to Christmas, many publishers introduce *hot-lines* – telephone numbers for the receipt of urgent orders which are then processed with unwonted despatch so that the books are in your shop in 24–48 hours. Why such services are laid on only at Christmas mystifies many booksellers. Perhaps it's the publishers' way of saying "We'd like you belly-aching booksellers to understand that we're perfectly capable of dealing with orders promptly, and the fact that most of the year we don't do so is simply that we don't care to. So there!" More probably it's an aspect of the paradox already noted (page 48) that the publisher offering a good service tends to come off worse than the publisher offering a bad one; only at Christmas, when large numbers of orders not fulfilled by a deadline are at risk of being lost for ever, do the interests of publisher and bookseller coincide.

TELEORDERING

Teleordering, run by Teleordering Ltd, is an electronic orders clearing system. To order by this method you need a computer terminal linked into the telephone system. All you do is type in the order number, ISBN and quantity required – no need for names, addresses, titles, authors or anything else. There are three levels of entry into teleordering.

For the largest bookshop

Major users, like the bookselling chains with centrally controlled ordering systems, can be provided with a direct computer link into Teleordering's central IBM bureau. This is unlikely to concern readers of the present guide.

For the medium size bookshop

The bookseller enters orders into the shop's computer at any time. They are automatically checked – for example, to ensure that the ISBN is a valid one – and stored. During the night, Teleordering's central mini-computer *polls* all the bookshop computers in the system – ie it calls them up via the telephone lines and collects all the orders which have been stored during the day. These are then sorted, processed against bibliographical, publisher and bookseller databases, and forwarded to the appropriate publishers, either directly into their computerised order processing systems, or as data to generate printed lists for manual processing. Non-participating publishers are sent print-outs of their orders in the first class post.

The following day the bookseller can get a confirming print-out from the terminal, showing the previous day's orders in expanded form – ie full publisher/author/title/price information is now presented. This not only provides a readable check on your orders, it also reports if you have tried, for example, to order an OP title or one which can't be traced.

The hard-disc terminal needed for the system costs the bookseller anything from £2,500 to £5,000, and the modem (ie the link to the telephone system) about £400. Annual maintenance costs £330 to £450. The teleordering software is £500 if Teleordering has also supplied the hardware, or £750 if not. Teleordering's joining fee ranges from £250 to £600 and the annual fee from £353 to £1,209, depending upon the number of order lines put through the system – the lower fee is for a daily order line capacity of 200 lines. All prices subject to VAT and as at 1988.

Though these are hefty costs, remember that computer hardware does not have to be dedicated to a single use. Much of your teleordering hardware should also be usable – but do check that it is before committing yourself – with *Bookbank*, for example, or for word processing or stock control or to do your book-keeping. Of course, you will need further software and possibly further pieces of peripheral equipment, but you shouldn't need to keep duplicating some of the more expensive pieces of hardware in your computerised set-up.

For the smaller bookshop: Teleordering Viewdata Service

The Viewdata Service is a little less convenient and a lot less costly than the service above. Instead of orders being stored on your terminal and then polled at night, they are entered by you directly into the central computer. To do this, you need a typical home computer plus monitor or TV and a link into British Telecom's Prestel service.

You dial up the central computer any time Monday to Saturday from 8 am to 10 pm and type in your orders. They are then processed as described above. You can call up the computer the following day to get displayed confirmation, with full bibliographical detail, of the orders you placed.

The joining fee for Teleordering Viewdata is £200; the annual fee is £175 for a shop with up to 7,500 order lines a year, or £230 for up to 10,000 order lines a year. Prestel's annual subscription is £72 – or £20 if you run the system at home. Prestel time charges and BT call charges for an average 100 order lines per week work out between £19 and £78 a year, depending upon the time and day you make your calls. All prices subject to VAT and as at 1988.

Though plainly requiring a greater cash outlay than a set of order forms, you should consider the Viewdata Service very carefully. Placing orders manually is labour-intensive, time-consuming and boring. You and your staff can probably use your skills to better effect than as copy clerks: Viewdata gives you the chance to do so.

JOURNEY ORDERS

All orders sent by the methods so far discussed are known as *direct orders*, and they are to be distinguished from orders given to publishers' reps who call at your shop. These latter orders are known as *journey orders* or *travellers' orders*.

The placing of a journey order may cause you no paperwork at all, the order being made out by the rep on his own stationery, which he then sends to his office for processing. Always make sure, however, that you are left a copy of the order and that the rep marks it with your own special order number, so that it may be filed in sequence with your direct orders.

Journey orders may be either stock orders or subscription orders. *Stock orders* are for the replacement of stock or for taking into stock for the first time titles not previously stocked. *Subscription orders* are for books not yet published. The winning of these pre-publication orders is an important part of a rep's job, as publishers like to see their books go off with a bang on publication day, and they cannot afford to wait until that day to start soliciting orders. By having reps start *subscribing* a book – ie taking subscription orders from booksellers – for some weeks, or possibly months, before it is due to be published, publishers give themselves the chance of assessing how many copies it is wise to print. Even so they often get it wrong, and it's not unknown for a publisher to have to order a reprint even before a book has gone on sale.

Journey orders in general and subscription orders in particular sometimes attract specially favourable terms from publishers.

Some reps carry car stock – especially at Christmas – so if the rep comes at the right time with the right books on board you could get the quickest delivery ever.

HOW THE SUPPLIER DEALS WITH YOUR ORDER

Ideally, the publisher or wholesaler will immediately pick the books you require from the warehouse, pack them and despatch them to you, either enclosing an invoice or sending one under separate cover. Towards the end of the following month you will receive a statement showing the total due for all the books supplied to you by the particular supplier in the last complete calendar month, together with details of any payment outstanding from previous months.

That, from your point of view, is the ideal. But a number of less than ideal responses are just as likely. The supplier may be unwilling to supply to you on credit, perhaps because of the smallness of the order or because earlier bills are still unpaid or because you have not formally opened an account. Whatever the reason, he will in these cases usually send you a pro forma invoice requesting pre-payment.

Whether he supplies to you on a credit or cash-with-order basis, the trade terms he allows you may fall short of what you consider to be either fair or reasonable. But unless you know of a wholesaler who can supply your order on better terms, there is nothing you can do about it beyond determining not to handle that publisher's books again – which may be a commercially unrealistic decision if the books sell well in your shop – or ensuring that future orders are made up to qualify for best terms. Indeed, as already suggested, you should check on terms in advance and if at all possible pace your ordering so that you always qualify for best terms. This is one of the few ways in which your profit margin is in some degree under your control.

Consideration of payment and trade terms apart, there may be other reasons why the supplier does not immediately despatch the books you require, the most common reason being the unavailability, temporary or permanent, of what you have ordered. The constantly changing availability of titles is one of the facts of book trade life, and it has given rise to abbreviated answers, which suppliers use when reporting to booksellers why particular titles ordered are not being supplied.

ANSWERS

The answers OP, RP and BDG have been referred to earlier (page 20); in the case of RP and BDG the supplier may further indicate the date when supplies will be available again – eg RP/March or less helpfully BDG/shortly – or he may draw attention to the fact that he cannot say when supplies will be available by adding the abbreviation ND, meaning no date can be given – eg RP/ND. An OP title which may be reprinted is TOP (temporarily out of print) – though such information is of very doubtful value; it just keeps you stringing along indefinitely. A title for which a new edition is in preparation is marked NE (new edition), and one which has not yet been published is marked either NP or NYP (not published/not yet published). Dates may be added as above. If a title is marked NK (not known) the publisher means that the title you require is not one he publishes; 'not ours' as an answer means the same thing. OO means 'on order'; OO/India, for example, means that the book you require is temporarily out of stock, but that further copies have been ordered from India. This situation arises when a UK publisher is acting as agent in this country for an overseas publisher; it can arise for a wholesaler at any time. Wholesalers also use the answer TOS for 'temporarily out of stock'.

These answers have developed over time and are not entirely standardised. BDG, for example, is sometimes given as just B, and you will meet other variations and even different answers altogether. To try to standardise things, the PA has recommended a brand new set of numerical answers to replace the traditional abbreviations. In the code – still not widely used – each of the digits 1 to 9 has a special meaning: *1* Not known; *2* On order to follow (date); *3* Binding (date); *4* Reprinting (date); *5* Not yet published; *6* New edition in preparation; *7* Reprint under consideration; *8* Out of print; *9* On order abroad.

Dues

When a book is temporarily unavailable, suppliers may indicate that they are recording your order for fulfilment at a later date. Such recorded orders are known as dues. If when you place an order you either want the book immediately or not at all, you should indicate this on your order by some such instruction as 'If unavailable please report but do not record dues.'

Keep a file of dues and check it regularly, chasing overdues and cancelling others that you or your customers have lost interest in.

DELIVERIES

The delivery method is usually at the discretion of the publisher or wholesaler. You can of course specify the delivery method you require, but will then almost invariably have to meet its full cost. See page 119 on orders sent direct from publisher to bookseller's customer.

For small parcels the postal service is frequently used. Larger ones go by commercial carriers. A few publishers and many wholesalers have their own van delivery services for the local trade. As already noted, reps sometimes carry car stock, especially at Christmas time. Cash-and-carry facilities may be found at a number of wholesalers' warehouses, and a declining number of publishers still offer a trade counter service to booksellers who call in person.

Checking deliveries in

Apart from unrecorded postal packages, you normally have to sign for deliveries. If a parcel is plainly damaged in some way, either refuse delivery or note the damage on the receipt before signing – eg 'parcel received damaged' or 'carton delivered badly dented on one side'.

Then do three things: (1) Check delivery contents against the invoice or delivery note or advice note. Notify the supplier immediately of any discrepancies and of any damage, whether already noted on the carrier's receipt or not. (2) Check delivery contents against your own order and again notify the supplier immediately of any errors or omissions. (3) Publication dates permitting (see page 215), get the books out on the shelves as soon as possible. Books in boxes on the office floor are not earning their keep; they're not even trying to.

Cyclic supply

Increasingly booksellers are ordering little and often. This is particularly true of those with computerised stock control and ordering systems which make it relatively easy to know what's needed and to place orders for it. Punitive terms apart, little-and-often is the most economical way of keeping the stock finely tuned to the shifting demands of the market. But as so often in the publishing–bookselling equation, a plus on one side means a minus on the other. Little-and-often may be good for the bookseller but for the publisher it means more work and more cost for the same volume of sales. Part of the stockholding burden is lifted from the bookseller and dumped back on the publisher.

Some publishers have reacted by introducing cyclic distribution systems. Instead of dealing with orders as they come in, they are held back, bookseller by bookseller or region by region, to be processed on fixed days – once a week perhaps – so turning little-and-often back into larger-and-less-often. If your orders are dealt with, say, on Mondays, anything coming in on any other day is in effect put aside until the following Monday. It's important to know if a publisher is working a cyclic distribution system and, if so, to allow orders to roll up in your office rather than his, sending them off in a batch to get there on the right day. Otherwise little-and-often may increase your work and cost with no corresponding improvement to the quality of your stock.

SPEEDING THE PROCESS

If you have an urgent order, send it in an urgent way. There's no point in marking your order VERY URGENT in big red letters if you send it in the second class post; and if you think no bookseller would ever do such a thing, spend a little time if you can in a publisher's office.

The quickest way of getting your order to the publisher or wholesaler is by phone or teleordering. The latter can have a particularly dramatic effect upon delivery times if orders get fed straight through to the supplier's computer. Type in an order this evening, and by the time the supplier's warehouse staff arrive for work tomorrow morning all the paperwork they need to get your order together and send it off will be waiting for them.

After the phone and teleordering, the next best method is a first class letter direct to the supplier. The other postal methods are plainly non-urgent.

But however speedily you get your order to the supplier, once there it's out of your hands, and if you come into bookselling you will have to learn to live with delivery delays. You will, however, get to know the typical lead times of different publishers and wholesalers and your stock control and ordering procedures will take account of them.

When accepting special orders from customers, avoid tarring all suppliers with the same brush by such a stock response as "We can get it for you but it will take six weeks." Most wholesalers and some publishers are very speedy in the service they give to booksellers, and if they are to be rewarded, and others encouraged to emulate them, booksellers should acknowledge their efficiency and not frighten off potential buyers of their books by a blanket prediction of prolonged delay.

SETTLING UP

The use of the BA's Booksellers Clearing House for the payment of bills has already been mentioned (page 93). An alternative service is offered by BOD. This works like BCH but offers a more extensive publisher list, and for an additional 20p plus VAT per publisher (in 1988), permits payments to be made to any UK publisher not on the standard list.

Chapter 6

Start-up and Running Costs

Questions uppermost in the mind of every would-be bookshop owner are *How much will it cost me?* and *How much will I make?* to both of which the truthful but unhelpful answer must be *It all depends*. Size, location, site, stockholding and so on will plainly have a major bearing on whether you need to find £50,000 or £500,000 to get started. And it's equally plain that a skilfully managed shop is likely to be more profitable than one allowed to blunder along from day to day.

But the questions have to be answered, and *It all depends* just won't do. At some stage you will have to draw up a detailed business plan, probably to present to your bank manager if you need to raise money, or just as a matter of business common sense if you are financing the venture from your own capital. But that stage may be many months off, and before deciding to embark upon even an investigation of possibilities, you need to have an idea, however imperfect, of what the costs and rewards of a bookshop might be. If the figures are discouraging, better not to start the project than to abandon it several months down the road after belatedly discovering its financial implications.

FINDING THE INFORMATION

To get helpful answers you have to put precise questions. There's no sensible answer to questions like *How much do bookshops cost these days?* but there is at least a tentative answer to questions like

How much will it cost to stock a 750 sq ft bookshop? What you need are facts and figures about bookshops already trading, by reference to which you can draw a financial profile of your own intended shop. Even so, some information – like the cost of premises or shopfitting – can be found only by direct and specific enquiry.

PREMISES

The cost of freehold premises, or the premium – if any – to be paid for a lease, defies generalisation. There are huge differences from place to place, often over a fairly small area. A knowledgeable local agent is the person to discuss such figures with once you have shortlisted the geographical areas that interest you.

You may, however, not want to buy a freehold, and the landlord or leaseholder may not be asking for a premium. While these costs, therefore, can be substantial, they are not an inevitable part of your initial outlay and no sensible figure can be attached to them at this stage. You must in due course remember to add them into your own calculations if they apply to the particular premises you have in mind.

SHOPFITTING

Shopfitting costs are another variable. The big chains currently reckon to spend anything from £40 to £80 per square foot on it – that covers structural alteration, shelving and other display units, carpets, lighting, new shop front, security systems and so on. At the other extreme, many a small independent, keeping structural alteration to a minimum, and concentrating resources on the functional rather than the decorative, have managed to get the whole thing done – and done professionally – for £12 to £15 per square foot. Those with confidence in their DIY skills have done it for even less.

But if one drew up a list of those features which typically distinguish the branch of a major bookselling group from the small independent, very high on that list would be the superior quality of shopfitting and design of the former compared to the latter. If the big chains are teaching us anything about the way to sell books, it is that a bookshop's *image* – of which shopfitting and design are such important components – contributes crucially to its success; it is not something to be attended to optionally if there's money left over.

There's more about the nature and importance of shopfitting in later chapters. For the present, let's say that you could easily spend as much as £35 per square foot turning an empty shell into a well designed bookshop ready for trading. This, at 1988 rates, is somewhere near the top of the range of what small independents are paying. But bear in mind the variability of costs already mentioned. As with the cost of premises, you must in due course take your own likely shopfitting costs into account; they may vary all the way from nothing at all – if you take over an existing bookshop, already satisfactorily fitted out – to a very substantial sum indeed.

RUNNING COSTS AND REWARDS

Property and shopfitting apart, most of the figures you need to make a provisional *generalised* calculation of your likely costs and rewards as a bookseller – ie without reference to a particular shop or a particular area – are not difficult to suggest.

Suppose you knew someone with a bookshop. If you could look at the accounts, you would learn how much was spent on rent, rates, staff, stock and so on, and also how much the owner was able to draw from the business for personal use. The figures would suggest what your costs and rewards might be in a similar shop. While no two bookshops are exactly alike, nor any two booksellers, the actual figures of an actual shop would at least help you to flesh out some likelihoods for your own proposed venture.

To allow for the possibility that your friend's shop might be untypical, it would be helpful to take your research a stage further. Suppose you knew several people with bookshops, and could get sight of the accounts of all them. By lumping them together, you could form an idea of costs and performance in general, and so avoid the misleading impression you might get from the freak results of any one of them.

In principle, the approach is a good one, but few intending booksellers have the right friends in the right numbers at the right time; and even friends have been known to shift about uneasily when asked to reveal their business figures. Fortunately, there is an alternative source of information that may be used in almost the same way: the annual *Charter Group Economic Survey*.

CHARTER GROUP ECONOMIC SURVEY

PRICE £25 IN 1988

Each year members of the BA's Charter Group are required to complete a confidential and detailed questionnaire based on the accounts of their latest complete financial year. The number of respondents varies from year to year but is typically about 330, and as some questionnaires relate to a group of shops the total number of shops represented is about 400.

Completed questionnaires are returned anonymously direct to the Manchester Business School where they are processed, and where statistical tables and charts are produced. Individual questionnaires are seen only by the researchers; the Survey itself publishes totals, ratios, averages and medians and does not identify individual shops. The Charter Group attaches such importance to the Survey that any Charter member failing without good cause to make an annual return is at risk of expulsion from the Group, and indeed a number have been expelled for this very reason.

For people not yet in the trade, the latest *Economic Survey* provides the most accessible insight into the detailed economics of running a bookshop. Short of the personal and obliging contacts already referred to, the Survey is the sole source of information.

Statistics present general rather than individual truths. We all know what is meant by the statement that the average family in a certain city has 2.7 children though we don't for a moment believe that any such family exists. The *Economic Survey* may similarly suggest the statistical characteristics of shops which have no counterparts in the real world, and in other ways too it presents figures which have to be interpreted with intelligent caution.

THE GREAT NET PROFIT MYSTERY

Look at Table 8 overleaf from the *Economic Survey*. One of its most depressing figures appears on the *Net (trading) profit %* line: 3.2 per cent in 1985, though improving over a five year view.

Ever since the Charter Group produced its first *Economic Survey* in 1965, critics have questioned the validity of the reported net profits. Can bookselling really be so unprofitable? Translated into pounds, 3.2 per cent means that the owner of a shop with a turnover of £100,000 a year is left with just £3,200 before tax. Arthur Young quotes the sceptics' description of the figures as 'too bad to be true'.

However, in determining what credence to attach to the Survey's net profit figures, a number of points need to be made:

- Net profit may not be the working owner's sole income from the business. He or she may also be drawing a salary, already included as a business expense under *Wages and salaries* earlier in the Table.

- Because of the different ways in which salaries, retained profits and dividends are taxed and the different pre-tax allowances for which they qualify, there is usually a tax advantage to be gained

TABLE 8

OVERALL BOOKSHOP RESULTS 1978–85

	1978	1979	1980	1981
Number of questionnaires analysed from booksellers	343	346	347	346
TOTAL NEW BOOK SALES				
£'000	103503	109700	122800	137500
Sales–other goods £'000	46199	52400	45750	64600
Total sales £'000	149702	162100	168550	202100
% Sales–new books–				
Retail*	65.4	67.3	70.0	69.3
Library*	10.1	10.4	10.4	9.0
Book Agents*	1.1	1.1	1.0	1.3
Schools*	9.7	8.6	9.0	8.4
	86.3	87.4	90.4	88.0
% Sales*–other goods	13.7	12.6	9.6	12.0
	100.0	*100.0*	*100.0*	*100.0*
*Gross Profit %**	*29.1*	*29.4*	29.8	*29.9*
TOTAL EXPENSES %*	25.4	26.1	26.8	27.9
(a) Wages and salaries %*	14.7	15.4	15.9	15.6
(b) Rent and rates %*	3.2	3.3	3.3	3.9
(c) Other working expenses %*	7.5	7.4	7.6	8.4
*Net (trading) profit %**	*3.7*	*3.3*	*3.0*	*2.0*
Net (trading) profit as % of operating assets	12.6	9.0	8.8	5.0
Number of times book stock turned over per annum	3.5	3.3	3.3	3.2
Sales per person employed (£)	21400	23700	27000	30500
Sales per sq. ft. of floor space (£)	75.8	85.0	91.5	97.7
% by which retail book stock written down to cost or valuation	40	40	40.0	38.6

by presenting a trading profit one way rather than another. It is by making the most tax-efficient decisions about presentation that accountants earn their keep.

For example, if on a turnover of £100,000 your bookshop achieves a trading surplus of £10,000, you could pay yourself a salary of £10,000 and show a zero per cent profit for the business; alternatively you could pay yourself nothing and show a profit of 10 per cent – or any other mix of salary and profit your accountant thought advantageous.

Source: *Charter Group Economic Survey 1985/86*

* *Figures expressed as % of total sales. Medians are used.*

1982	1983	1984	1985	
326	330	320	320	Number of questionnaires analysed from booksellers
				TOTAL NEW BOOK SALES
146900	163400	175100	191900	£'000
172000	180000	236700	259800	Sales–other goods £'000
318900	343400	411800	451700	Total sales £'000
				% Sales–new books–
70.2	69.8	70.3	71.4	Retail*
8.7	7.7	9.5	9.4	Library*
1.1	1.2	1.4	1.6	Book Agents*
7.9	9.3	9.4	9.0	Schools*
87.9	88.0	90.6	91.4	
12.1	12.0	9.4	8.6	% Sales*–other goods
100.0	*100.0*	*100.0*	*100.0*	
30.3	*30.2*	*30.5*	*30.6*	*Gross Profit %**
28.4	28.2	27.8	27.3	**TOTAL EXPENSES** %*
15.7	15.0	14.9	14.7	(a) Wages and salaries %*
4.0	4.2	4.2	4.3	(b) Rent and rates %*
8.7	9.0	8.7	8.3	(c) Other working expenses %*
1.9	*2.0*	*2.7*	*3.2*	*Net (trading) profit %**
5.3	6.0	7.3	8.1	Net (trading) profit as % of operating assets
3.2	3.2	3.0	3.1	Number of times book stock turned over per annum
32900	34700	36200	39700	Sales per person employed (£)
109	117	120	130	Sales per sq. ft. of floor space (£)
40	39.8	39.8	39.7	% by which retail book stock written down to cost or valuation

- It may be possible to charge to the business as pre-tax expenses some costs which in part at least accrue to the personal benefit of the owner – running a company car, for example – and which therefore quite legitimately depress the declared profit of the business without increasing to the same extent the owner's taxable salary.
- To many outsiders, running a bookshop of one's own looks to be a most attractive way of life. Some people come into the business –

and stay in it – more for pleasure than profit. With private means or a spouse earning a salary elsewhere, the fortunate few can indulge themselves in what may be called *hobby bookselling* – possibly giving a highly professional and valuable service to the public but making very little for themselves in hard cash. Any Charter bookshops run on these lines will naturally pull down the Survey's average net profit figures.

- When all is said and done, the inescapable truth is that bookselling is not a very profitable activity for the small independent trader. *Bookselling News* reported in its July 1987 issue that the International Booksellers Federation (IBF) produced its own *IBF Economic Survey* for the first time in 1986, comparing the profitability of bookselling in eleven different countries. The best figures came from New Zealand (8 per cent), Denmark (5.4 per cent) and Australia (5 per cent). The worst came from Canada (0.7 per cent), the Netherlands (0.9 per cent) and Austria (1.8 per cent). So Britain's net profit figures of 3.2 per cent in 1985 are, comparatively speaking, not all that good but not all that bad either.

The Charter Group's net profit figures turn out not to be such a great mystery after all. They must be read with a realistic appreciation of how businesses, and in particular small owner-managed businesses, arrive at the bottom line of their accounts. More of this later in the chapter.

PURPOSES OF THE SURVEY

The Survey serves three broad purposes. First, to present an annual picture of the trade, permitting year-on-year comparisons so that trends may be detected. Second, to be a yardstick against which existing traders may measure their own performances and identify areas for improvement. Third, to help intending bookshop owners put provisional figures into their business plans.

Year-on-year comparisons

Trade trends are as important to intending booksellers as to existing ones. While nothing is for ever, the expectation that tomorrow will be like today, only more so, is right more often than wrong. Data relating to past years has predictive as well as historical value. The best way of knowing where you're going is to look where you've been, check where you are now, and imagine yourself continuing along the same path into the future. Statisticians call this *extrapolation*. In this way, the *Economic Survey* can tell you something of how the trade is likely to be in future years.

Look at Table 8 again. This gives overall results for the period 1978–1985. The statistical snapshots of individual years, viewed in sequence, clearly show the trends in some values and the flatness of others. Note, by the way, that most of the key figures in the Survey are *ratios* – ie they express the relationship between two values – and these automatically discount inflation unless the ratio itself is expressed in pounds.

We can see that rent and rates have been a continuously increasing burden for booksellers in the eight years surveyed: in 1978 they cost 3.2 per cent of total sales while in 1985 they had reached 4.3 per cent. These figures represent real increases in cost, and extrapolation gives every reason to fear that further increases will take place in the future. On the other hand, while the sales per person employed rose over the same period from £21,400 to £39,700, these figures represent no real increase at all. They are not adjusted for inflation, and with a calculator you can work out for yourself that sales per person employed in 1985 represent the same fraction of total new book sales as they did in 1978. There has been, therefore, no improvement in staff productivity, though the Table does show that booksellers have managed to rein back wages and salaries to their 1978 levels after they threatened to gallop away in the early 1980s.

A yardstick for existing traders

Once you have your own shop, you can measure your achievements against those of colleagues in the trade as indicated in the Survey tables – not merely the net profit figures but all the detailed sales and cost ratios which lie behind the net profit. If you find, for example, that your sales per person employed are decidedly lower than the average, you will want to investigate why this should be so. Is it that you're employing too many people? Or that staff are tied up in labour-intensive tasks – like writing out large numbers of orders – when a change of method or technology would give them more time to deal directly with customers and so improve sales? Or is the price mix of your stock wrong – too many low-priced books and not enough high-priced ones for gift buyers who want to splurge? Or what? The Survey draws your attention to the questions; it is for you to find the answers.

Provisional figures for intending booksellers

The *Economic Survey* as crystal ball is its main use for readers of the present guide. The method will be demonstrated using data from the 1987 Survey, which covered the period 1985/86. Note that because businesses are necessarily in arrears with their annual returns, the latest Survey always relates to a period between 12 and 24 months earlier. To make your own calculations, buy a copy of the latest Survey from the BA. It comes out in late March.

PRESENTATION OF DATA IN THE SURVEY

The Survey contains a number of tables and charts, each presenting its own perspective on some aspect of the data, together with a commentary which interprets the data, particularly drawing attention to trends and reversals of trends. We have seen how Table 8, for example, permits broad year-on-year comparisons for the trade as a whole. While of great interest, this sort of table is not especially helpful for the intending bookshop owner because its figures are based upon all the returned questionnaires in the Survey – those of the smallest village booksellers, the largest high street shops, and everything in between. Of the 320 respondents in the 1985/86 Survey, by the way, 16 had an annual turnover below £50,000 while 32 had an annual turnover above a million pounds.

More helpful for the intending bookshop owner would be an analysis of the data by reference to turnover, so that larger shops were separated from smaller ones, and you could read off the figures that relate to the size of shop you had in mind. Just such an analysis is included in the Survey – shown here as Table 9 on page 138.

SALES AND PROFITABILITY BY SIZE OF OUTLET

Table 9 is, for our present purpose, the Survey's main table. Notice that each of the six size divisions is further analysed into three categories of roughly equal size by reference to the net profits achieved: the least profitable (*low*), the averagely profitable (*average*), and the most profitable (*high*).

ANOTHER LOOK AT NET PROFIT

Look at the *Net (trading) profit* line in Table 9. It is worth noting straight away that in all but the Super-large division there are significant numbers of businesses with no net profit at all (see also Figure 3 on page 102), and these lead to an average net loss for the *low* achievers as a whole. But once these businesses are removed from the figures, the average net profits of the remainder improve markedly. The *high* achievers in each category go from 7.2 per cent to 11.1 per cent – much healthier figures. What the Table seems to be saying is that reasonable returns are not impossible to achieve in bookselling – whatever the size of the shop – but that they are not achieved automatically.

Table 9 also allows us to remove one of the possible distortions present in Table 8 where, as already noted, the amount of a working owner's salary – if any – could not be identified. Table 9 not only gives us a *Wages and salaries* figure but also, under Detailed Cost Ratios, *Working directors' and proprietors' basic salaries* and their *Pension Contributions* charged to the business.

It was noted earlier that the attribution of a trading surplus to the owner's salary or the shop's profit is, to an extent, at the discretion of the accountant. So by adding together the owner's salary and the declared net profit, we come closer to the real amount of money that a working owner can take out of the business. Look at the *average* Medium category, for example. The working owner benefits from a salary of 3.8 per cent and a pension contribution of 0.5 per cent – a total of 4.3 per cent; add to this the declared net trading profit of 2.6 per cent, and you have a grand total of 6.9 per cent. And it is this last figure which most accurately reflects the sum the working owner can take out of the business: £6,900 before tax for every £100,000 of turnover.

This still leaves us with unquantifiable distortions. A shop run by a husband and wife, for example, may, for the purposes of the accounts, show one of the spouses as owner and the other as employee, and their joint earnings may be rather more respectable than anything we can deduce from the Survey figures. Nevertheless, the above way of calculating how much a working owner can take out of the business is probably as near to the generalised truth as we can get.

FINANCIAL PROFILE OF YOUR PROPOSED BOOKSHOP

You hope of course that your shop will be among the high achievers. But as a newcomer to the trade, you may think it prudent to expect to perform only averagely in the early years. And the same prudence will probably lead you to plan a business large enough to be commercially viable but small enough to allow you to exercise moment-by-moment control. These assumptions point to a business in the *average* Small/Medium category of Table 9. And this is the category upon which figures will be based for the purpose of the worked examples below, though if you wish to make different assumptions, the same approach will work using the figures in any one of the other categories.

There are various starting points for the calculation, depending

TABLE 9

BOOKSHOP SALES AND PROFITABILITY BY SIZE OF OUTLET

BOOKSALES	SMALL Below £91,000			SMALL/MEDIUM £91,000-£146,000			MEDIUM £146,000-£211,000		
Net Profit Category	Low	*Average*	High	Low	*Average*	High	Low	*Average*	Hig
Number in Category	17	18	18	18	17	18	17	18	18
SALES RATIOS									
New book sales %	93.2	*76.7*	76.8	87.5	*72.2*	78.7	83.8	*81.5*	85.0
*(a) Retail	87.2	*90.1*	89.9	82.8	*40.1*	84.1	85.0	*79.3*	86.8
*(b) Library	3.2	*2.8*	1.8	4.0	*4.5*	3.3	3.7	*6.5*	1.7
*(c) Book Agents	0.2	*5.5*	4.3	0.3	*0.9*	1.0	0	*0.2*	1.7
*(d) Schools	9.4	*1.0*	4.0	12.9	*4.5*	11.6	11.3	*14.0*	9.8
Other goods sales %	6.8	*23.3*	23.2	12.5	*27.8*	21.3	16.2	*18.5*	15.0
PROFIT + COST RATIOS									
Gross Profit %	26.8	*30.9*	33.6	29.1	*31.3*	33.8	30.8	*29.6*	31.6
Total Expenses %	37.3	*30.6*	26.4	32.2	*27.0*	22.7	38.5	*27.0*	23.3
(a) Wages and salaries	16.0	*15.3*	13.5	16.3	*14.6*	12.3	17.2	*14.3*	13.6
(b) Rent and rates	7.6	*5.5*	5.3	5.8	*4.5*	3.5	9.4	*4.7*	4.2
(c) Other working expenses	13.7	*9.8*	7.6	10.1	*7.9*	6.9	11.9	*8.0*	5.5
Net (trading) profit %	(10.5)	*0.3*	7.2	(3.1)	*4.3*	11.1	(7.7)	*2.6*	8.3
OPERATING RATIOS									
Stock turn (books)	2.2	*2.3*	2.5	4.5	*3.2*	2.5	2.6	*3.5*	3.4
% by which retail stock written down to cost or valuation	35.3	*37.6*	37.8	37.3	*36.4*	37.0	41.7	*42.5*	40.9
Sales per person employed (£)	28900	*30900*	34300	37400	*45700*	41500	37000	*38500*	45800
Sales per sq.ft. (£)	87	*107*	102	122	*114*	120	129	*108*	163
DETAILED COST RATIOS									
Wages, salaries, NHI of staff %	10.1	*11.6*	10.9	10.8	*10.2*	9.6	13.1	*9.8*	8.6
Pension contributions for staff (other than NHI) %	0.1	*0.2*	0.3	0.1	*0.3*	0.3	0.3	*0.2*	0.4
Working directors' and proprietors' basic salaries and NHI only %	5.7	*3.4*	1.8	4.6	*3.6*	2.2	3.6	*3.8*	3.8
Pension Contributions to directors and proprietors (other than NHI) %	0.1	*0.1*	0.5	0.8	*0.5*	0.2	0.2	*0.5*	0.8
Rent %	5.8	*4.5*	4.0	3.9	*3.1*	2.3	6.8	*3.6*	2.6
Rates (incl. water & sewerage) %	1.8	*1.0*	1.3	1.9	*1.4*	1.2	2.6	*1.1*	1.6
Gas, electricity %	0.9	*1.0*	0.7	0.7	*0.2*	0.6	0.7	*0.6*	0.5
Telephone %	0.6	*0.6*	0.5	0.5	*0.4*	0.4	0.4	*0.4*	0.4
Postage and carriage charges %	0.7	*0.6*	0.5	0.5	*0.6*	0.4	0.4	*0.4*	0.6
Printing and stationery %	0.5	*0.4*	0.5	0.4	*0.5*	0.4	0.4	*0.4*	0.4
Publicity and advertising %	0.3	*0.4*	0.3	0.8	*0.4*	0.5	0.9	*0.4*	0.4
Repairs, renewals & maintenance %	1.1	*0.6*	0.4	0.4	*0.4*	0.6	1.1	*0.4*	0.4
Vehicle running & travelling costs %	1.6	*1.0*	0.6	1.2	*0.7*	0.7	0.7	*0.7*	0.4
Interest paid %	2.7	*0.8*	0.1	1.3	*0.3*	0.7	1.0	*1.3*	0.4
Bank charges (excl. interest), audit and accountancy %	2.5	*1.3*	1.3	1.4	*1.2*	1.1	1.1	*0.9*	0.8
All other working expenses (excl. depreciation) %	1.2	*2.0*	1.8	1.1	*1.1*	0.1	2.9	*1.2*	0.4
Depreciation & write-offs %	1.6	*1.1*	0.9	1.8	*1.1*	1.4	2.3	*1.3*	0.8

upon how deeply committed you are to particular characteristics of your intended shop. Here are two worked examples of how the Table 9 figures can be used: Example One assumes a certain required income, Example Two assumes premises of a given floor area.

Source: *Charter Group Economic Survey 1985/86*

** % of new book sales. Averages are used.*

MEDIUM/LARGE £211,000-£335,000			LARGE £335,000-£1,000,000			SUPER-LARGE £1,000,000 or over			BOOKSALES
Low	*Average*	High	Low	*Average*	High	Low	*Average*	High	*Net Profit Category*
20	16	18	17	20	19	4	5	8	Number in Category
									SALES RATIOS
80.3	*90.1*	83.0	93.9	*83.6*	84.4	95.9	*59.0*	79.8	New book sales %
75.1	*73.1*	90.8	77.6	*71.4*	81.6	68.0	*92.9*	87.7	*(a) Retail
9.3	*8.8*	5.4	11.9	*13.9*	14.3	30.5	*5.1*	12.3	*(b) Library
3.7	*1.1*	1.7	2.0	*0.4*	0	0.4	*0.3*	0	*(c) Book Agents
11.9	*17.0*	2.1	8.5	*14.3*	4.1	1.1	*1.7*	0	*(d) Schools
19.7	*9.9*	17.0	6.1	*16.4*	15.6	4.1	*41.0*	20.2	Other goods sales %
									PROFIT + COST RATIOS
28.7	*26.7*	31.5	28.6	*28.9*	33.1	29.4	*30.6*	33.3	*Gross Profit %*
31.4	*23.4*	23.3	31.7	*25.7*	25.0	28.7	*26.2*	25.1	Total Expenses %
16.5	*14.2*	12.5	16.7	*13.1*	14.5	16.0	*15.2*	13.6	(a) Wages and salaries
5.6	*2.9*	4.7	5.7	*3.1*	3.5	3.3	*3.2*	4.3	(b) Rent and rates
9.3	*6.3*	6.1	9.3	*7.5*	7.0	9.4	*7.8*	7.2	(c) Other working expenses
(2.7)	*3.3*	8.2	(3.1)	*3.2*	8.1	0.7	*4.4*	8.2	*Net (trading) profit %*
									OPERATING RATIOS
3.8	*3.7*	3.6	3.7	*3.5*	4.3	4.1	*4.6*	4.1	Stock turn (books)
41.1	*42.2*	38.6	41.7	*38.3*	37.6	35.5	*41.8*	43.7	% by which retail stock written down to cost or valuation
44900	*47600*	50900	46200	*46700*	48600	37500	*65700*	57600	Sales per person employed (£)
157	*173*	176	156	*200*	172	140	*269*	209	Sales per sq.ft. (£)
									DETAILED COST RATIOS
10.3	*9.0*	10.5	13.0	*11.3*	12.0	14.3	*12.0*	12.3	Wages, salaries, NHI of staff %
0.4	*0.1*	0.2	0.6	*0.5*	0.7	0.4	*0.8*	0.4	Pension contributions for staff (other than NHI) %
5.6	*4.6*	1.4	2.5	*2.8*	1.4	1.3	*2.2*	0.9	Working directors' and proprietors' basic salaries and NHI only %
0.2	*0.5*	0.4	0.6	*0.5*	0.4	0	*0.2*	0	Pension Contributions to directors and proprietors (other than NHI) %
4.1	*2.2*	3.2	4.3	*2.2*	2.7	2.0	*2.2*	2.9	Rent %
1.5	*0.7*	1.5	1.4	*0.9*	0.8	1.3	*1.0*	3.7	Rates (incl. water & sewerage) %
0.6	*0.5*	0.5	0.6	*0.5*	0.5	0.5	*1.7*	0.6	Gas, electricity %
0.5	*0.4*	0.3	0.4	*0.3*	0.3	0.3	*0.2*	0.2	Telephone %
0.4	*0.4*	0.6	1.4	*0.5*	0.4	0.8	*0.7*	1.1	Postage and carriage charges %
0.4	*0.4*	0.3	0.4	*0.5*	0.3	0.5	*0.4*	0.3	Printing and stationery %
0.5	*0.4*	0.5	0.7	*0.5*	0.4	0.6	*0.8*	0.7	Publicity and advertising %
0.6	*0.4*	0.5	0.6	*0.6*	0.7	0.4	*0.7*	0.8	Repairs, renewals & maintenance %
0.9	*0.7*	0.3	0.7	*0.6*	0.4	0.5	*0.4*	0.3	Vehicle running & travelling costs %
1.2	*0.2*	0.2	1.2	*0.4*	0.2	0.4	*0.1*	0.2	Interest paid %
0.9	*0.8*	0.6	0.8	*0.7*	0.7	0.5	*0.4*	1.0	Bank charges (excl. interest), audit and accountancy %
2.1	*1.0*	1.5	1.3	*1.7*	2.2	3.2	*1.4*	0.2	All other working expenses (excl. depreciation) %
1.2	*1.1*	0.8	1.2	*1.2*	0.9	1.7	*1.0*	0.8	Depreciation & write-offs %

EXAMPLE ONE: AIMING AT A SPECIFIED PROFIT

(1) Name your target income. How much – or, more realistically, how little – will you be content to draw from the business year by year? Take a three year view and think of a number. Suppose that you decide upon an income of £10,000 a year as your target.

(2) Sales. What volume of sales will you need to achieve the target income? What annual turnover is implied by an income of £10,000 a year? The *average* Small/Medium category shows net profits of 4.3 per cent, to which, as explained earlier, must be added the working owner's salary and pension contribution benefit – ie 4.3 + 3.6 + 0.5 = 8.4 per cent. The question therefore becomes: Of what sum is £10,000 8.4 per cent? Answer: £119,047. Call it £120,000. That's the annual turnover to aim for.

(3) Shop size. What size shop will you need to produce sales of £120,000 a year? The Table gives a *Sales per sq ft* figure of £114 and that implies a sales area of 1,052 sq ft to produce £120,000. Call it 1,000 sq ft.

(4) Stock investment. The Table suggests a stockturn of 3.2, which implies that annual sales of £120,000 require an average stock value at retail prices of £37,500 (ie £120,000 ÷ 3.2). If you get 35 per cent discount, that in turn implies a stock investment of £24,375. Call it £24,000.

(5) Staff. Could you manage a shop of this size? The Table gives *Sales per person employed* as £45,700. So you'll need the equivalent of approximately 2.6 people – for example, yourself, one other full timer and someone else working about half time.

(6) Rent and rates. What sort of rent and rates should you be prepared to pay for your premises? The Table suggests 4.5 per cent – ie £5,400 (but remember that rising trend we've already noticed).

(7) Etcetera. You can see that once you settle upon an annual sales figure, all sorts of other figures can be deduced from the Table. At this stage, the above figures are among the most important, but if you wish you can go on to calculate typical expenditure on bank charges, telephone, gas and electricity and so on.

EXAMPLE TWO: STARTING WITH THE SHOP

(1) What size is the shop? If you already have a property in mind, you will want to estimate its potential for use as a bookshop. The Table won't help you to judge the merits of the shop's location (see page 169 for that), but it can give you an idea of its potential if the location *is* otherwise suitable. The starting point this time is the shop's size.

The physical dimensions of a shop set limits on its commercial potential because you can display only so many books in a given space and accommodate only so many customers. You may not be able to put precise figures on these limits, but once they are reached, further development will require further premises. You may be able to expand sideways by getting the shop next door, but that would be a lucky chance you couldn't rely upon. The likelier choice would be between staying put with a stunted business or moving to larger premises on an untried site; the former may lock you into an inadequately profitable business, the latter presents you with start-up problems all over again. It is important, therefore, to get an idea of what you can hope to achieve in a given space.

Suppose you have 750 sq ft available.

(2) Sales. The figure of £114 for sales per sq ft suggests that annual sales might be £85,500.

(3) Income. Using the same 8.4 per cent ratio as in Example One above, your income as owner-manager may be estimated at £7,182 – call it £7,200.

(4) Stock investment. With stockturn at 3.2, a turnover of £85,500 implies an average stock value at retail prices of £26,718. Call it £27,000. This implies a stock investment at trade prices of about £17,500.

(5) Staff. The Table suggests – using the *Sales per person employed* figure – that you should manage comfortably with just yourself and the equivalent of one other full timer.

(6) Rent and rates. With specific premises in mind, you already know the rent and rates. The Table suggests that they should total £3,847 for your £85,500 level of turnover. If the known rent and rates differ from this figure, then your predicted income will either benefit from the shortfall or suffer from the added cost.

(7) Etcetera. As in Example One, you can now go on to use the Table to estimate various other business costs if you wish.

RELIABILITY AND VALIDITY OF THE CALCULATIONS

Practising booksellers looking at the above calculations are likely to be scornful. Their own stockturn is nothing like the figure used; the sales per square foot bear no relation to anything remotely in their experience; the sales per person employed should be put forward for the next top fiction award; rent and rates at that level! – you must be joking; and so on.

Indeed, look at other figures in Table 9. Stockturn, for example, varies between 2.2 in the *low* Small category up to 4.6 in the *average*

Super-large category; and the same two categories show a range of sales per square foot from £87 to £269. Rent and rates vary from 2.9 per cent in the *average* Medium/large category to 9.4 per cent in the *low* Medium category. Since all these figures are averages, the individual returns upon which they are based must include figures which are even lower and even higher than anything appearing in the Table. There are huge variations in performance from bookshop to bookshop. It must be admitted, too, that some of the detailed figures produced by the Survey in successive years show such marked changes that one suspects they may be indicating rather more about the nature of the Survey and its basis of compilation than about the real world of bookselling in the high street. But if we content ourselves with such observations as these, we are right back with the *It all depends* answer which does nothing to help would-be bookshop owners start upon the task of converting dreams into the facts and figures needed for serious evaluation.

The *Economic Survey* may be an imperfect tool for the purpose, but it is the best we have. You might find it an interesting exercise to repeat your calculations using successively the figures from two or more different columns, thus getting an idea of the spread of possibility. You might also like to see how your figures work out if you use the Arthur Young recommendations of minimum targets for booksellers to aim at: a stockturn of between 4.5 and 5, and sales per square foot between £170 and £250. Repeat all your calculations, too, with figures from your copy of the latest *Economic Survey*.

Putting all these alternative calculations into the reckoning, you arrive at a profile which defines the limits of likelihood rather than one which purports to be the specific truth. This is perhaps the best compromise between the unhelpfulness of *It all depends* and the specious precision of a single set of figures.

CAPITAL REQUIREMENTS

So, setting aside the ifs and buts, how much to start and run your bookshop?

START-UP COSTS

Before you can open your shop door for the first time to let in the eager throng, this is the minimum set-up you need:

- premises;
- shopfittings;
- plant, equipment and tools of the trade;
- stock;
- sundry.

Suppose that the figures in Example One apply to you: you need a 1,000 sq ft shop with a turnover of £120,000 a year. Of the five elements in the minimum set-up, you are so far only able to put a figure on stock at £24,000. Shopfitting costs we know to be variable, but let's cautiously use the £35 per sq ft figure mentioned earlier, and provisionally earmark £35,000 for the purpose. The cost of acquiring premises can be nothing at all or a great deal – it's impossible to generalise. You will have to add the figure into your calculations after direct enquiry.

Plant, equipment and tools of the trade include everything from a car or van, to computers, cash registers, microfiche readers, bibliographies and so on. Again, the costs are variable. In time, you will have to work them out in detail for yourself. At this early stage, earmark £7,000 under this heading.

Sundry costs are anything else not yet covered: legal fees, rent payable in advance, insurance, stationery and everything else needed in the business. Leave yourself money also for the unexpected. Earmark, say, £4,000 under this heading.

Total the tentative start-up cost of your 1,000 sq ft shop and it comes to £70,000 – plus the cost of the freehold or lease premium, if any. Go through the same calculation for the 750 sq ft shop, and the start-up cost is something like £52,500.

None of the above assumptions or deductions is gospel. They are intended only to give you a first idea of the possible costs and rewards of a bookshop, and to suggest how you might make preliminary calculations based on your own circumstances and assumptions, and using the latest published figures. Just as soon, however, as you feel convinced, on your own calculations, that a bookshop looks to be a feasible idea for you, find yourself a good accountant and discuss the whole thing with him or her.

RUNNING COSTS

Once you start trading, money starts coming in, though probably not at the same pace as bills fall due for payment. Indeed, in the first year or so, it would be no surprise if you traded at a loss. Few businesses, however well managed, move straight into profit. And even shops running profitably can be short of cash from time to time. Like that of most retailing trades, bookselling revenue peaks at Christmas, while bills are spread more evenly over the whole year.

You therefore need to be able to call on reserves of money for running the business even when it has started trading. Another £10,000 for this would be prudent. It may not be necessary to have this sum sitting as cash in an account; an overdraft facility at the bank may be the best way of ensuring an adequacy of working capital.

CAN IT BE DONE ON LESS?

The expectation must be that the lower the investment, the lower the return. If £70,000 might produce an annual income of £10,000, and £52,500 an annual income of £7,200, lower investments must be expected to produce proportionately lower incomes. Of course, you might beat the predictions, but the smaller the business, the less able it is to develop a successful momentum: limited space, stock, staff and so on are all handicaps difficult to overcome.

People *have* succeeded in building thriving bookshops from small beginnings with tiny capital. But it is difficult enough even with larger capital, so the outlook for the shoestring operation is not good.

As in all fields, the greatest economies are possible where the greatest expenditure is made. You're bound to look very carefully at shopfitting costs, though you must avoid the mistake of thinking that shopfitting is merely cosmetic. As far as the public is concerned, the shop's appearance *is* the shop. There probably is scope, however, for implementing a shopfitting plan in stages, though it makes sense to have the master plan from the start.

What about going concerns?

A going concern is only worth buying if it is trading profitably. But if it *is* trading profitably, and if the stock *is* of good saleable quality, and if the shop fitments and equipment *do* have useful life left in them, then the vendor will certainly be looking to sell for a sum rather higher than the mere asset value of the business. So while taking over a going concern may have other attractions (see page 167), the saving of investment capital is not one of them.

IS IT ALL WORTH IT?

The pleasure and satisfaction you take in running your own bookshop can't be quantified. You must consult your own feelings. Here we simply look at the monetary implications.

Using the Example One figures again – but you will of course do the calculation with your own figures – it seems you might need capital of about £70,000 to have a chance of making £10,000 a year as a working owner.

You either have to borrow the £70,000 or use your own savings, or a mix of the two. To borrow money, you have to pay interest. To use your own money, you have to forgo the interest you would earn if you left it on deposit, say, in a building society.

Most new businesses are started with a mix of personal savings and borrowed money. But for the purpose of the illustration, suppose you borrowed the whole £70,000 for five years at 12 per cent. The first year's interest alone would come to £8,400 and the repayment of capital would be a further £14,000. As the debt is paid off, so the interest repayments reduce, but it remains a major burden on the business until finally cleared at the end of the fifth year.

If you rely entirely on your own savings, and remove your £70,000 from where it is earning, say, 7 per cent interest, then you forgo £4,900 a year in interest in order to get, as working owner, £10,000 a year as earned – and taxable – income. The whole exercise, if you reach your target, leaves you (before tax) £5,100 better off after a year's full time work than if you had done no work at all and left your money on deposit.

Some of your start-up costs remain as assets in the business, but these assets are only realisable if you can find a willing buyer. Don't rely upon being able to sell your shop as a going concern a few years hence unless it is significantly more profitable than anything the *Economic Survey* seems to hold out as a possibility.

Chapter 7

Stock Control

We saw in the last chapter that a bookseller aiming at a fairly modest income may need stock worth about £38,000 at retail prices or £24,000 at trade prices. You get a lot of books for that money, and keeping track of what you've sold and what you haven't sold, and deciding what to do in either case, is a major headache.

At the average book price figures suggested in Chapter 3 (page 74), £38,000 would buy about 10,000 paperbacks or 2,900 hardbacks. A bookshop with a fairly typical mix might have by value 60 per cent paperbacks and 40 per cent hardbacks – say, £23,000 of paperbacks (about 6,000 books) and £15,000 of hardbacks (about 1,200 books). Some of the better sellers would be held in multiple copies but a lot of the stock would be singles. So a £38,000 stock might be made up of something like 5,000 titles and 7,200 volumes.

There is an element of grabbing figures out of the air in all of this, and if you make different assumptions you will come up with different answers. Try the calculation for yourself, using your own proposed stock value, mix and today's average prices. You can see that even in a small bookshop the number of titles, each requiring your individual judgement – to buy or not to buy, one or many, to hold or return – is substantial. Happy the non-specialist who need only ask the wholesaler's rep to fill up the fifty feet of shelving in the corner of the shop and leave it at that. For you, as a specialist bookseller, each title must be individually chosen and its fortunes individually monitored. That's the stock control problem.

TIME IS MONEY

Whatever the size of your bookshop, a large part of your capital will be tied up in stock. You can't get your hands on that money again until the books are sold. The quicker they sell, the harder your money works. It is not just the discount that matters, but also the time it takes to earn it.

Suppose you take two £10 net books into stock at the start of the year, Book A at 25 per cent discount, Book B at 35 per cent. How do the two books compare as commercial propositions if Book A sells at the rate of one every two months and Book B at the rate of one every four months?

At the start of the year you invest £7.50 in one copy of the low discount Book A. By the end of two months you have sold it, recovered your £7.50 and made a profit of £2.50 besides. You re-invest your £7.50 to buy a replacement copy, and by the end of another two months you have once again recovered your outlay plus another £2.50 profit. You continue like this throughout the year, recycling the same £7.50 every other month. In cash terms, you end the year with total profits of £15 and your original £7.50 intact. Your cash has grown by 200 per cent: each £1 invested in stock has earned a gross profit of £2 over the year.

Now do the same calculation for the high discount Book B which sells one copy every four months. This time you invest only £6.50 at the start of the year, and this is the sum you recover and reinvest every fourth month. In cash terms, you end the year with total profits of £10.50 and your original £6.50 intact. Your cash has grown by 162 per cent: each £1 invested in stock has earned a gross profit of £1.62 over the year.

So the low discount book has earned significantly more than the high discount book: £2 against £1.62 for each £1 of stock investment. Once again, work it out for yourself. Think of other discounts, prices and rates of sale, and note the effect upon annual gross profit.

If every £1 of your stock investment at trade prices of, say, £24,000 did as well as Book A, your annual gross profit would be £48,000; if it did only as well as Book B, your annual gross profit would be £38,880. The difference of over £9,000 would be represented, pound for pound, in the amount of money you could pay yourself at the end of the year. If on the Book B figures you could draw, say, £8,000, then on the Book A figures you could draw over £17,000. Alternatively, you could achieve the same turnover and the same income for a lower stock investment.

Of course, such calculations are a tidy simplification of the real world of stock investment, but they do reflect the importance of time in the financial equation. The temptation is to focus on the question of discount – conveniently precise and known in advance – and to ignore the time component which lies uncertainly in the future.

The standard way of expressing the time component in stock management is stockturn (see page 103) and much of your effort as a bookseller will be directed to maintaining it at least and improving it if possible. The mechanism for doing so is stock control.

ROLE OF STOCK CONTROL IN BOOKSHOP MANAGEMENT

The above figures make clear both the desirability and the difficulty of effective stock control: desirable because of the greater profit potential, and difficult because of the large number of titles to be managed and the small number – often one only – of each title stocked. This is how Anne Williams of *Wordstock* – one of the trade's computerised stock control systems – puts it: "Most people who want to own a bookshop dream of a pleasantly book-drenched environment; a good stock control system sees that the dream doesn't die young under a mass of semi-legible paperwork and unpayable bills."

Look at the matter of numbers in a little more detail. Although for any given shop the *number* of titles stocked may not vary greatly from month to month, the *make-up* of the stock will vary because of continuously changing title availability – that is, old books going out of print and new ones being published. A shop with a fairly steady stock of 9,000 titles, for example, may during the course of a year drop 2,000 titles hitherto stocked and take on a further 2,000 titles never stocked before.

KNOWING WHAT'S GOING ON

Suppose you open a brand new shop with 6,000 titles. Business is brisk in the first week and a good number of books get sold. But which books? How do you know which titles to reorder? How do you know how many of each to reorder? How, in the course of time, do you decide which books *not* to reorder because they are such slow sellers? And how – and when – do you identify which titles are such a dead loss that you will try to return them to the supplier for credit?

Some booksellers do it all by memory and intuition. They feel they know their stock so well and are so involved in day-to-day selling that they have a shrewd idea of their stock position at any moment, and can almost instinctively judge what to order, when to order, how many to order and what to return. Though widely practised by small independent booksellers, this memory/intuition method is a long way from the ideal. It can only work tolerably well in a one-person shop with very limited sales.

If you do the stock control inside your own head like this, you make yourself indispensable. That may do wonders for your self-importance but it locks you personally and permanently into continuous stock-watching. You only have to be out of the shop for a day or two – or even an hour or two – and you begin to lose track of what's happening. And anyway, can you really know of all your thousands of titles which ones have sold and how quickly, which ones haven't sold and how long they've been in stock – to say nothing of the question of discounts, delivery times, minimum order requirements and so on?

Without some sort of formal stock control system, you manage your business by hunches and lower your limits of potential commercial success.

SERVANT NOT MASTER

You use various aids in your business to help you make or implement management decisions – *WBIP*, the telephone, a wholesaler's catalogue, a desk calculator, the BA's Buyer's Guides, a book of order forms and so on. A stock control system is just such an aid: a management tool which helps you make timely and sensible decisions about your stock.

Even the most sophisticated electronic systems do not relieve you of your managerial responsibility. It is not a question of whether you use a stock control system on the one hand or make decisions for yourself on the other. The decisions are always yours; no system can replace the skilful judgement of a good bookseller. What it *can* do is alert you to the need for a decision and provide you with the information to make it. The point needs to be stressed because there are still booksellers who regard formal stock control systems as a challenge to their professional self-respect. The attitude is perverse. A stock control system is an aid to skilled management, not a substitute for it.

KEY COMPONENTS OF STOCK CONTROL

The basic questions a stock control system must answer are (1) Which books are selling? (2) Which books aren't selling?

You need to know which books are selling so that you can

order replacement stock without delay. However much you may try to encourage customers to ask for what they want, most people don't ask for what they can't see. You will never know how much business you've lost by failing to maintain wanted titles in stock.

You need to know which books *aren't* selling so that you can return them for credit if possible, or, failing that, sell them off at bargain prices under the NBA rules. However skilful a buyer you are, some of your purchases will fail to sell. Unless you do something about these non-sellers, they gradually silt up the system, reducing your cash flow and therefore the amount available for spending on saleable stock.

All the other questions answered by stock control systems – *How fast is it selling?, How long has it been in stock?, How do we get best terms on the title?* and so on – are elaborations of the two basic questions, and give the detailed information you need to make a judgement and implement it.

To get answers to the basic questions, you must either monitor shop sales so that you know what has been sold, or check shelf stock from time to time in order to deduce what has been sold.

Whether by observation or deduction, the mere noting of stock movements is not itself a stock control system, though a necessary part of one. The information obtained has to be checked against previous stock levels in order to determine how quickly or slowly a title is selling, how many replacement copies, if any, should be ordered, or how many remaining copies, if any, should be returned. There has therefore to be a master file of everything taken into stock with which the current position can be compared.

So the key components of stock control are: (1) a sales record of each title in the shop; (2) routines for keeping the record up to date; (3) a system for alerting the bookseller when decisions are needed; (4) making and implementing the decisions.

A formal stock control system provides the first three components; your skill provides the fourth.

MANUAL *v* COMPUTERISED SYSTEMS

More than twenty years ago, Gerald Bartlett in *Stock Control in Bookselling* (Hutchinson) – still well worth reading though now long out of print – wrote that "The essence of stock control is to have the right book in the right place at the right time, and not to have the wrong book at any time." Technology has moved on but that central truth remains the same. When you come to evaluate different methods of stock control you should never lose sight of what it's all about.

The more sophisticated the system, the more useful information it provides and the more promptly it provides it. Information from the best of the computerised systems is up to date to the very second, and available in various forms to suit your requirements of the moment. Manual systems can give prompt news of individual sales, but in other ways are much slower and far less flexible.

It is only recently that the size, capacity and price of computer systems have brought electronic stock control within sight of the small independent bookshop. Within sight but not yet, perhaps, within reach of any but the largest of the small independents – say, with a turnover approaching £250,000. But the situation is changing fast and when you come to plan your own shop in detail, you should look very hard at the available computerised systems and not dismiss them out of hand as too costly or complex. Computerised stock control must be the preferred system if your volume of business justifies it.

COST

Stock control systems cost money to buy, set up and maintain. These costs have to be more than covered by resultant savings in stock investment or increased profits on turnover. Any system worthy of the name should achieve these ends, though the benefits of the more expensive systems may take time to come through.

Manual systems

The initial outlay for a manual stock control system is very low. You need nothing more costly or complex than record cards and boxes to file them in – and not all systems need even those. There is, however, a hidden cost which has always put limits on the usefulness of manual stock control: staff time. Manual systems can be depressingly labour-intensive. It's not much of a triumph to save, say, £2,000 a year by improved stock control, if it costs £2,500 of staff time to do it. Because of the sheer chore of manual systems, they tend to be compromises between the ideal and the practicable. A less than thorough system which can be maintained through slack and busy times alike is preferable to a theoretically perfect one which collapses through neglect as soon as the shop fills up with customers.

Computerised systems

Set-up costs (in 1988) for computerised stock control are in the range £2,500–£10,000, with annual running and maintenance costs of about £500. Most of the cost is for the hardware – computer, monitor, hard disc system, floppy disc system, printer – and, as already pointed out in the comments on *Bookbank* and teleordering, these pieces of equipment need not be dedicated to specific tasks but, with appropriate software, will do a variety of tasks. Indeed, with the right hardware and software connexions (*interfaces* in the jargon), the different tasks can be integrated so that each can access the data and facilities of the others. There is little doubt that this is where the future lies. Get a copy of the BA's *Bookshop Computer Guide* for information on the possibilities.

If you opt for computerised stock control, it is important to get a system designed specifically for the peculiarities of bookselling; general retail systems which you have to tailor to your own needs are not worth considering, whatever the price. Bookshop systems currently on the market include *Bookshop* (AND Software Ltd), *Booksolve* (Diamond Epos Systems), *BORIS* (Applitek Books) and *Wordstock* (Wordstock Software Ltd).

MANUAL STOCK CONTROL SYSTEMS OUTLINED

Most manual stock control systems are based upon stock cards. These may be used to create a master file, or as card-in-book records, or as display stock reorder signals.

MASTER FILE SYSTEM

A master file contains a record card for each title in the system – which may mean something less than each title in the shop (see below). The information typically included on the card is:

- author, publisher, ISBN and price;
- subject category, indicating where the book is shelved;
- quantity in stock at different dates;
- when ordered;
- when received into stock;
- supplier, if other than the publisher;
- trade terms and conditions.

Other helpful detail may be noted too – eg 'Serialised on BBC1 Jan/Feb 1988' or 'Book club edition published April 1989'. Notice that all of this is purely factual. It informs: it does not instruct. It provides the information you need to make a decision about reordering or returning, plus the necessary detail – ISBN, supplier etc – for you to take action.

The only entries you might put on the card which have the appearance of instructions are the reorder level and the recommended order quantity. *Reorder level* is the number of remaining

FIGURE 5

BA STOCK CONTROL CARD *Actual size 6 × 4 inches*

STOCK CONTROL CARD – DO NOT REMOVE

AUTHOR:		PUBLISHER:	
TITLE:		ISBN	
PUB. CATEGORY	REORDER LEVEL	MAX. STOCK:	PRICE:

TV	FILM	RADIO	O U	G C E	C S E	SECTION:

DATE	STOCK	Quantity ordered	DATE ordered (or O/No.)	DATE received (or Report)	SALES	DATE	STOCK	Quantity ordered	DATE ordered (or O/No.)	DATE received (or Report)	SALES

copies which, being reached, alerts you to consider reordering. *Recommended order quantity* suggests the number to reorder, taking account of typical rates of sale, trade terms, suppliers' lead times and so on. Both figures are guides not instructions.

The BA's standard stock control card (see Figure 5) shows a typical card layout. Though less convenient, you can of course use blank record cards, available from any stationer's, or any other stationery you wish. Paper slips are not to be recommended for the file as they quickly become worn and tatty.

There is a lot of tedious writing or typing to be done to set up the file, and it does not become usable until a readily identifiable category of the stock has been completely recorded. You might, for example, start by putting only your hardback fiction on file, or children's books or reference books. This section-by-section approach allows you to put your stock control system into place by degrees, and start to reap benefits from it, albeit partially, at an early date.

Updating the file

The file is updated by regularly checking shelf stock (see below), recording date and quantity of books ordered, books delivered, books reported RP, TOS and so on. For every new title taken into stock, a new card must be prepared; for every title dropped, the card must be removed and either destroyed or, more usefully, put into a 'discontinued' file which in time builds up into a helpful record of past titles and sales experience.

Checking shelf stock

A sectioned master file, with the cards arranged alphabetically by author within section, facilitates stock checking – one of the basic routines for keeping the record up to date. To stock-check your Gardening books, for example, you take the cards in the Gardening file and write in the date and numbers in stock as you check the Gardening shelves title by title. Apart from one or two special displays, the books will be shelved in the same order as the cards are arranged. The system permits the checking of small sections of the stock at slack times. The job is never-ending. Once you've finished checking the Yachting and Zoology sections, for example, you start back again on the Art section, Biography, Children's Books and so on.

If there is more than one pair of hands to spare, different staff can be simultaneously checking different sections.

Stock decisions

Once a section is checked, the cards arrive on your desk for review: this is how the system alerts you to the need for decisions. If you include reorder level and recommended order quantities on the cards, your work may be speeded up, but you must beware of blindly relying upon what are, after all, historical judgements which may no longer be valid. The figures are perhaps of most use to your staff if at times during your absence they have to make stock decisions.

Review the cards by considering each title's stock position. Compare the number currently in stock with the number at the last stock check. Note the time lapse between ordering stock and receiving it – the lead time. Pay particular attention to the dates of receipt and checking so that you can assess the title's rate of sale. If it's too slow, should you ask the supplier to accept all of or some of your stock of the title back for credit? If the title is selling satisfactorily, have you enough copies in stock to see you through to the next stock check? If not, how many should you order?

Key figures in the calculation are *rate of sale* and *supplier's lead time*. If, for example, you're selling an average of 2 copies a week of Title X, and the lead time is 3 weeks, you plainly cannot delay reordering beyond the time when stock levels have fallen to 6; otherwise you risk going out of stock before fresh supplies arrive. Even so, waiting till you're down to 6 may be cutting it a bit fine, since real customers and real suppliers don't behave with arithmetical precision; perhaps it would be wiser to reorder when numbers fall no further than 7 or 8, thus allowing a safety margin. Notice, however, that the more you insure against the out-of-stock risk, the more adverse the implications for your stockturn.

Frequency of ordering also crucially affects the calculation. Safety margins apart, it rarely makes sense to stock more copies than you expect to sell in a period equal to the supplier's lead time: if you can get what you need from the supplier on three weeks' notice, for example, why order four weeks ahead? On the other hand, it can make sense to stock *fewer* copies than you need to cover the lead time, provided your frequency of ordering permits. In theory, stocks of Title X in the example above would be adequately maintained by ordering 2 copies every week; the weekly delivery would match your weekly sales, and stock levels need never exceed 2 copies – or 3 or 4, to allow a safety margin. But frequency of ordering depends upon frequency of stock checking – it would plainly be dangerous nonsense to reorder without first checking current stock levels – and this is the real bottleneck in effective stock management. It also explains why computerised systems, giving moment-by-moment stock information, can lead to startlingly better stockturns than manual systems.

Both reorder level and recommended order quantity, then, relate not only to rate of sale and lead time, but also to stock checking frequency. The calculation must take account, too, of the minimum order needed to get the supplier's best terms – and this may mean that other of the suppliers' titles have to be checked and ordered at the same time. And on top of the whole thing sits the major imponderable: will historical rates of sale be maintained, reduced or improved? Making stock decisions is like walking a tightrope: ordering too many can be as disastrous as ordering too few. And you have to make just such decisions regularly and successfully for every single title in the shop.

Stock information

Occasionally it will happen that, despite your best efforts, a title will be found to be out of stock when a customer asks for it. The record card now becomes the means of investigating how this has come about and possibly to take remedial action to see that it doesn't happen again. The card will show whether you have under-ordered, whether the rate of sale has suddenly increased, whether a delivery is overdue and whether the supplier has been or should be chased up, whether the supplier has already informed you of the reason for delayed supply, and so on.

Advantages of the master file system

The main advantage of a master file system is that it works. It ensures you take stock of your position regularly, topping up and weeding out as needed.

Stock checking as a continuous exercise slotted into slack periods is an efficient use of your own and your staff's time. As a spin-off it encourages and maintains familiarity with the stock – something which ensures that customers get a better and more knowledgeable service when they seek advice. Put new members of staff on to stock checking as early as possible; it's not a difficult task, the odd mistakes are not disastrous, and there's no better way for a new assistant to learn what's in stock and where it's to be found.

The system works best in a bookshop which maintains a fairly stable list of titles. A religious bookshop, for example, may stock the same range of bibles, commentaries, hymn books, prayer books and standard texts for years at a time, with only a relatively small number of short-life titles.

Disadvantages

As already pointed out, the setting up and maintenance of the system is labour-intensive. It is not the stock checking that's the main problem, but the origination and updating of the cards in the office. At busy times you may find that you can't get freshly delivered stock out onto the shelves because the cards haven't been prepared or updated. Yet busy times are precisely when you *need* to get stock out as quickly as possible. If you cut corners by putting the books out straight away, leaving card updating from delivery notes till later, you risk building up a backlog of unwritten cards, with all sorts of confusions arising during stock checking, or stock checking itself being held back pending card updating.

Even if you manage to keep the cards up to date, your stock knowledge is always behindhand because of the intervals between stock checks. The busier you are, the faster your stock is turning over, the less time you have for stock checking and the less effectively you control the stock.

If a lot of your stock is ephemeral – for example, a selection of doctor/nurse romances from this month's list with a fresh lot of titles to replace them next month – the work of card preparation is almost certainly more trouble than it's worth.

When it comes to making a judgement about what, how many and when to reorder or return, your decisions, though based upon hard information, are still impressionistic. The complex mix of rate of sale, supplier's lead time, price and terms of supply may all be identified or calculated from the record but it isn't practicable to work out the detailed mathematics as you review each one. It is bound to be a matter of looking at the card and getting a gut feeling of what action to take.

CARD-IN-BOOK RECORDS

In this system, the stock card, instead of being held in a master file, is placed in the book itself, to be removed at the cash desk when the book is sold. Thus the record automatically alerts you to the need to make a stock decision; you don't need to await stock checks before knowing what has been sold. Each day you review the day's sales, decide about reordering and update the cards, holding them in an office file until fresh stock arrives and the cards are placed in the books again.

Some wholesalers supply such cards free of charge with all orders. In these cases the 'cards' are normally computer print-out slips showing title, author, publisher, price, ISBN and date of supply. Similar cards are obtainable from some major publishers.

Advantages

Sales information is always up to date and reorder decisions can be made daily. If you use the free wholesaler-supplied cards you have no set-up or maintenance costs or chores at all. Even if you have no other form of stock control, you should certainly take advantage of this wholesaler service. You will at least be exercising control over what is likely to be the most active part of your stock.

Disadvantages

If you have to prepare the cards yourself, the system is labour-intensive. At busy times, you haven't even the unsatisfactory option of putting new stock out and writing up the cards later. The system fails if a book reaches the cash desk without a card in it; the sale would be unknown to the system and the title would never be reordered unless its absence were discovered in some other way.

With one card per book, you build up a sales history only of those titles you stock singly, and only then if you make a point of putting the same card, updated, into the replacement book when it arrives. The only way of maintaining a sales history of titles stocked in multiple copies is to have a card-in-book system *and* a master file, using the card-in-book as the means of keeping track of sales without the need for continuous stock checking.

However, stock checks would still be needed to discover which titles are *not* selling, although such checks may be limited to one a month, for example, and need not involve checking each title against the master file, but only examining the card in each book to see how long it's been on the shelves (but see also *Ageing the stock* below).

DISPLAY STOCK REORDER SIGNALS

This is a way of getting an automatic reminder to reorder and so avoid the need for frequent stock checking. It is a system for titles stocked in quantity and held in fixed displays. A stock card, written up in the usual way, is placed behind or beneath the displayed books, so that it is revealed when the last copy has sold.

A rather more sophisticated version of the system involves deciding upon a reorder level and holding the appropriate number of copies in reserve. As soon as the revealed card signals that the main stock has sold out, the reserve stock is put in place and further copies are ordered from the supplier.

Advantages

It is a very easy system to work and uses negligible staff time. The second version above ensures that popular titles remain continuously in stock. Large numbers of titles can be managed successfully in this way with a minimum of effort.

Disadvantages

The first version above is crude and unavoidably leaves you out of stock between ordering and delivery. The second version makes demands on stockroom space; and if you really have such space available, couldn't you develop it to better advantage by expanding your shop sales area and stocking more titles?

For a shop which has the bulk of its stock in singles, twos or threes, the system is pretty hopeless. Unless all books are rigidly and permanently regimented in particular display positions, the cards easily become separated from the titles they refer to. And it doesn't help to put the card *in* the bottom book because you and your staff, knowing that cards are to be found only in *some* books, are likely to become negligent about looking for them in any. At busy times, cards will be sold along with books and the system will break down. Nor can customers be relied on to take the top copy of a display. They often go to the trouble of pulling out a copy from the back or the bottom with the half-formed idea that it will somehow be in more pristine condition. You could well find yourself selling 'the last copy' first of all.

The system, as far as it works at all, monitors sales only. Shelf stock checks are still needed to identify the titles which are not selling or are selling too slowly.

SOME OTHER POINTS

You can see that manual systems all fall short of perfection one way or another, and you may in the end concoct a hybrid system for yourself, using a selection of ideas which commend themselves to you and which you believe you could happily work. Here are a few more ideas to think about.

Ageing the stock

A non-card way of *ageing* books – ie of knowing when they came into stock – is to pencil very lightly a code letter, say, inside the back cover to indicate the date of purchase. This might be A for January, B for February, C for March and so on. Examination of shelf stock will at any time enable you to sort the dead wood from the living trees.

Sales monitoring

While card-in-book systems are to be recommended if the wholesaler supplies the prepared cards to you free of charge, the chore of doing them yourself is considerable.

There are various ways of recording the sales of books without cards. The carbons of detailed written receipts would serve as such a record; but the system is laborious and at busy times becomes an irritation for customers and assistants alike. Alternatively, titles may be briefly noted on a sales sheet – just enough detail to make them recognisable. This is less laborious, less time-consuming, but still easily skimped or neglected at busy times. Open to the same objection, though more convenient for sorting at the end of the day, is the use of sales *slips* rather than sheets – one slip per title. Yet another method, faster at the point of sale but more awkward at the end of the day, is to speak the titles into a tape recorder at the cash desk.

A messy compromise may be the best option. Use the wholesaler's card-in-book when provided; write a brief sales slip if there is no card-in-book and if there is time to do so without inconveniencing your customer; use the tape recorder when you're rushed.

Theft

One of the less savoury aspects of retail life is shoplifting. Would you notice if one £10 book vanished from your £40,000 of stock? Probably not. It seems trivial enough. But suppose it happens every day. Would any single one of those thefts be any more noticeable? Presumably not. Yet they would add up to more than £3,000 a year at retail prices or – and this is what really matters – to about £2,000 of your capital investment. What that means is that if your business, but for the thieves, could have paid you £10,000 at the end of the year, it will in the event be able to pay you only £8,000. That's not an over-simplification; it's the truth.

Knowing the extent of your shoplifting problem won't cure it, but it will let you know if it is serious enough to require additional security measures (see page 186).

Neither a master file nor sales monitoring nor stock checking will by themselves identify thefts, but all three together will. If you know your stock level at a given date from the master file card, sales monitoring lets you deduce how many copies of a given title should still be on the shelves, and stock checking will either confirm the figure or reveal a theft problem.

MINIMAL MANUAL STOCK CONTROL SYSTEM

Stock ageing and the compromise method of sales monitoring are the minimum controls which will enable you to manage your stock in a moderately informed way. They have the merit of being so undemanding that the temptation to neglect them can normally be resisted. Unfortunately, such minimal control will not reveal thefts – which you may only get hints of, many months into the future, when you calculate your annual gross profit figures and find them to be suspiciously low.

COMPUTERISED STOCK CONTROL SYSTEMS OUTLINED

As soon as you can afford it, go for computerised stock control. As a management tool, it is unparalleled. The current explosive growth of the big bookselling chains is in part attributable to the computer. For the first time in bookselling history, managers can actually know moment by moment what their stock position is, both overall and by title. They don't have to wait for the next stock check or the accountants' annual report to discover what happened last month or last year: they know today what's happening today. Companies switching from manual to computerised systems have typically found themselves able to offer a better stock range to their customers at the same time as holding lower stocks than formerly – in other words, they get a better return on their investment. If it works for them, it can work for you.

COMPONENT PARTS OF COMPUTERISED STOCK CONTROL

As already stated, these are exactly the same for electronic as for manual systems. The questions to be answered and the judgements to be made are also the same. The difference lies in the way the raw data is fed into the system and the speed and varied formats in which answers are presented to you for evaluation.

Starting a manual system is largely a matter of getting hold of stock cards and deciding for yourself how you will use them to best advantage. Computerised systems, however, normally come as ready-made commercial packages with most of the structural detail already present; what you can do with any given system is predetermined by its design. The account of computerised systems below does not relate to any particular one of the currently available commercial packages, but is intended to show the sort of facilities such systems typically offer; some may offer more, some less. Make sure you see a system up and running before buying it so that you know it will do what you want it to do.

MASTER FILE

The master file is the heart of a computerised system, as it is of any thorough-going manual system. It is the complete record of all titles in stock, with the history of each.

In a manual system you can only get to the information by finding the card it's written on, and you can only find the card if you know where it's filed. If you're looking for *The Merchant of Venice*, you would need to know you could find it in the Drama section under *Shakespeare*. In a computerised system, however, you could find it just by looking up *Merchant of Venice*; you wouldn't need to know it was in the Drama section; you wouldn't need to know it was by Shakespeare. Indeed the system will allow you to find it as easily from its ISBN or abbreviated title or from most other features present in the record.

Even more important than this simple way of accessing individual records are the tailor-made reports that the system will produce for you based on a range of records. Specify your requirements – eg a list of all biographies first stocked in the last year; all orders outstanding for more than ten days; all books unsold for more than four months, listed by publisher and, within publishers, by author; a complete list of titles in the Astronomy section listed in order of price; the same listed in order of author; a list of publishers in order of the discounts they give you; and so on. One of the system's strengths is its ability to retrieve and collate information in a virtually limitless number of ways.

All information can be displayed on your monitor screen or printed out. This means that you can not only investigate your stock in a variety of ways for stock control purposes, but can also create booklists for particular promotions or even to meet the requirements of particular customers: a list of children's hardback fiction under £7, all titles in stock by or about Thomas Hardy, all books to do with cats, your hundred best sellers in the past year, and so on.

Perhaps most important is the way the system will perform *calculations* upon a specified range of records. This means you can ask for a list of publishers with whom you have spent more than £1,000 in the past 12 months; the total value of special customer orders in March; stock order values for each month of the year; and so on.

Creating the master file

Setting the system up in the first place can involve a great deal of work. Details of your entire stock, title by title, need to be entered into the system. The number of titles any given system can handle mainly relates to disc storage capacity: most of the off-the-peg commercial packages for independent bookshops can be set up to deal with anything between 2,000 and 20,000 titles – though systems can be produced that will cope with any number you care to think of.

Once set up, the system is little more problem to maintain with, say, 9,000 titles in it than with only 5,000: there is no advantage in running the system below capacity. If you computerise, you must computerise the whole stock: it makes no sense to do it partially or piecemeal as you might with a manual system.

So a database of every single stock title, author, publisher, ISBN, price, etc has to be created before the system can be effectively used. The basic and most laborious way of doing this is by sitting at the keyboard and typing in all the data, title by title, in the electronic equivalent of filling in stock cards. But there are quicker ways you may be able to use:

- The system supplier may be able to introduce you to another bookseller already using the system, and you may, for a fee, be able to get a copy on disc of that bookseller's title database. Of course, your own stock will not be a precise match but if both of you are, for example, general booksellers there is likely to be a substantial overlap of titles. It is very little work to delete from the file any titles you are not stocking, and no more work than it would have been anyway to add titles that are not already there. For a new bookseller, there is the added advantage that an existing bookshop's stock list acts as a useful guide to titles you might yourself consider purchasing.
- If you are a subscriber to Whitaker's *Bookbank*, you already have a title database of all books in print. Your stock control system should – correctly interfaced – be able to copy into your own stock master file any titles present in *Bookbank*. Instead of having to type in all the details yourself, you need merely in effect say *Yes* or *No* to each of the titles in *Bookbank* in order to create your own master file.
- Another way of using *Bookbank* – though again your system supplier must provide the interface – is to enter abbreviated information of all your stock titles – say, just the ISBNs – the full data for which may then be located in *Bookbank* and copied over to your own file as above.
- Even keying in ISBNs can be avoided if you have a bar-code reader which will electronically enter the ISBN into the computer by reading the bar-code which publishers are increasingly printing on the back covers of their books (see page 35).

Updating the file

Records have to be originated for new titles as they're taken into stock. As above, this is a matter of keying in the data or lifting it off an existing database.

Numbers of copies ordered and received must be individually added to the master file, together with suppliers' reports on unfulfilled orders.

Sales are put into the file either by keying in data collected as in a manual system – ie by stock checks, card-in-book methods or noting the details of books sold at the point of sale – or by reading them directly into the system with a bar-code reader. This latter is known as an electronic point of sale system (EPOS). EPOS captures book sales data at the cash desk, rings up the correct price (automatically retrieved from the system's database via the bar-code ISBN), prints out a detailed receipt for the customer, records the sale and updates the database. This means, among other things, that the current stock position, moment by moment, is known to the system.

SOME OTHER POINTS

As indicated before, the full advantage of computerisation comes from integrating, via the computer, various bookshop routines. The same information which updates the stock database can be used by other packages such as sales and purchase ledger systems and teleordering.

Order quantities

Computerised systems can automatically calculate the rate of sale per title and the supplier's lead time, and so arrive at a recommended order quantity for a specified period. Of course, you have to exercise your own skill in deciding whether to act on the recommendation, but the starting point for your judgement is a reliable and precise arithmetical calculation.

Easy access of detailed information

Because of the lightning speed of computers, you can interrogate the system any number of times in any number of ways to extract up-to-date information. Routines that are too cumbersome to be done manually with any frequency can be done without difficulty as often as you like on the computer.

You can investigate the value of different sections of your stock in relation to their sales. You might find, for example, that while Geology accounts for 2 per cent of your stock investment, it produces only 1 per cent of your sales. Or that Classical Fiction, occupying 5 per cent of your sales area is making only 2 per cent of your turnover. Figures like these should lead you to reconsider your stock mix. You may decide that the image you want your shop to have necessitates these imbalances, or that it is, after all, quite impossible for every section of your bookshop to be equally profitable. On the other hand, you may think it appropriate to invest more in the more profitable sections of your stock and less in the less profitable.

The decision must always be yours. But the computer, as a management tool, enables you to see easily and swiftly what is actually going on in your business. You move away from the hunch, the gut feeling and the impression towards a system which allows you to make intelligent choices on the basis of precise information.

Theft

As with manual systems, theft is only revealed by the comparison of shelf stock with the stock record. But it is easy enough to get a print-out of the numbers and titles of any particular section in your shop, so regular stock checks can be made in slack times to identify the extent of the theft problem, if any.

Multiple access

As your business grows, a number of your staff may need to access the system at the same time. You may have more than one cash register, each with its own bar-code reader inputting data to the system moment by moment. You may yourself be working in the back room deciding on the day's orders or making more long-term calculations about stock range and mix. There should be no problem in providing each user with a terminal and immediate access to the stored data without in any way interfering with the other users accessing the data at the same time.

Chapter 8

Choosing Premises

There are two ways of getting a bookshop: you either buy an existing one or start from scratch in empty premises.

Specialist bookshops for sale are rarely found anywhere except the classified columns of *The Bookseller*, and there are not usually more than two or three a week even there. You can place advertising yourself in the Businesses Wanted column, but don't expect to be overwhelmed by replies. The market after all is a small one: only about 2,000 specialist bookshops are trading altogether.

If you're in the market for a going concern, it could be worth looking through the past several months' issues of *The Bookseller*. Some vendors may just insert a single advertisement, fail to attract a buyer, and then do nothing more for a year or so, though still interested in selling. Others will have found a buyer who, perhaps months later, pulls out of the deal, leaving the shop on the market again but not yet readvertised.

Non-specialist bookshops are more widely advertised in the Businesses for Sale columns of the national and local press, and may be found on the books of business transfer agents.

If you're looking for empty premises in which to start a shop you first need to narrow your search to one or more areas which you believe could support a bookshop of the kind you are planning. Then find who the most active retail property agents are in those areas – look at advertising in the local press, check Yellow Pages, sound out other retailers – and visit them to discuss your requirements and seek their advice. Because of the way property agents work – taking a commission on sale from the seller or landlord – consultations cost you nothing and you gain access to detailed and constantly updated information about the local retail property market almost impossible to come by in any other way.

GOING CONCERNS

The advantage of taking over a going concern is that everything is in place and you are not forced into early decisions about shopfitting, stock range, bibliographical tools and so on, nor do you have the task of initiating business relationships with suppliers, staff and customers. To some extent you can let the business ride while you learn how things are done; you can take your time in deciding how far, if at all, the inherited ways of running the business might be developed, modified or changed altogether. A going concern offers you a degree of certainty. The bookshop should be as busy in your first week as it was in the former owner's last week. The business records, analysed by your accountant, should give you a pretty good idea of what to expect in the year ahead by way of turnover, gross profit and the amount you can take out for yourself.

There is a price to pay for all of this. A going concern normally costs more than the value of its physical assets, an additional payment typically being required for the *goodwill* – which is more or less the expectation that the bookshop's record of profitability will be maintained in the future. That expectation, of course, comes with no guarantee of fulfilment.

Vendors tend to have exaggerated ideas of the value of their shops, fixtures, fittings and other assets. You should be particularly careful about how the stock is valued; it is almost certainly not worth to you the same as it cost the present owner. Make sure you take over only the recently bought and active stock, and let the vendor dispose of the old stock however he chooses. If the stock control system does not distinguish between the old stock and the new, you might do better to take none of it and buy in fresh stock yourself. But if you do that, why not go the whole way and start from scratch in empty premises?

You might be offered the stock at a seemingly generous *written down value* – that is, an amount calculated as an arbitrary percentage off the stock's total value at retail prices. It might seem that the chance to buy the stock at, say, a 40 or 45 per cent discount must be a bargain since suppliers' discounts rarely exceed 35 per cent. But the only acceptable written-down value of an unsaleable book is zero – the thing's worthless – and insofar as the stock includes unsaleable books, any valuation above zero is not generosity on the vendor's side but charity on yours.

Stock apart, the detailed pros and cons of going concerns versus starting from scratch, and how to value the worth and evaluate the merit of a going concern, are general retailing matters rather than anything specifically concerned with the book trade. As such they are beyond the scope of the present guide, and readers seeking information and advice on these subjects should refer to such books as A. St J. Price's *Buying a Shop* (Kogan Page) and P. Levene's *How to Start and Run Your Own Shop* (Graham & Trotman).

The rest of this chapter assumes you will be starting from scratch, though most of the matters considered will be of concern to you however you get your shop.

TO BUY OR RENT

Whether you hold your bookshop premises leasehold or freehold is a matter which may turn out to be critically important to the success or failure of your business venture but, like the question of going concerns, it doesn't lend itself to discussion in book trade terms. When you buy freehold premises, you may be investing substantially more in the property than in the bookshop. The advantage to you as a bookseller is your security of tenure and freedom from the risk of rent increases, which, moving in line with property values rather than book trade margins, have been known to squeeze the life out of formerly profitable bookshops. By contrast, someone owning a freehold may run a barely profitable bookshop for many years and then sell out at a handsome profit. Though they may not like to think of it in this way, bookselling freeholders are often enough in the property business with a bookshop as an interesting sideline.

The holder of a long lease is sometimes in a similar position, the balance of a lease acquiring value if the rent payable under its terms is below current market levels. Hence you may be asked to pay a premium to acquire a lease, and if you in due course become a seller, you may be able to ask for a premium yourself. But all leases are wasting assets and only the very longest may safely be regarded as investments.

The conclusion must be: buy a freehold if you can. If your finances can withstand the initial capital shock, your bookselling career will be altogether more comfortable. But for the purposes of this chapter, the assumption is that you will be renting – which is what most booksellers in fact do.

STARTING FROM SCRATCH

You have total flexibility when you start from scratch. You are not limited to the handful of specialist bookshops that are on the market at the time you happen to be looking. You are free to consider opening a bookshop of any size and character anywhere in the country.

In Chapter 6 you saw how to sketch a financial profile of your intended shop, and what inferences might be drawn about floor area, staffing levels, and so on. Take the profile as the starting point of your search for suitable premises. It gives you an idea of the sort of money you'll need and the size of shop you should be looking for.

The profile, useful in its definition of possibilities, is something of an abstraction. Though based upon the performances of real bookshops, the figures are not to be read as a firm prediction that a new shop with characteristics A, B and C will necessarily achieve performance figures X, Y and Z. You can't open a shop on an uninhabited island and expect sales of £120,000 a year merely because the floor space happens to measure 1,000 sq ft. The *Economic Survey* figures give an idea of achievable averages; as to whether you will achieve them – or do even better or rather worse – has much to do with the siting of your premises in relation to your customers and competitors, and the rent and rates you have to pay for those premises.

These are the matters to weigh up when choosing a site for your bookshop: custom, competition, rent and rates. Unfortunately, they tend to pull in different directions. The site that offers multitudes of customers, no competitors, a peppercorn rent and low rates has yet to be found. But though your final choice will inevitably be a compromise, it may not be the self-evident compromise you might jump at if you fail to think through the possibilities.

LOCATION: GENERAL CONSIDERATIONS

Choosing a site for your bookshop is both the most difficult and most crucial of your early trade decisions, perhaps of *all* your trade decisions. If the site is wrong, nothing else can be right.

Maximise your chances of making the right decision by favouring those towns and parts of the country that you already know well. The more familiar you are with an area, the better able you are to judge its potential and the merits of particular sites within it. You will know, without research, which shopping areas are improving and which declining; you will know the shopping habits of the local people; you may know of planned developments which will raise the attractiveness of a particular shopping area in the next couple of years, though current rentals and property prices still reflect the situation today.

If you either need or want to consider areas you are unfamiliar with, be prepared to put in a lot of research. Study the map. Check the population figures in the catchment area – that is, the population of both the town itself plus that of the outlying areas whose inhabitants routinely come into the town to do their shopping. Consider the profile of the population – wealth, house ownership, family size, age range and so on. The presence – or absence – of such amenities as theatres, art galleries, museums and colleges of further or higher education give important clues to the cultural disposition of the area.

Discuss the area with as many knowledgeable locals as you can get into conversation with – certainly with the leading retail property agent. Go to the local Planning Department to see what changes and developments are in the pipeline. Spend as much time as you can just walking the streets at different times of day and, ideally, at different times of year, to see how many people there are about and how busy the shops are. Look at the shops of all the booksellers, specialist and non-specialist, in your chosen area and in neighbouring areas. Assess the volume of book business in the catchment area and guess at how much of it is accounted for by those already trading – remember the £13 per capita expenditure on books noted earlier (page 41), and the estimated 30 per cent of it which goes through the specialist book trade (see Table 5 on page 50).

CUSTOMERS

Customers come mainly from among the people who pass the shop while going about their daily affairs, and to a lesser extent from those who positively seek the shop out. The former may be considered local, even if only temporarily local as, for example, holiday makers; the latter may come from further afield.

Using the £13 figure mentioned above – but remember that this related to 1986 statistics – you can calculate the size of population needed in the locality to produce a given potential value of book business if, as most general booksellers, you are entirely dependent on local trade. Suppose you're aiming at a turnover of £120,000 a year. That seems to imply a population of about 9,000 (ie £120,000 ÷ £13); but if only 30 per cent of the new book market goes through the specialist bookshops, the local population would need to be nearer 30,000 – and that, on the highly optimistic assumption, that you could win all the available business.

As always, the figures must be treated cautiously. It is not a law of nature that 30 per cent of book purchases are made in specialist bookshops. That was merely an estimated national average for 1985. And if you look at the breakdown of the figures in Table 5, you will see that the small independents' share of the market is put at 8 per cent and declining – and that would imply a required population exceeding 115,000 for your £120,000 a year..

The figures must not be read as absolute truths. If in a given area there are *no* small independent bookshops, then *none* of the local book business will be going to this sector. If there are no branches of any of the large bookshop chains within the catchment area, then the estimated 17 per cent of the business which might be expected to go to them is theoretically available for other bookshops.

Any analysis of the figures is so hedged about with qualifications that you might be tempted to ignore them altogether. But imperfect though the figures are, it would be foolish not to try to deduce what they are saying about the location you are considering, even if you conclude that there are other more persuasive indicators which you decide to follow.

The very least you must look for is a catchment area with enough available bookselling business to give you the chance of hitting your chosen sales target. Available business is to be judged by considering the theoretical maximum book business in the area – ie head count of the population multiplied by the per person expenditure on books – and then estimating (1) the share of that business not already held by outlets currently trading, and (2) the amount of business you might take from the current traders because of the superiority of your location, stock range, quality of service or whatever. It will never be more than a guess, but it can at least be an informed guess if you know or research the area thoroughly and do a few simple sums.

COMPETITORS

Most retailers would like to trade in a major shopping area of a major centre of population: that's where the business is. Wherever you see such a major shopping area, the big bookselling chains will either already be trading or are likely to move in at a future date. The demand for sites in such places ensures that rents are much higher, space for space, than in the less favoured shopping areas. At first it looks as if your choice is between moderate rents with little competition but not much business, and a high level of business with certain competition and exorbitant rents.

We'll return to the question of rents later (page 176). For the moment, consider the problem of competition. What should be your attitude to it? Should you aim to be as close to the major shopping position in a major town as you can afford, or go for a site in so plainly secondary a position that you feel confident of being unchallenged by the presence or future arrival of a major competitor?

Surviving the competition

The local bookselling competition comes in three forms: other small independents, the non-specialist chains and CTNs – W.H. Smith, John Menzies and so on – and the specialist bookselling chains.

If there is already a small independent bookshop trading in your chosen location, it is probably best to go away and look somewhere else, unless either the existing shop or yours is an exclusively speciality bookshop (see below). There are so many places to be found where small independents are *not* already trading that there seems little point in opening on the doorstep of one that is. How close a site may be thought to constitute 'the doorstep' of an existing shop is a matter for debate, but your calculations about the population in the catchment area and the theoretical size of the local book business will probably reveal whether a new shop would encroach on someone else's territory or genuinely fill a gap in the market.

Most booksellers agree that the non-specialist chains are not a serious challenge to the specialist independent. Individual branches may have a good selection of books, and collectively account for about a third of the entire book trade, but by and large they are not perceived by the public as 'real' bookshops.

The competition to worry about most comes from the big specialist bookselling chains. The public is in no doubt that these are 'real' bookshops, and very good ones too. Tim Waterstone, founder and managing director of the bookshop chain that bears his name, has put it like this: "The point about general bookselling is that somebody who is prepared to take a much bigger site and have a much bigger stock is going to win at the end of the day. People want to see a vast amount of books in front of them. That's what general bookselling is about."

All else being equal, then, a big branch of a major bookselling chain will pull business away from a neighbouring small independent bookshop. But the crucial phrase is 'all else being equal' – that is, if you are offering a similar range of books and a similar quality of service from a similarly located shop. The salvation of

TABLE 10 Source: BA membership records mid-1988

BA MEMBERS WITH SUBJECT SPECIALITIES *Corporate membership 3260*

(a) alphabetical order		*(b) numerical order*	
169	Art & architecture	760	Children's
88	Astrology/occult	526	Maps/atlases/travel/guides
275	Biography	510	Religion & theology
122	Business, management & commerce	457	Fiction
760	Children's	404	Cookery & home economics
68	Cinema	355	Gardening
100	Computer technology	330	Reference books
404	Cookery & home economics	315	Natural history
304	Crafts & hobbies	304	Crafts & hobbies
244	DIY	275	Biography
87	Drama	272	Health & Fitness
66	Economics	249	Music
62	Education science	246	Photography
55	Engineering	244	DIY
457	Fiction	232	Military
100	Foreign languages	172	Poetry
355	Gardening	169	Art & architecture
272	Health & Fitness	127	Sports
124	History	124	History
82	Law	122	Business, management & commerce
526	Maps/atlases/travel/guides	116	Women's studies
85	Medical sciences	112	Secondary school books
232	Military	102	University textbooks
249	Music	100	Computer technology
315	Natural history	100	Foreign languages
88	Philosophy	100	Science fiction
246	Photography	96	Primary school books
172	Poetry	91	Sociology
77	Political science	88	Astrology/occult
96	Primary school books	88	Philosophy
88	Psychology	88	Psychology
330	Reference books	87	Drama
510	Religion & theology	85	Medical sciences
100	Science fiction	82	Law
112	Secondary school books	77	Political science
91	Sociology	68	Cinema
127	Sports	66	Economics
102	University textbooks	62	Education science
116	Women's studies	55	Engineering

the independent bookseller must lie in ensuring that all else is *not* equal. Somehow you must find a competitive edge.

GEOGRAPHY

Perhaps the simplest way of competing is in a sense not to compete at all: to choose a location – for example, a small town or village – which the big bookselling chains would consider too small to be worth considering. Roughly speaking, a catchment area of fewer than 150,000 people would be unlikely to excite much interest among the major chains unless it had other things in its favour – heavy tourist traffic, for example, or a local university.

So to keep *geographically* clear of the serious competition you might look for an area large enough for your ambitions but too small for the big chains. Catchment areas in the range 20,000–100,000 are the ones to consider, though you will need to out-perform the average achievements of the trade as a whole if you are to make yourself a satisfactory living from the lower end of that population range. And the nearer you approach the upper end, the less certain you can feel that the competition won't move in after all, especially if your own shop thrives and therefore proves the existence of a significant book-buying public in the locality.

SPECIALISATION

Specialisation offers another way of dealing with the competitive threat. To the extent that your bookshop covers a section of the market in depth while the competition offers a broad coverage of the market as a whole, you side-step the direct confrontation. But don't underestimate the problems. There is not much point in being on the high street if, as a matter of policy, you major in a subject category that the high street isn't interested in. Table 10 on page 173 shows the subject specialities of the BA membership.

It rarely makes sense to specialise *exclusively* because if you restrict your entire stock to a narrow speciality, you effectively reduce the number of your potential customers to a small section of the already limited number of people who buy books.

The safest way to specialise is *within* the shop: build up a speciality section on theatre or chess or anthropology or whatever, and aim to become an acknowledged authority on the available literature in your chosen subject. But keep your basic stock range in the mainstream of the general bookshop trade so that you don't lose the bread-and-butter sales – the bestsellers, the fast sellers and the steady sellers – on which most sound bookshop businesses are based.

A bolder but far riskier strategy is to choose a popular subject speciality and set your sights on the 70 per cent or so of the population who are not normally 'bookshop people' at all. By trading as *Cookery Bookshop*, for example, or *Sports Bookshop*, you might reach a market that the competition is missing altogether. But you must be confident that the specialist market is sufficiently large and *accessible to you*, given the location of your shop, to compensate for the loss of general trade from among book buyers not interested in your speciality. If this is the sort of bookshop you want to run, then a slightly off-centre site would probably do very nicely, and other bookshops in the area need be no cause for concern. A speciality bookshop of this kind can be strengthened by a sideline stock of appropriate non-book goods. Mail order too (see page 222), enabling you to cast your customer net nationwide, may be worth considering, though for the bookshop to succeed, it will almost certainly need a secure local base.

Some degree of specialism, then, may help you to survive the competition in a prime or near-prime position. But the real attraction of a speciality is that enthusiasts will take the trouble to seek you out, and you can therefore consider a secondary or even tertiary trading position with consequent savings in rent and rates.

Children's bookselling and religious bookselling. Two specialisms which can, in some locations, provide a sufficiency of business all by themselves are children's bookselling and religious bookselling, though in a small shop it may be difficult to offer a more interesting stock range than that found in the corresponding subject section of a branch shop of a large bookselling chain. So as a means of getting an edge over the competition, these specialisms, from a *stock* point of view alone, are to be viewed cautiously.

Such specialisms, however, have an appeal of their own. Booksellers engaged in children's or religious bookselling are often passionately committed to the wide dissemination of their chosen literature, and their shops frequently play an active role in the local community, with a social importance transcending their commercial function. But, in the end, a business has to pay its way in pounds and pence, without which no amount of social importance will save it from bankruptcy. As with all proposed specialisms, you must do your sums carefully, but if the figures come out right and these are subject areas in which you have a genuine interest and specialist knowledge, they are certainly worth considering.

SERVICE

Service is the least costly and most effective way for the small bookseller to compete. However well managed the branch of a major bookselling chain may be, a branch manager is never the same as a working owner. For the manager, the shop is a thing apart; for you, it's everything.

The attractiveness of a bookshop depends upon far more than its stock of books. It relates also to the structure of the premises, the shopfittings, the design and decoration of the shop, the way books are displayed, the lighting, the attitude of the staff and so on: these all contribute to the *ambience* of your shop. The books themselves are the goods; all these other things are part of the service.

The bookselling chains necessarily have a corporate image that each branch conforms to; the manager and staff are to some extent actors performing on a set designed at head office, and playing though a script written remotely, often with little or no input from themselves. By contrast, you as owner-manager are producer, director, designer, script-writer and lead player. You can impose your personality on every aspect of the shop – indeed it is very difficult to avoid doing so – and it is this that can make the quality of service of a small independent bookshop so different from that of a local branch of a bookselling chain. If customers can 'feel' the character, the personality and the quality of your shop – and if they like it – they will tend to come to you rather than to the competition. It's a subtle thing, difficult to describe, and recognised subliminally rather than head on. But it's real, and it is something that you as owner-manager can give to your shop, while the salaried manager in the branch bookshop across the way has nothing to offer but his professionalism.

At the level of immediate practicalities, service is a matter of allowing your customers to browse, unpressured, while approachable staff are discreetly on hand to offer helpful and knowledgeable advice; it's a readiness to track down unstocked titles and positively to welcome special orders.

A small independent offering a first-class service has every chance of holding its place in the high street even if a competitor moves in down the road. Of course, you wouldn't choose to open next door to an established major bookshop, but if you get there first and build up a reputation for service over the years – knowing your customers, having wide-ranging contacts in the local community, being prepared to put yourself out to win business and keep it – then you should be in a strong position to survive a later challenge.

RENT AND RATES

It is probably rent and rates more than anxiety to avoid the competition that lead many booksellers to take secondary locations or out-of-town sites. There is no doubt that some very successful bookshops may be found in such places. But if you would rather be in or near the town centre, don't rule yourself out by assuming that the rent and rates *must* be impossible.

At the time of writing, major reforms to the rating system are in train, but quite how they will affect the relative expensiveness of different sites and different areas is not yet clear. Readers can only be advised to keep an eye on the reforms and their implementation, and to watch the market. It is the level of rents, however, that is likely to remain the major consideration in site acquisition, because even under the reformed system rateable values will be pegged to rental values.

Rent variations

Rents are, of course, higher in prime positions than in secondary ones, but they do vary from shop to shop even in a small area. The landlord has to pitch the rent at a level that reflects the general attractiveness of the specific site to potential traders. Two shops next door to each other, and each offering the same sales area of, say, 20 ft × 45 ft, are likely to command different rentals if one of them has the larger dimension parallel to the street, with perhaps two separate entrances, while the other has the smaller dimension parallel to the street, and only one entrance. Despite their identical floor space, the shop with the wider frontage has more than double the amount of *presence* on the street. Furthermore, customers have an observable reluctance to go *deep* into a shop, and shopkeepers, of whatever trade, find the zone of the shop that fronts the street at ground floor level produces proportionately more sales than the zones that lie further back or are on other floors. So for a similar square footage, wide-and-shallow generally commands a higher rental than narrow-and-deep. (See also *Zoning* below.) For you as a bookseller, however, narrow-and-deep is by no means to be despised. Indeed, because the most space-efficient way of displaying books is upon shelves against walls, you might note that the three internal walls of the deep 20 ft × 45 ft shop provide a 110 ft run of wall while those of the wide shop of the same dimensions provide only 85 ft.

Some shops may have such awkward features as to render them unusable by a number of trades, most of which favour a large open space offering the maximum freedom to shopfitting designers. A bookshop, however, can turn to advantage some of the most unpromising structural features, exploiting them for their charm and character – back to ambience again.

Bookshops aren't supermarkets where customers want to buy their prewrapped sanitised products as quickly as possible and then get out again. They are places where people come to browse and relax and indulge themselves in the leisurely process of choosing and buying. More than most retail outlets, bookshops are a part of the leisure industry, and the quirky, oddly shaped shop can enhance rather than diminish the pleasure of the experience. And the good news is that these same oddly shaped premises may well be available at a lower rental than the bland, clean-lined shop next door.

Booksellers' final advantage is that they *are* booksellers. The developer of a new shopping area, whether a simple parade on the high street or a whole complex in a new precinct, knows that the success of the development depends upon the collective attractiveness of the shops within it. A good bookshop gives character and style to a shopping area, and you may find that you can negotiate a favourable rental in a new shopping centre if the planners want a bookshop and recognise some of the low profit margin problems of the independent book trade.

What all this comes to is that you should not, on the grounds of assumed high rentals, rule out premises in major shopping areas. Talk over the possibilities with the local retail property agents. A 'live' agent will know of available sites at an early date; if you wait for 'To let' boards to appear, you are likely to miss the most interesting propositions. If there are particular new shopping developments that you would like to get into, contact the development manager. Above all, do not assume that because particular sites are on offer at impossibly high rents that all sites in the area will be similarly exorbitant. There *are* bargains to be had, and a site which is less than prime but still in a major shopping area could well fit both your budget and your ambitions.

Zoning

As you investigate the property market, you may come upon references to *Zone A values*. Retail property dealers have developed this way of indicating the comparative rental values of shops of different shapes and orientations. The method takes account of the fact, already noted, that a shop's best selling area is on the ground floor at the front. The first twenty feet depth of this area is called *Zone A*, the twenty feet behind it *Zone B* and the twenty feet behind that *Zone C*. The method then assumes that for a given square footage, Zone A is worth twice Zone B, four times Zone C and eight times anything else.

Imagine two shops, both 20 ft × 80 ft – ie both offering 1,600 sq ft of selling space. With respect to the street, however, one of them is wide and shallow while the other is narrow and deep; and the wide shop's rental is £20,000 a year, while the narrow shop's rental is £9,450 a year. Which is the better value?

The professionals work it out like this:

The wide shop, being only 20 ft deep, is all Zone A. The rental per square foot per year is £20,000 divided by 1,600 sq ft: that comes to £12.50. The rental is described as *£12.50 Zone A*.

The narrow shop, though the same nominal size as the other one, has only a quarter of its area in Zone A. The front 400 sq ft (ie 20 ft × 20 ft) is Zone A, the 400 sq ft behind it is Zone B, the next 400 sq ft is Zone C, and there is a final block of 400 sq ft behind that. As Zone B is deemed to be worth only half Zone A, Zone B's 400 sq ft is equivalent to only 200 sq ft of Zone A. By similar calculation, Zone C's 400 sq ft is equivalent to 100 sq ft of Zone A, and the 400 sq ft right at the back of the shop is equivalent to no more than 50 sq ft of Zone A. So *in terms of Zone A*, the area of the narrow shop can be thought of as 400 + 200 + 100 + 50 sq ft = 750 sq ft. Using the zoning method, then, the rental *per Zone-A-equivalent square foot* is £9,450 divided by 750 sq ft: that comes to £12.60. The narrow shop's rental is described as *£12.60 Zone A*.

You can see that by expressing the rentals of both shops in terms of Zone A, the value-for-money comparison is easily made. The wide shop – all else being equal – looks to be marginally better value: £12.50 Zone A compared with £12.60 Zone A. Even so, of course, you'll need to find £20,000 a year for the wide shop but less than half of that for the narrow one. A Rolls Royce may be better value than the banger on offer from the man in the pub, but if you haven't the money for the Rolls; the banger it has to be. As far as bookshops are concerned, the trick is to find premises at an affordable rent with a strong, though probably narrow, Zone A, and then to work at making the low-zoned areas of the shop sell as hard as possible.

Future of the high street

There is an interesting by-product of the development of shopping precincts and major out-of-town shopping centres which is so marked a feature of contemporary retailing. Because many leading retailers are migrating from the high street to these newer locations, the pressure on high street rentals may in places be starting to ease. Although you won't want to take premises in a manifestly declining area, it may be that the old high street *won't* decline but will become the home of smaller-scale retailing in which the independent bookseller will fit very well. And remember that communications, access, residents and so on do not all vanish overnight when the big names move out.

THE SPECIFIC SITE

Whatever type of bookshop you plan to have in whatever location, the time comes when there is a specific site on offer, and you have to decide whether this is the one to take. Presumably the rent is acceptable to you; if it isn't, there's nothing further to consider unless and until you can negotiate a lower figure. What needs to be judged is whether the premises, both internally and externally, have the right characteristics to help you exploit the book business in your catchment area.

EXTERNALLY

A general bookshop needs a high volume of pedestrian traffic, not just in the general area but actually going past the shop. Anything that directs the traffic flow past your shop is a plus; anything that blocks it is a minus. Pedestrian crossings, traffic lights, bus stops, major stores – features like these are magnets deflecting the flow of people towards one direction and away from another. There are sometimes main routes that pedestrians take from the car park or the bus terminus or the railway station in order to get into a shopping centre. Indeed, wherever you look, despite the freedom there may be for people to move randomly, they may be observed to favour certain fixed – though often invisible – channels. You want your shop to be where the channels flow – not just a few yards round the corner or on the other side of the street. Of course, you are unlikely to get or be able to afford the prime site, but you must be noticeably present where the shoppers are.

A speciality bookshop, as has already been mentioned, can be acceptably sited in a secondary position, but anything too tucked away and out of sight is to be avoided unless you're pinning all your hopes on mail orders.

Level access to the shop is better than steps up or down – the latter will discourage people with prams or shopping trolleys and those with walking difficulties.

The shop frontage should permit an adequate amount of display to announce your presence to passers-by and to show selected stock. The window is how you cry your wares to the public. And unless you're stuck with an old-fashioned window closed off from the shop, it is also the means by which people can see into the shop and feel tempted to enter. Many people are wary of going into a shop if they can't see what it's like before committing themselves to crossing the threshold.

INTERNALLY

It is preferable to have the sales area limited to the ground floor. For reasons of security, you will at all times need at least one member of staff on each of your sales floors. If the premises are multi-level, bear in mind that customers find stairs down to a basement less daunting than stairs up to a first floor.

In multi-level premises, make sure that all the floors are strong enough for commercial loading and that there are separate fire exits at each level. Indeed in any premises, fire and smoke security alarms may need to be installed if not already there – an important point to bear in mind if you're the first tenant in new premises; they're not cheap. If any floors you intend to use as sales areas have not previously been used for retailing – perhaps they have been offices or domestic accommodation – you will need local authority permission for *change of use* unless that has already been granted. Confirm the position before committing yourself to anything; approval for a change of use is not given automatically.

If you have the choice, it is usually better to let the vendor dispose of any non-bookshop fixtures and fittings rather than buy them yourself and hope they can be incorporated into a bookshop design. You might take advice on this from a design consultant (see below).

The significance of the shape and orientation of the sales area has already been discussed. As a general principle, note that narrow-and-deep rectangles always provide more wall space than squares of an equal floor area. In irregularly shaped areas, consider the usable wall space rather than the nominal square footage.

What you're looking for most of all is *selling space*. You only need a very limited amount of backroom space for office work, unpacking and so on. You certainly don't need anything much larger than a walk-in cupboard as a stockroom. You'll probably use it only for holding customers' special orders and for titles subject to a publication date embargo (see page 215); everything else should be out on display.

DESIGNERS

Designers can do wonders with all sorts of premises – putting in false ceilings, ripping out old walls, constructing new ones – but the more suitable the shell you start with, the lower your shopfitting costs are likely to be.

If you are planning to use professional design help, contact the designer *before* committing yourself to particular premises. Now is the time when you can walk away from costly structural problems by just crossing the premises off your list of possibles, so now is the time when professional advice can be most valuable. Designers – for a fee of course – can help not only with the detail of internal design but also with all the stages of setting up the shop, from acquiring the premises to getting local authority permissions, instructing builders, and so on.

Insight Design Services, a design consultancy, will deal with quick queries by phone free of charge to BA members. They also offer a full consultancy service at commercial rates.

Chapter 9

Countdown to Opening Day

Between finding the premises and opening the doors to your first customer there is much to do and even more to think about. During this relatively brief period the business foundations are laid: the physical structure and appearance of the fitted shop are determined, management routines are set in place, policy decisions are made about stock, staffing, security and so on, and, as far as possible, future problems are thought through and responses planned to meet them. The decisions to be made and tasks to be done come mainly under the headings of business basics, bookshop basics, shopfitting, opening stock purchase and publicity.

BUSINESS BASICS

Those matters common to all business are outside the scope of this book, but you will have to deal with them at this stage if you have not already done so. You will need to: contact professional advisers – solicitor, accountant, bank manager; draw up a business plan to present to the bank or other possible providers of finance; decide on the legal status of your business – sole trader, partnership or limited company; contact the local tax and VAT offices; establish a book-keeping system; engage any staff you need; and so on.

If you're new to business, it is certainly worth reading one or more of the many books now available for business beginners. Dare one say that unless you are near a bookshop with a business speciality, you'll probably find it more profitable to browse in the business section of your local library? In addition to the titles mentioned in the last chapter (page 168), you might look for M.J. Morris's *Starting a Successful Small Business*, Clive Woodcock's *The Guardian Guide to Running a Small Business*, Colin Barrow's *Financial Management for the Small Business* (all three published by Kogan Page) and the latter author's *New Small Business Guide* (BBC Books). Of particular interest is the unhelpfully named *Credo Planning*, available free of charge from your nearest Midland Bank; this is a pack of three booklets for intending business people. Among other things, it gives detailed practical advice on how to draw up a business plan and cash flow forecast, and provides the stationery you need to do it.

See if a local college runs courses for business beginners. For general business help and guidance, including information about current schemes designed to give support and sometimes financial help to people setting up on their own for the first time, contact your nearest Small Firms Service – a Department of Employment agency with a specific responsibility for providing guidance and information to new and small businesses: dial 100 and ask for Freefone Enterprise. Also look up Business Enterprise Agencies in Yellow Pages for local schemes.

SECURITY

Though security is plainly a general business matter, its importance is so easily overlooked by the intending bookshop owner that certain points must be stressed. There may be only a tiny minority of thieves in the community, but they cause substantial losses to traders of all kinds. Regrettably, thieves do not go around like comic-strip villains with sacks prominently marked 'swag' slung over their shoulders. They look just like you and me, and the distasteful implication of this is that everyone is potentially suspect.

Shoplifting

The devastating effect upon net profits of seemingly trivial thefts by shoplifters has already been mentioned (page 160). Unpleasant though it is, you must be tough when you catch a thief; otherwise the word gets around that you're a soft touch, and your shop risks becoming a happy hunting ground for local criminals who know they're in danger of nothing more than being told to go away and not be naughty in future. For them, it's opportunity without risk: for you, it's a hiding to nothing.

The unpleasant business of apprehending a shoplifter is the responsibility of the person who sees the crime committed, and strict routines must be followed to ensure that no innocent person is falsely accused and no guilty person escapes justice on a technicality. Volumatic Ltd are security specialists who supply a number of free checklists on retail security matters which are of particular interest to the bookseller. This is their advice on apprehending a shoplifter:

1 It is important that you actually see the thief take at least one item.
2 Remember, you may need to testify that the item taken was in fact your property or the property of the shop.
3 If possible, notice where the thief conceals the item. Concealment contributes greatly towards establishing that the suspect intended to steal and did not merely 'forget to pay'.
4 Make sure that the suspect does not pass the item on to a colleague or, if he thinks he is under surveillance, get rid of the item somewhere in the shop.
5 Do not have a break in your surveillance.
6 Check that the suspect does not pay for the item. It is not sufficient to ask the cashier if payment was made.
7 While suspects can, if necessary, be apprehended within the shop, it is always a good, commonsense approach to permit the suspect to leave the shop before your apprehension.
8 Be polite but firm. Ask the suspect to accompany you back to the shop. Then call the police.

Other theft

Though shoplifting is the form of theft we all think of as the typical shop crime, it accounts for only about a quarter of retail thefts. Here are some other forms you need to guard against, any one of which will damage your business and some of which, unchecked, could drive you out of business altogether. Burglary, breaking-and-entering, staff theft of books for themselves or their friends, staff sale of books below price to friends, staff under-ringing sales and pocketing the difference, short stock deliveries – packages missing or books missing within packages, bills submitted for books that haven't been supplied, suppliers' invoices wrongly totalled, purchases made with worthless cheques or stolen credit cards, cash snatched from tills or on its journey to the bank.

Your insurance will cover some but not all of these losses. You may be protected from the consequences of some cheque and credit card frauds if you scrupulously follow the routines laid down by the card companies. The most insidious thefts are those that could be genuine errors, and these are also the easiest to overlook.

Take precautions

Be adequately insured (see page 99). Scrupulously check all deliveries, all invoices, all statements. See that your stock control system is able to reveal discrepancies between what is and what ought to be on the shelves, and that your sales monitoring system reveals discrepancies between what is and what ought to be in the day's takings. Always take up references before employing someone; a phone call on the lines of "If this person applied to rejoin your company, would you take him back?" will often reveal more, via hesitancy and a careful searching for words, than a request for a written reference. Don't let large sums of cash accumulate in the till; you only need enough to be able to give change. Fit convex anti-theft mirrors in the shop to allow staff to keep an eye on otherwise obscured areas. Be particularly watchful when groups of children come into the shop. Fit intruder alarms. Avoid taking money to the bank at regular times or by regular routes. Consider getting a special anti-theft cash carrying case: if snatched, an alarm goes off and a dye pours over the case contents, rendering them useless to anyone but the rightful owner.

BOOKSHOP BASICS

Put in an application to join the BA as soon as you have secured bookshop premises. Take out a subscription to *The Bookseller*. Decide on your main bibliographical material and buy it or take out subscriptions accordingly.

WHEN TO OPEN

As much as a third of the year's trade may be concentrated into the few weeks before Christmas, so if there is any choice in the matter, start trading before Christmas rather than after it. The early summer is usually the quietest period.

For a newcomer to bookselling, July or August are good months to start as you can find your feet before the busiest time of the year, and then be buoyed along by increasing levels of trade as Christmas approaches.

In practice, you may have only marginal control over the timing of opening day. You cannot know in advance how long it will take you to find suitable premises, and once those premises are yours and you're having to pay rent, rates, insurance and so on, it must make sense to open and start trading as soon as you can, however theoretically inopportune the time of year.

Sometimes, however, it is possible to negotiate a rent-free *fitting-out period* with the landlord, during which time you get the shopfitting done. This may enable you to choose a convenient opening date. You can typically expect a delay of two or three months between acquiring premises and getting them ready for trading.

All these considerations, of course, apply to bookshops started from scratch. If you are taking over a going concern, you may start trading the very day after the vendor ceased trading, or there may be no more than two or three days during which the shop is closed for stocktaking and other procedures associated with the handing over of the business. The exact date of take-over of a going concern is naturally a matter for negotiation, but if it is to be some time during the winter months, make sure that you're the one who gets the benefit of the Christmas trade.

MANAGEMENT AND CONTROL SYSTEMS

You have to make a policy decision on whether to favour electronic or manual systems. It is important to have an overall, coherent plan even if you implement it only by stages. Changing systems once you have started trading is difficult and disruptive unless you build into your original system preparation for later changes.

Electronic systems particularly must be planned with care. The traditional small business approach of muddling through and cobbling something together just won't work with the new technology. However much flexibility may be written into computerised systems, they still tend to be unyielding at the edges. If, for example, the card in a manual filing system is found to be inconveniently small for the information that has to go on it, you can always let the words spill into the margin or use smaller handwriting than normal. But if a computerised filing system has been programmed to accept no more than, say, twenty letters in a given entry, then once you've entered your twenty letters – that's it.

Further, a human being can always mediate between incompatible manual systems for relatively little extra time-cost because they are so time-costly anyway. In a manual system you might use *WBIP* to trace a book and then copy the information onto an order form: the two separate systems of title checking and order processing are linked by the human being. But if you check titles in *Bookbank* and place orders via teleordering, the two systems must be interfaced electronically if you are to avoid having manually to retrieve the information from the one system in order to feed it manually into the other. With no interface, it would be like running a high-speed train on two unconnected tracks, having to manhandle it from line to line halfway through the journey. You only get the full advantage from electronic systems when they can pass data and instructions to each other without manual intervention.

Coherent planning of electronic systems will also keep your hardware costs down. If you hope in due course to introduce computerised stock control, but at first use a computer only for book-keeping, it may be worth choosing the computer with an eye to its future compatibility with the stock control system even if a short-term saving could be made by getting something good enough to run the book-keeping suite of programs but nothing else.

Stock control is the central management activity in bookselling, and other systems generally connect to it like the spokes of a wheel. If you hope to take the electronic route to controlling your business, it is a good idea to investigate the stock control systems first.

Stationery

If money is really short, you can get by with very little specially printed stationery. A rubber stamp with your shop's name and address can be pressed into service for most purposes. However, see pages 96–99 for the sort of trade stationery you can buy from the BA and which you will either have to get printed for yourself or improvise on rubber-stamped blank sheets if you don't.

Practise any necessary economies first with your purely internal stationery – paperwork generated within the shop for your own use – then with trade stationery used to communicate with suppliers and colleagues, and only as a last resort with stationery that gets into your customers' hands. Any stationery that goes to your customers has a public relations job to do as well as serving the specific function of the moment; it's part of your shop's image. Whatever safety-pins and sticky tape you use to hold the set together behind the scenes, out there by the footlights everything should look polished and professional.

CREDIT, CREDIT CARDS AND OTHER PLASTIC

Some booksellers estimate that 25 per cent or more of their sales are paid for by credit card, and you can see from Table 11 that credit cards are accepted by about half the BA membership. In addition to a joining fee of £50, the main companies – Visa and Access – charge booksellers between 2.25 per cent and 5 per cent of each transaction's value by way of commission. Actual charges are a matter for negotiation between bookseller and credit card company, but in practice most booksellers seem to pay 4 per cent to Access and 4.5 per cent to Visa.

TABLE 11 Source: BA membership records mid-1988

BA MEMBERS OFFERING SPECIAL SERVICES *Corporate membership 3260*

(a) alphabetical order		*(b) numerical order*	
1736	Credit cards	2150	Customers' special orders
2150	Customers' special orders	1736	Credit cards
572	Library supply	816	Post-A-book
775	Mail order	775	Mail order
289	OU set book stockist	765	School book supply
215	Out of print search	572	Library supply
816	Post-A-book	289	OU set book stockist
161	Production of catalogues	215	Out pf print search
765	School book supply	161	Production of catalogues

With bookselling profit margins so tight, these are punishing rates. On a typical credit card sale of £15.50, something between 62p and 70p goes to the company; and although the percentage is calculated on the net price, it actually comes out of the gross profit, which reduces from an expected £5.40 to £4.78 or less. It's as if your trade discount were cut from 35 per cent to 30½ or 31 per cent.

Yet most booksellers are convinced that the acceptance of credit cards generates business and customer goodwill. One might expect that a number of impulse purchases (see page 214) would be lost if the customer couldn't pay by card, and the same would be true of telephone orders and some mail orders. On balance you will probably decide to apply to join the schemes and try to negotiate the best terms you can.

Monthly accounts

To an extent, credit card schemes render unnecessary the old system of offering monthly accounts to regular customers. A credit card payment should be totally secure for you, while giving the customer all the advantages – and more – of a monthly account.

However, monthly accounts do have certain advantages: there's no commission to pay on the customer's transactions, the customer is tied into a special relationship with your shop, and you can include further promotional material when mailing the customer's monthly statement. The disadvantages are the need to check the customer's creditworthiness, the administrative work in dealing with the account, and the bad debt risk.

Credit cards or no, you will still have to supply on credit to any institutional customers you have, but your worst risk there is of being paid late rather than not being paid at all.

If you decide to offer monthly accounts to individual customers, you *must* take up references from the customer's bank and from other traders with whom the customer already deals on account. Don't allow would-be account customers to hustle you into supplying on credit before you have had time to take up references. The people most impatient with the formalities are the very ones to be checked out with the greatest care.

Cheque guarantee cards

The bookseller doesn't have to subscribe to any scheme before accepting a cheque up to £50 backed by a cheque guarantee card. Follow the instructions on the card and payment should be secure. Be very wary of accepting a non-guaranteed cheque.

Debit cards

Debit cards are the usual standard-shaped pieces of plastic but they are designed for use as cheque substitutes. As in a credit card transaction, the retailer completes a voucher which the customer signs. For customers, the difference from credit card transactions is that payment is deducted from their current bank accounts just as if they had written out cheques. For retailers, the difference is that there is a fixed charge per transaction – typically 20p for booksellers – instead of the credit card percentage charge.

At the time of writing, only one debit card system is in operation – Barclays Connect – but other banks have announced plans to introduce them soon.

One advantage of the debit card over the bank-card guaranteed cheque is that the customers can spend up to the amount available in their current accounts. There is no £50 limit.

Further developments

Card-swipe machines are becoming more widely used in retail transactions. The customer's plastic card is *wiped* through the machine, which is online to the card company's central computer, and the transaction is automatically authorised or refused; if authorised, a receipt for the customer to sign is automatically printed out.

At present, Barclaycard's PDQ system uses card-swipe machines and accepts Visa credit cards. In the near future, we can expect the equivalent of cash transactions to use a similar system: the customer's account being instantly debited and the retailer's account instantly credited. This instantaneous transfer of funds already has its own ugly acronym – EFTPOS: Electronic Funds Transfer at Point of Sale.

Further details of these and other electronic marvels are included in the BA's *Bookshop Computer Guide*.

SHOPFITTING

Shopfitting involves substantially more than just putting in shelving runs. Depending on the premises, it may require structural alteration, fitting false ceilings, changing the lighting system, carpeting, decorating, installing security devices, replacing or rebuilding the shop front and so on. Various local authority permissions may be required for the work to be undertaken and to ensure that regulations – building control, fire safety, planning permission, advertising control, etc – are complied with.

There are four approaches to shopfitting: DIY, mainly DIY, using shopfitters, using design consultants.

DIY

If you're confident enough of your design, building and decorating skills, you can draw up your own plans, buy in whatever fixtures you need, and install everything yourself. This is undoubtedly the cheapest option. Shops of a few hundred square feet may cost you less than £3,000 to get ready for trading. The practicality of doing the shopfitting yourself relates as much to the structure and condition of the premises to start with as to your own DIY skills.

Modular bookshop shelving is readily available (see *Shopfitters* below) but is rather more expensive than fixed shelving or the sort of all-purpose DIY shelving you might put up yourself.

Some major publishers – particularly paperback publishers – may be willing to make a contribution to the cost of shelving in return for your undertaking to mount a permanent display of their titles. Other publishers may be able to supply display equipment – spinners, plinths, dumpbins and so on to accommodate their own titles. Don't be afraid of sounding out the publishers to see what they can offer (see also page 197 on contacting reps).

The disadvantage of DIY shopfitting is that it risks looking like what it is: well-meaning but amateurish – qualities that have characterised and bedevilled the small independent bookshop for so long.

MAINLY DIY

This is a matter of instructing local builders to carry out work to your specifications. The plans and designs are largely yours, and you may independently buy in shelving and display units, but most of the installation work, decorating and so on are done by the builders. All the above comments on DIY shopfitting apply. Costs should still be low, but the work is likely to lack the polish and professionalism of experienced shopfitters to the book trade.

SHOPFITTERS

If you look in the Business Supplies column of *The Bookseller*, you will find details of suppliers of bookshop shelving and display equipment. These firms are also able to supply a total shopfitting service, designing complete layouts using their own products. The end results are pleasing and professional. The shelving and display units are constructed as modules which may be arranged in various ways to create a unified design. The merit of a modular system is that it can be easily modified or expanded at a later date.

The BA can supply information on a wide range of specialist book trade suppliers of shopfitting and display equipment.

DESIGN CONSULTANTS

Using a bookshop design consultant (see page 181) is the top-of-the-range option, likely to produce the best results but at the greatest *immediate* cost. Long term, today's greatest cost may prove to be the best value-for-money investment. Good design enhances the appeal of your shop and ultimately shows up, year by year, in the net profits. Shelving system A which costs twice as much as shelving system B may have three times the useful life.

A consultant, uncommitted to particular builders or display equipment manufacturers, has no interest in recommending anything other than the most appropriate solution to a problem. If you wish, all of the work can be put into the consultant's hands – not merely drawing plans and proposing fittings, but everything from securing local authority permissions to instructing builders and supervising installation work. Alternatively, you can buy in the consultant's expertise for any particular part of the work – just the design plans, for example – which you then implement independently.

In the matter of structural alteration rather than bookshop fitments, a good local architect is also worth consulting.

SHOPFITTING CONSIDERATIONS

Whether you buy in expertise or do it all yourself, the same matters have to be considered. Here are some of the things to bear in mind:

- The ultimate objective of all bookshop activities is to make a profit. The contributions that shopfitting makes to this objective are (a) the creation of a shop that people are attracted to enter and enjoy being in once they have entered; and (b) the maximising of the shop's useful selling space.

- The big retailing chains – both booksellers and major retailers in general – have demonstrated the importance of *image* in attracting and retaining customers. Shops with similar ranges of products at similar prices are often perceived as significantly different by their customers because of the image they present. Just as people 'say' things about themselves by the clothes they wear and the way they speak and move, so shops say things about *themselves* by their decor, lighting, layout and so on.

  Your choice as a bookseller is not whether your shop will or will not have an image. It can't help having one. The choice is between making a deliberate decision as to what that image shall be, and then expressing it through all facets of the shop's design, or allowing the image to come about as the unplanned consequence of piecemeal decisions. The latter tends to be characterless at best and messy at worst; avoid it.

- However splendid the interior of your shop, no one will ever know until they come in. It's generally a mistake to refurbish the inside of a shop while leaving its front looking exactly as before. Make sure that passers-by *know* that changes have taken place. Change excites interest; sameness isn't even noticed.

- Walls are the best places for shelving, but shelving that is too high for the average adult to reach is effectively storage space, not selling space.

- Shelving and display units in a central floor area should not normally be more than 54 inches high. At this level, your view across the shop is unimpeded – an important deterrent to shoplifting – and customers can similarly look around and get a sense of the shop's layout.

  You can allow central shelving to go as high as 60 inches provided you raise the level of the cash desk by a six inch step so that staff can maintain visual supervision of the shop.

  Anything above 60 inches for central shelving makes for a shoplifters' paradise, effectively converting an open sales area into a number of screened hideaways.

- Central shelving creates corridors between itself and the wall shelving or the next row of central shelving. Leave pathways open between corridors so that customers can circulate freely when something catches their attention across the way. Avoid a continuous run of central shelving for more than about 12 feet.

- The distance between wall shelving and central shelving should not be less than about 40 inches if customers are to have room to pass freely and to lean over to reach for books on lower shelves. If you can spare the space, a distance of 48 inches is to be preferred.
- The side window of a narrow and deep corner shop is normally best treated either completely or largely as another wall. The latter is achieved by leaving one or more gaps between sets of shelves or by putting a set of low shelves between the high shelves, in effect defining a restricted window area through which people in the street can see into the shop. Leaving an entire side window *as* window inevitably reduces the floor area available for shelving and display within the shop.

STOCK

For a shop to be seriously thought of as a bookshop, it must deal exclusively or mainly in books. But as you doubtless appreciate by now, it is not easy to run such a shop profitably. You may find it more satisfying to use your expertise to recommend precisely the right book for a discerning customer, but you get a much better return on your money when you sell a piece of coloured card printed with doggerel to celebrate yet another Special Day that the greetings card publishers have succeeded in writing into the public or private calendar. While 35p is your typical profit margin in every pound customers spend on books, it's more likely to be 50p in every pound they spend on cards.

NON-BOOK STOCK

Many bookshops take in greetings cards, stationery and other non-book goods as a way of leavening the business and getting more people into the shop (see Table 12). But where do you stop? If instead of a set of bookshelves, you put in a card display, you may well boost your profits. So why not have even fewer bookshelves and sell fancy paper as well, and some children's games, and maybe a jigsaw puzzle or two? And why not diversify into digital watches and personal stereos? The point is this: if you allow non-book items to encroach too far into your shop, you're at risk of edging yourself out of specialist bookselling altogether. No shame in that, of course, but do make a conscious policy decision on the matter.

TABLE 12 Source: BA membership records mid-1988

BA MEMBERS STOCKING GOODS OTHER THAN NEW BOOKS *Corporate membership 3260*

(a) alphabetical order		*(b) numerical order*	
356	Computer hardware	2127	Greetings cards
402	Computer software	1607	Stationery
2127	Greetings cards	955	Remainder books
931	Records/cassettes (music)	931	Records/cassettes (music)
955	Remainder books	525	Video cassettes
269	Secondhand books	402	Computer software
1607	Stationery	356	Computer hardware
525	Video cassettes	269	Secondhand books

Look at the *Other goods sales %* line in Table 9 on page 138. Most specialist booksellers take rather less than 20 per cent of their turnover on other goods. That category, by the way, covers everything except new books, and therefore includes remainders, secondhand books, and so-called talking books – ie book readings on audio cassettes. Significantly, the lowest net profits are shown mostly by shops with the lowest sale of other goods.

It is eminently sensible to try to sweeten the profits with a few non-book lines, and to use them also to attract non-book buyers into the shop, but keep a close eye on the ratio of book to non-book sales if your main ambition is to be a specialist bookseller.

Some book wholesalers also stock non-book lines – check the *Directory of Book Publishers and Wholesalers* – but you may prefer to buy your non-book stock from a local general wholesaler or a specialist national wholesaler or manufacturer. Trace local wholesalers from Yellow Pages, and national suppliers from the appropriate trade journals. You will find classified lists of trade journals in, for example, *Willing's Press Guide* (Thomas Skinner Directories). Relevant trade fairs are also an important and convenient source of non-book merchandise; look for trade fair announcements in the appropriate trade journals.

So make your policy decision and, if appropriate, lay in the goods.

NEW BOOK STOCK

Buying the opening book stock is less daunting than it looks at first. It's certainly not a matter of ploughing through a list of 440,000 titles and putting ticks or crosses beside them. Without experience to guide you, there's not a lot of point in agonising too precisely over every last title. However painstakingly chosen, your opening stock is bound to contain surprises: books you consider to be of indifferent quality which sell well, and others you regard highly which don't sell at all. The broader your stock range, the greater the opportunity for customer preferences to reveal themselves. Then in future weeks and months as you replenish and return, expand this section and run down that, you slowly refine your stock profile so that it matches more and more closely your customers' known requirements.

Rather more daunting is the business of actually shelving the opening stock when it arrives. Several thousand books needing to be unpacked, checked in and put out on display can take many days to deal with, depending upon how much thought you have given to subject layout and how many reliable pairs of hands you can call upon to help. Ideally, the books move straight from the boxes to their final shelved positions. In practice, you're likely to find some subject sections overflowing, with the consequent need to move books, already shelved, along to new positions. Ah well, it's all experience. You'll probably be more efficient by the time you open your second shop.

As to the composition of the opening stock, it's generally best to take advantage of the available experience of others, and limit your own input to editing the recommended list by adding or deleting the odd title.

You will by now have decided how much you have to spend and whether you will be operating as a general bookshop, a general bookshop with one or more subject specialisms, or a speciality bookshop. These decisions being made, you can approach publishers or wholesalers and seek their advice on the fine detail of your opening selection.

Wholesalers

General booksellers can, with advantage, buy most if not all of their opening stock from a good wholesaler. The wholesaler's stock, you remember, represents an experienced bookseller's evaluation of what the market will buy, and the wholesaler's record of sales is a useful indicator of the relative popularity of different titles.

At the time of writing, Hammick's, one of the major book wholesalers, offers a Recommended Opening Stock Service (ROSS) specifically aimed at new bookshops. The bookseller indicates how much money is available for opening stock, and the wholesaler's computer produces a detailed list of recommended titles and quantities. If required, you can get a print-out of the wholesaler's entire stock, classified by subject, and listed within subjects in descending order of sales. You are free to edit the ROSS list, adding or deleting titles and varying the numbers; but the major part of the work is done by the wholesaler, who delivers the finally selected stock in a single consignment, the books pre-sorted by subject, ready for unpacking straight onto the shelves. Additionally, extended credit and special returns arrangements are included in the deal.

Other wholesalers may be able to provide a similar service even if they don't market it as a specially named package. Address enquiries to wholesalers listed in the latest *Directory of Book Publishers and Wholesalers.*

Publishers

If you decide to buy your stock in whole or part direct from publishers – perhaps because your subject speciality is inadequately covered by the wholesalers – you can still approach the problem in a similar way. Choose the publishers whose books you feel should be represented in your shop, decide the varying amounts you want to spend with each of them, and then invite them to recommend which titles you should stock and in what quantities.

REPS

A bookseller's most helpful contact with a publisher is normally the publisher's representative – the rep. Once your shop is trading, reps will call on you to show you their latest titles, keep you informed about forthcoming ones, make sure you haven't overlooked any of their backlist titles which they believe would sell in your shop and – not least – update you with the latest gossip going the rounds of the trade.

Drop a line to *The Bookseller* telling them when you plan to open, and ask if they will mention the fact in their weekly Trade Notes section, adding that you would like to receive publishers' catalogues in whatever subjects interest you and would also be pleased to see *by appointment* any reps who might wish to call; give your phone number so they can ring you up first.

You can also approach the reps directly. A call to a publisher's local rep to fix a time for him or her to visit is often the easiest and quickest way of making contact with a publisher for the first time. All members of the Book Publishers' Representatives' Association are listed in the *BPRA Handbook*, published annually (price £4 in 1988) and available from the BA. It comprises an alphabetical listing of reps – names, addresses, telephone numbers, and the firms they represent – plus an alphabetical listing of publishers, identifying which of their reps cover which areas of the country.

In addition to being able to recommend an opening stock of their titles, reps can also help you with sales aids and other hints and advice, and ultimately – if reluctantly – with returns.

PUBLICITY

Various forms of advertising and promotion are considered in the next chapter. The real rewards of publicity come long-term, and publicity itself is a continuing rather than a once-for-all exercise. Be wary of spending good money in an attempt to make a big splash in a short time. Regard any opening publicity as the start of a steady selling of your bookshop to the public; it is something to be continued tomorrow and the day after, and the day after that. There's really no way that you can send your business off with such a big publicity push that the momentum will carry you through to long-term success. Concentrating all your efforts and all your promotional money on Day One is only likely to leave you feeling hung over on Day Two.

A high street shop being fitted out and stocked in readiness for opening day is its own advertisement. Don't keep the windows boarded up or whited out while the preparations go forward. Take advantage of the public's natural curiosity; you're running a live 2–3 month serial, and it costs you nothing extra to keep the passers-by entertained as the story unfolds from empty shell to opening day. "I wonder who's taken that shop on the high street", "They were putting in a new front window today", "I do hope it's not going to be *another* estate agent", "I saw lots of shelving being fitted yesterday", "Have you seen? They've just put the name up! It's going to be a bookshop! Yippee!"

A little formal advertising may be worth while, but don't spend too much on it. Put a display ad in the local paper announcing your opening day, stock range (list the subjects), special services (Book Tokens, credit cards, Post-A-Book, etc), opening times, address and telephone number. Perhaps one or more publishers will share the costs with you in return for a plug for their titles. Remember, however, that today's paper could be lining the budgie's cage tomorrow, and it's normally best to spread your advertising budget over smaller ads and a longer period rather than blueing it all on one announcement of short life and uncertain impact.

A leaflet drop (see also page 206) to the households in the catchment area is also worth considering, but is subject to the same qualifications.

Whatever paid advertising you decide upon, try to include in it some special offer (see page 204) rather than limiting yourself merely to making an announcement.

There's much to be said for a low-key opening if you're new to bookselling and to business. You'll have excitement enough just finding your feet in those early days. The last thing you want is to attract a large number of people into your shop and then be unable to serve them satisfactorily because you and your staff are inexperienced and uncertain. Why not have a launching party just for a few friends to cheer you on your way, and reserve a larger and more public celebration for your first anniversary by which time you'll have settled in, know what's what, and probably be able to make a much better guess of what will pull the customers in? And, of course, by then you'll have something to celebrate.

Chapter 10

Selling Books

During the countdown to opening day, all is calculation, guesswork and hope. The moment you open your doors to the public, you start to learn the truth. The customer, until now a figment of your imagination, actually walks in and buys something or, more probably, browses round the shelves while you try to maintain an air of discreet nonchalance, and then either asks for something you haven't got or leaves without saying a word.

The first truth you learn is that most 'customers' don't buy anything. Research has shown that two out of three people who go into a bookshop leave it again anything up to twenty minutes or more later without having made a purchase. More about this below (page 213). The second truth is that most people walking past your shop do precisely that: only a minority come in for their twenty minutes of free browsing. The third truth restates the first two in so self-evident a fashion that some booksellers acknowledge it only dismissively and never think to do anything about it: while only one in three of those who come into your shop buys something, none of those who *don't* come into your shop buys anything at all. The significance of this is that insofar as bookselling is about book*selling*, your task falls under two quite separate heads: (1) Getting people into the shop, and (2) Selling to them once they're in.

The temptation is to devote all your selling skills to the second part of the task – that's the bit that actually *feels* like selling: no doubt about it, if the customer hands you some money and you hand the customer a book, you've made a sale. Yet if you could achieve a high level of success with the first part of the task – getting people into the shop – the second part would to some extent look after itself. After all, similar reasoning lies behind your preference for a prime site if you can afford it: the expectation is that where there are more people there will be more sales.

It is instructive to take a quick look at the approach used by sellers in another field. Some insurance salesmen settle down to a day's work with a list of *prospects* they ring up to try to make appointments at which insurance needs are discussed and hopefully a policy sold. A given salesman may succeed in making appointments with only, say, five people in every fifty he telephones, and then go on to make a sale to an average of only one of those five – at first sight, a depressingly low level of success. But if his one sale per fifty prospects actually makes him a living, he can keep his spirits up by viewing the job statistically. The expectation that working through a list of fifty names will produce one sale allows him to think of each of those names as one-fiftieth of the way towards success, whatever the outcome of the particular phone call or interview. The crucial task is keeping the prospects list topped up. If he looks after *that*, the rest more or less looks after itself.

Many a bookseller will bridle at being likened, however remotely, to an insurance salesman. But selling is selling; its basic principles relate to the activity, not to the trade. If you can increase the number of people who cross the threshold of your bookshop, you can expect by that means alone to increase your turnover. These people are *your* list of prospects, and you must work at creating and maintaining it.

GETTING PEOPLE INTO THE SHOP

Booksellers typically spend very little on publicity and advertising – 0.4 per cent of turnover is fairly common even among Charter Group members (see Table 9 on page 138), and that's less than £500 a year on a turnover of £120,000. According to other figures, referred to by a speaker at the BA's 1987 Conference, whereas retailers in general in 1985 spent £5.80 on advertising for every £1,000 of turnover, booksellers spent just 12p per £1,000 of turnover! The exclamation mark is irresistible.

Doubtless the NBA accounts in part for this low level of positive promotion. The argument is that if a book costs the same wherever it's bought, there's not much point in your advertising a given title as the customer would have no greater reason to buy it from you than from any other bookseller. Your expensive ad in the local paper announcing that film star X's thrilling biography is now available in your shop is as likely to increase sales at the nearest W.H. Smith as it is to increase your own sales. The only certain beneficiary of specific title advertising – if there are any beneficiaries at all – is the publisher of that title, and that indeed is why most book advertising is undertaken by publishers and not by booksellers. But that should not mean that you just wait passively in your bookshop hoping that someone else's publicity will spin off a few customers in your direction. If you want the business, you've got to go for it. Here are some ideas.

LOCAL PRESS ADVERTISING

Remember that the NBA restricts price competition only on net books. Remainders and other non-net books such as specially published *bargain books* – usually OP titles reprinted by new publishers and offered at prices substantially below the original net prices – give the bookseller the chance to make the same kind of money-saving appeal that other high street retailers seem to find so successful: *'The XYZ Health Food Encyclopaedia' originally published at £19.95, now only £4.95 – limited stocks – first come first served – at The Bookshop, High Street . . . .*

The object of such advertising as this, and indeed of all promotion, is not merely to sell the specific proposition but also to attract people who might not otherwise come into your shop. Once there, they may buy other books too, and most significantly of all, may become regular customers. The success of such promotions is not to be measured only in terms of immediate profit. If a £50 advertisement in the local press produces gross profits of £50 on the sale of the specific title, the narrow judgement is that nothing worthwhile has been achieved. But what really matters is the wider and continuing effect on customer numbers and spending produced by the advertisement. Even a single extra regular customer is of value to your business: an ad which covers its cost and produces a 'profit' of one regular customer must be rated a success.

EVALUATING THE SUCCESS OF ADVERTISING

Judging the long-term effects of advertising is difficult and uncertain, because you can never know in advance what a newly acquired customer will be worth to you in future months and years. Nor can you be certain that any increase in profits, year on year, is attributable to your advertising or would have taken place anyway. But it is often possible to evaluate the short-term response fairly precisely, and that will at least show up the marked successes and the total failures.

What is needed is some means of distinguishing customers you would have had anyway from those who come in response to a particular promotion. The simplest way is to encourage the latter to identify themselves by offering some sort of inducement – eg *Bring this advertisement with you on your next visit to The Bookshop and claim your free copy of our Summer Bargains Catalogue.* You might even think of building up a mailing list by asking respondents to complete a name-and-address coupon and tick off special subject interests (but see page 222 on mail order). Or what about offering a small prize in a simple competition? – *Guess how many titles were in stock at 9 am on 1st June* or *These were our five bestselling titles last month: can you list them in order of numbers sold? A £10 Book Token to the first correct answer opened on 30th June.* Use your ingenuity. There are any number of ways of getting advertisement respondents to reveal themselves if you make it worth their while, and the cost to you of making it worth their while need only be a small addition to the basic advertising cost.

Once again the NBA constrains you to tread warily because anything that might be construed as a cut-price offer of a net book will bring the wrath of the trade upon your head. The most obvious and tempting offers – eg *10 per cent off your next purchase if you clip the coupon and bring it with you* – have to be avoided unless specifically related to your non-net titles. But then why not concoct something that *does* relate only to one or more of your non-net titles? Or, if you deal also in non-book products, why not make an offer related to *those*? Remember the objective is simply to get bodies into your shop and then to identify what has brought them there.

Once you have a method of identifying advertisement respondents, you can easily work out how much advertising money you have had to pay for each potential customer, and you can compare this with the average amount the respondents actually spend on the particular visit to your shop.

You must try to build measuring devices like this into all your publicity and advertising so that you have some means of knowing, at least at the extremes, which sort of promotions are worth repeating and which are not. The principle is that anything that *can* be measured *should* be measured. Indeed, when choosing between equally attractive promotional strategies, always favour the one which will produce the more analysable results. Unless you're able to measure the effectiveness of your advertising expenditure, you're just blundering about in the dark, throwing money at an invisible target. With that sort of behaviour, even 12p per £1,000 is reckless extravagance.

LET YOUR ADVERTISING *PROPOSE*, NOT MERELY ANNOUNCE

Don't be paralysed by the fear that specific title advertising will put business into other bookshops. All that matters to you is that your return on advertising money should be satisfactory. And if it is, you're not made any poorer by the fact that others may be getting a spin-off benefit they haven't paid for.

An advertisement merely announcing that your shop is a bookshop and has lots of splendid books may remind old customers of your existence, but it does nothing to tempt them into making a fresh visit; as for non-customers, such an advertisement scarcely penetrates their awareness. By contrast, an advertisement which includes specific offers is a double promotion: it reminds people of your existence at the same time as making suggestions to which they can react immediately – "That sounds the perfect present for Auntie Flo", "Could be the very thing I've been after for years", "At that price it must be worth going to have a look at it".

If you're thinking of advertising one or more titles of a particular publisher, you may find the publisher willing to meet part of the bill. This not only reduces your expenses, it may also give you access to more professional advertising copy than you could either devise or commission yourself.

SIGNING SESSIONS

Getting an author to visit your shop to autograph copies of his or her books is worth doing occasionally. Choose a well-known author who can easily be recognised. Signing session flops are embarrassing for everyone. Few sights are as unhappy as an author, pen poised, never asked to sign a book, but occasionally mistaken for a supernumerary shop assistant by someone wanting a Book Token. A successful session, however, can shift a good number of the author's books, and it also brings into your shop more people than would normally be there – some of whom may be newcomers who will turn into regular customers.

One advantage of a signing session is that there is no risk of competitors' benefitting from your efforts. The most ubiquitous authors can only be in one place at a time, and if they are signing books in your shop, the advantage is all yours and can't spill over to the competition.

Signing sessions need not be expensive to arrange. Depending on time and location, you may need to lunch or dine your author, arrange overnight accommodation and meet out-of-pocket expenses. But it is a publicity session for the author too, and you may be quite sure that every time he or she signs a customer's purchase, a talking cash register whispers something like "Another 55p royalty in the bag, old thing."

To get an author, contact the publisher with your proposal or try the author direct. Ask the publisher for help with a proportion of your special advertising costs to publicise the event in local papers or on local radio. The publisher may be able to provide posters, showcards and other display material for the occasion. Have cheap handbills printed to give advance notice of the session to your customers, and offer to put signed copies aside for anyone unable to attend the signing in person, which should of course be timed to ensure a large number of likely buyers; for most signings this will be late morning or early afternoon on a Saturday.

Once the session is over, you could ask your author to sign some or all of the rest of your unsold stock of his or her work; this could enhance the appeal of the books, particularly as gifts, in the weeks to come. You must, of course, be confident that the books will indeed sell, as publishers are unlikely to accept signed copies back as returns.

PERSONAL APPEARANCES OF FICTIONAL CHARACTERS

Publishers of children's books often have character costumes for loan or hire. All you have to provide is a body to go inside the costume, and *voilà!* you can proudly present the special guest appearance of whichever much-loved character you wish to feature. It can be great fun. Even the children enjoy it. And provided you haven't mistakenly allowed your cashier to wear the costume, your takings may also be up on the day.

As with signing sessions, it is important to get the event well publicised. Make sure the local schools and any mother/children groups in your catchment area know about it.

BARGAIN SALES

The National Book Sale provides an opportunity to do what most non-bookselling retailers are able to do all the year round – sell off old stock for whatever it will fetch. See Appendix B for the regulations.

But you don't have to restrict yourself to a once-a-year sale. Put on a sale at any time of year to suit the circumstances of your own shop. Of course, the NBA prevents you from putting in your slow-moving titles unless you've had them in stock for over twelve months and you satisfy certain other conditions, but you can make an attractive sale out of remainders and bargain books and even the odd non-net book that's overstayed its welcome.

Everyone loves a bargain, but don't stint on your advertising. You won't pull in extra customers unless you get the message across to the public out there that you are having a sale. While it is always a good idea to have a table of remainders and bargain books, unless you proclaim the fact publicly, you are not giving yourself the chance of increasing your number of customers.

House-to-house leaflet drops can be a cheap and effective way of getting the message to the public. Have the leaflets professionally designed and printed; you don't want them looking like a scrappy invitation to a jumble sale. The Post Office delivers unaddressed items along with the mail in its Household Delivery Service; local leaflet distributors are listed in Yellow Pages under 'Circular and sample distributors'.

THE SHOP WINDOW

The shop window is your permanent advertising space, and you're paying for it in rent and rates whether you use it creatively and aggressively or just let it fill up with a tired and random display of this and that. Only tantalising inches the other side of the window are non-customers whose only reason for not coming into the shop is that nothing has stirred their desire to do so. You can't physically waylay them and haul them in but a good window display can be almost as effective.

Change your window frequently and *obviously*. Discreet and subtle improvements go unremarked. For those regular passers-by who are not yet your customers, your shop merges into the unnoticed ordinariness of the street unless new and striking displays grab their attention.

Avoid giving your window over to scruffy notices announcing mums' coffee mornings, bring-and-buy sales, hamsters looking for loving homes, and all the rest. If you want to provide a notice board for the local community – and that can be a cheap and effective way of winning favour with potential customers – then literally provide a notice board. Site it either within the shop or in some otherwise unusable part of the window, but make sure that all notices are kept strictly within the confines of the board or the untidy amateurism inseparable from such notices will slowly erode the professionalism of your own displays.

Remember also that people like to be able to see into a shop before entering. Don't let your window displays block off the view from the street into the interior. A window display can occupy the low foreground while the attractive layout of books within the shop can be thought of as an extended though separate window display.

Thematic displays

General booksellers have one great advantage over other retailers: there is no area of human interest unrepresented in books. Whereas the shoe shop can do nothing but display shoes, and the DIY shop is stuck with cans of paint and the like, a bookshop can focus on any subject under the sun. You can have a window this fortnight on poetry, next fortnight on sport, the fortnight after on traditional crafts – and so on. Try matching your displays to public preoccupations of the moment, national or local.

Where appropriate, borrow props from other shops to liven the displays and provide different shapes to relieve the rectangularity of the books. A well-written card acknowledging the loan of the props will give the other retailer some free advertising while you benefit from the extra interest of the display. If you're doing a window on music books, for example, borrow one or more musical instruments from a local music shop and incorporate them into the display, noting that 'The musical instruments are by courtesy of The XYZ Music Shop'.

Tie-ins with films at local cinemas or plays at local theatres are also possible. Part of your display can give publicity to the cinema or theatre, and they in return may find a space for you to put a display of books – or even a stand in the foyer where you could sell them before, during or after the performance.

By highlighting different subjects at different times in your window displays, you increase your chance of attracting people who may never have thought that a bookshop would contain anything of interest to them. Non-book buyers – and remember that means most of the population – tend to assume that the subject range of books is limited – literary, intellectual, obscure, dull – and that bookshops therefore are alien places not worth exploring. Your special subject windows can prove them wrong, to both their advantage and yours.

Window dressing is an art, and if you haven't got the necessary flair yourself, you might make a point of looking for it when you come to employ staff. Alternatively, you could use a freelance window-dresser. Look for someone in Yellow Pages. One way of covering the cost of professional window-dressing may be to lease part of your window area to a particular publisher, perhaps on a regular monthly basis or from time to time to different publishers on a one-off basis. Sound out the publisher's rep, or contact the sales manager to see if they're interested.

Non-book stock

If appropriate, use your non-book stock to pull people into the shop. Have your greetings cards display, for example, easily visible from the street so that non-book buyers may be tempted in and, once there, may browse round the books as well as the cards.

CONTACTS IN THE LOCAL COMMUNITY

Make yourself known in the local community. Contact local schools and offer to run a book stall at PTA evenings or open days or any other appropriate occasions. Contact all local clubs and associations with similar propositions – ie that you will put on a display, at their premises, of a selection of titles of particular interest to their membership. Offer to give talks about reading, books, bookshops, the book trade or whatever – and make sure you have a selection of relevant books with you for people to buy.

Consider taking a stand at local events – stamp fairs, flower shows, antiques fairs, etc. Publishers may be prepared to supply stock on consignment for these special promotions, so you need not depend solely on your normal stock nor need you risk special stock investment.

Don't overlook the local business community. Books are bought not only by associations like the local chamber of commerce but also by individual companies, especially the larger ones, who may have their own small libraries and spend a considerable sum each year on directories, reference books and publications covering their own business areas. Direct mail key personnel in local companies: send details of desk reference books, training handbooks, management guides, relevant HMSO publications – eg on recent legislation of business interest – and follow up with a phone call a week or so later to see what interest you have aroused and to press your advantage further.

Book Tokens are much used as prizes by schools and other organisations: keep reminding them that you can supply their wants at a moment's notice. A few hundred poundsworth of Tokens distributed as prizes among local schoolchildren can bring a whole host of eager new customers into your shop.

School bookshops

The schools and the book trade have a common interest in wishing to foster a love of books and reading among children. Not all children have parents who introduce them to the pleasures of bookshop browsing, but in many schools there are enthusiastic teachers who supervise school bookshops where children may taste the delight and acquire the habit and – who knows? – even buy the odd book. Many school bookshops are run by publishers selling their own titles into the schools, but they can also be run by local booksellers, who are naturally able to offer the titles of a range of publishers.

Near the start of term, the responsible teacher comes to your shop, makes a selection of stock off your shelves, noting titles and quantities on a reconciliation sheet – one copy for you, one copy for the teacher – and then takes them away to form the stock of the school bookshop. Not later than the end of term, the teacher returns with unsold books, the reconciliation sheet marked up to show what has been sold, and the amount due for the sales. Damaged or soiled books must of course also be paid for.

If the school has a Book Agent's Licence naming you as supplier (see Appendix D) – and this is the recommended way of operating – you can allow them a discount, even off net books: 10 per cent is typical. Strictly speaking, however, a Licence isn't needed as you are effectively wholesaling books to another bookseller. But in that case, it's your responsibility to see that the school understands that (1) any discount is for themselves as *sellers*, (2) no discount is allowable under this arrangement for books which are for the school's own use, and (3) the full net price must be charged to any child buying a net book.

You will find that different schools produce very different results, though it is difficult to tell in advance which will do well and which won't. Much depends upon the teacher running the bookshop and the importance that the head and other staff attach to the venture. It is, in any event, unlikely to be a major money-spinner for you. You are having to finance the stock while it is in the schools, and you may meanwhile need to order further copies of titles for your own shop stock only to find that these same titles are returned unsold by the schools at the end of term.

The whole thing is best regarded as a public relations exercise. You build up goodwill with the schools, the children, the parents, the teachers; and provided you can ensure that they know that you are the ultimate provider of the stock and the service – see that advertising bookmarks, for example, are given away with all sales (see page 224) – you can hope that it will bring more people into your shop. If viewed in immediate commercial terms you manage to do no more than break even, it may nevertheless be worthwhile as a way of promoting your shop. But you must regularly assess the position to make sure that you're not investing more time and money in the activity than the unquantifiable spin-offs may warrant.

Institutional business

The supply of books to public libraries and schools has traditionally formed part of the specialist bookshop's business. You can see from Table 9 on page 138 that library and schools business between then typically account for between 10 and 20 per cent of Charter booksellers' new book sales. This is, however, a percentage of turnover; the percentage contribution to gross profits is likely to be rather less. School text books, after all, have a very low profit margin even before customers extract further discounts from the bookseller; and schools and libraries holding the appropriate licences (see page 70) will expect 10 per cent off everything.

Gross profits on institutional business are likely to come within the range 7½ to 25 per cent. Since, as you can see from Table 9, gross profits overall hover around the 30 per cent mark, it is clear that institutional business helps to pull gross profits down from the 35 per cent typically produced by across-the-counter net sales.

Institutional supply is an increasingly treacherous area for the independent bookseller. Compared with the sale of stock off your shelves to the general public, it is more labour-intensive, less financially rewarding, and far less reliable as a continuing source of revenue. However, institutional business is worth going for if you can slot it into the slack times without incurring extra expense or needing to take on extra staff. This way you have a chance of squeezing a bit more profit out of your existing resources, and the fact that it produces a lower level of profit than the rest of your business doesn't matter. It would only matter if you needed to forgo more profitable business in order to free resources to service the less profitable business. Furthermore, since institutional business necessarily increases the volume of business you place with your suppliers, it gives you more leverage when it comes to negotiating better terms.

But the main reason for discussing institutional business here is the higher profile it can give your shop in the local community. The schools, the libraries, the teachers, the librarians – all are, we hope, impressed by the standard of service you provide; and some will therefore come to your shop for their personal wants and, when the occasion arises, recommend others to do so.

EDITORIAL MENTION IN THE LOCAL MEDIA

A publicity idea worth considering is to suggest to your local paper or radio station that they run a Bestsellers of the Week/Month list, based on information you provide, each published list to be accompanied by an acknowledgement of its source, thus giving your shop free and regular publicity.

Even more attractive is a regular column in the local press or airtime on local radio in which you review and discuss a selection of current titles. The by-line, naming you and your shop, can be worth far more than any paid-for advertising.

Don't overlook the newsworthiness of things that happen in your shop. If you're installing some of the latest book trade technology, send a brief press release about it to the local papers; they may do a feature on it. If you're opening a new children's section or having a signing session or giving a talk or running a competition or whatever – do a press release. A single A4 sheet cleanly typed on one side only with double-line spacing is all that's needed; a paper interested in your information might well lift copy, word for word, from your press release, so compose it with that possibility in mind. Most of the time your efforts will be ignored, but when they're not, a lot of useful business might come your way from the publicity which costs you no more than the price of a sheet of paper, an envelope, a postage stamp and a little inspiration.

LITERARY LUNCHEONS

Organising events like literary luncheons – or dinners – takes time. Plan at least six months ahead to give yourself time to book speakers, venues, caterers, and to sell tickets. It is a good idea to propose that your local paper sponsors the occasion jointly with your shop. It makes useful publicity for them too. And while you look after the organisation, they are ideally placed to handle the publicity, both before and after the event.

SELLING TO PEOPLE IN THE SHOP

Fittings, design, layout, lighting, signage and so on all contribute to the convenience and attractiveness of your bookshop. Though you will have built some flexibility into your original plans (see page 144), it's a flexibility to be exploited on a time-scale of weeks or months rather than minutes and hours. Giving a good impression on the shorter time-scale is a matter of freshness, tidiness, full shelves and pleasantly helpful staff. A token uniform for staff can be part of your shop's image, and serves the practical purpose of helping customers identify staff. Simple slip-over tops with the shop's name, or even just prominently worn badges, could be suitable.

Whenever there is time to spare, you and your staff should be tidying and adjusting the stock on the shelves. Spine-out books – ie those displayed library fashion with only the spines showing – should be held comfortably upright by the books to each side or by other supports; they should be neither wedged in, making removal and replacement difficult, nor falling over at an angle on an overspaced display. As books are sold from spine-out displays, shelves can be kept looking comfortably full by turning one or more of the remaining books face forward.

Most books sell more readily when displayed face forward, but face-forward displays naturally take up more space than spine-out ones and if all your books were displayed face forward, your stock range would perforce be more limited. A mix of spine out and face forward adds variety to your displays and helps you cope with shifting stock levels without either having gaps on the shelves or books languishing undisplayed in a stock room. Choose the most popular books and those with the most attractive covers for face-forward display.

BROWSERS AND BUYERS

About 25 per cent of the people who go into a bookshop have in mind a specific book they wish to buy. Another 25 per cent are looking for something to buy on a particular subject or by a particular author. The remaining 50 per cent have nothing particular in mind at all; indeed some of them may have gone into the shop to buy a non-book product. Any given individual may on one bookshop visit be in one category and on another visit in another category. All the people in the bookshop are therefore potential buyers, though at any particular time some are more immediately motivated to purchase than others.

The above figures come from *Lost Book Sales*, a survey undertaken jointly by the PA's Book Marketing Council and the BA. Published in 1980, and still in print, its findings are as valid today as they were then. The main purpose of the survey was to discover the value and number of sales lost because of booksellers' inability to fulfil customers' requirements. As a by-product, it produced a range of other fascinating statistical information – for example, the popularity for bookshop visits of different days and times of day (see Table 13) is both interesting and in some respects surprising –

TABLE 13 Source: *Lost Book Sales*, 1980

DISTRIBUTION OF BOOKSHOP VISITORS BY TIME *51 bookshops*

	TOTAL %	*MON* %	*TUES* %	*WED* %	*THURS* %	*FRI* %	*SAT* %
TOTAL	100.0	9.8	17.6	24.9	9.0	17.6	21.2
before 10.00	9.7	0.6	2.5	1.9	0.7	1.9	2.1
10.01–11.00	13.9	1.0	2.4	3.3	1.3	2.2	3.6
11.01–12.00	16.3	1.8	2.5	3.9	1.5	2.8	3.8
12.01–1.00	15.9	1.8	2.8	4.3	1.4	2.7	3.0
1.01–2.00	13.5	1.5	2.0	3.4	1.4	2.6	2.5
2.01–3.00	13.1	1.4	2.0	3.6	1.2	2.1	2.9
3.01–4.00	10.7	1.1	1.8	2.4	0.9	2.0	2.4
4.01–5.00	6.9	0.6	1.6	2.1	0.5	1.2	0.9
after 5.00	*	*	*	*	*	*	*

* less than 0.1% *Slight discrepancies due to rounding*

and it presented a picture of the typical make-up of bookshop sales, highlighting areas offering scope for improvement by well directed selling techniques. It estimated – at 1980 prices – that turnover of an extra £30 million a year was there for the making.

Customer categories: Definites, Possibles, Browsers

Lost Book Sales put customers into three categories: those looking for a particular book (the *Definites*), those looking for something on a particular subject or by a particular author (the *Possibles*), and those not thinking of buying a book at all (the *Browsers*). The survey found that about half of all bookshop customers are Browsers, a quarter are Definites and a quarter are Possibles.

Who buys what?

Here are some of the findings of the *Lost Book Sales* survey:

- For every 1,000 people going into a bookshop, 670 leave without buying anything. 130 Definites buy 165 books, 110 Possibles buy 162 books, 90 Browsers buy 129 books. 1,000 people in the shop thus generate a sale of 456 books.
- About 50 per cent of the Definites and Possibles leave without buying anything, as do over 80 per cent of the Browsers.
- The commonest reasons why Definites leave without the book they came in for are that it is not stocked or is out of stock

(together these account for 50 per cent of the non-purchases) or that it cannot be traced (22 per cent of the non-purchases).

- Of those deciding not to make a purchase even after finding the book they came in for (13 per cent of the Definites and 7 per cent of the Possibles) about 1 person in 3 rejects the book because it's too expensive.
- For every £1,000 spent, £590 comes from Definites and Possibles buying books they had planned to buy. The remaining £410 comes from *impulse purchases* – unplanned purchases of books the customer just happens to notice in the shop – of which £88 comes from Definites, £75 from Possibles and £247 from Browsers.
- Impulse purchases are made by 45 per cent of book buyers, accounting for 47 per cent of book sales by unit and 41 per cent of book sales by value.
- Of the planned purchases, 50 per cent by value are paperbacks; of the impulse purchases, 62 per cent by value are paperbacks.
- An estimated one third of books are bought as presents. Of these, 59 per cent are paperbacks, 41 per cent are hardbacks.
- Of all books sold, 82 per cent are paperbacks.
- Among the Possibles who can't find the book they want, only 1 in 5 seeks help from bookshop staff; the rest just look around.
- About 56 per cent of people who go into a bookshop stay for up to 10 minutes; about 32 per cent stay for 11–20 minutes; about 12 per cent stay for over 20 minutes.

CATERING FOR DIFFERENT CUSTOMERS

The above facts and figures suggest what you can expect in your own shop. Successfully selling to customers requires an appreciation of their different needs, interests and motivations. Selling to someone who comes in to browse without any intention of buying clearly requires a different approach from selling to someone who comes in with a shopping list of titles.

Selling to the Definites

Plainly, you maximise your chances of selling to the Definites by having in stock the books they're looking for. We saw in Chapter 1 the impossibility of stocking everything in print or even coming anywhere near it. The books most Definites are looking for, however, have not been selected by perusing a list of 440,000 or so titles; they are far more likely to have been chosen from the much smaller number of titles being currently promoted or discussed in the media. And these same titles, of course, are the ones most likely to trigger a response when noticed by Possibles and Browsers. An important objective of your stocking policy, therefore, is to anticipate demand: see page 104 for more on evaluating titles for stock.

PUBLICATION DATE EMBARGO

It is ironical that in a trade where it requires such skill – and luck – to stock what the customers want that there should be times when you've got what they want and yet may not sell it to them.

That bizarre situation arises like this: When a book is to be published, the publisher announces a publication date (shown also on the invoice) before which it may not be sold or offered to the public even if the bookseller has received his supplies of the new title. This principle is regarded by most of the book trade as an important element in the maintenance of an orderly market.

It is not always possible for publishers to supply all their bookshop customers simultaneously with stocks of a new title. Apart from the uncertainties of delivery services, there is the sheer size of the distribution problem. For a major title, the publisher's warehouse may have to spread its packing and despatch of books over an extended period, possibly even of weeks. If booksellers were permitted to display and sell the books as they received supplies, the result might be that one shop was doing a roaring trade in the title while another was telling customers that the book wasn't yet available. This is similar to the position that can arise at the end of a print run (see page 21), but this time, with co-operation and goodwill, it can be overcome.

By specifying a publication date, publishers ensure that a given title goes on sale simultaneously throughout the country, and they can gear the publicity campaign to that date. Campaigns have to be carefully orchestrated as large sums of money may be spent on them – money which will be wasted if the book isn't in the shops when the customer's enthusiasm has been whetted. Press reviews, radio and television interviews with the author, extracts published in newspapers and magazines – all of these, plus the more conventional space advertising, must be timed to climax at the publication date.

Early selling – that is, breaking the publication date embargo – surfaces as a contentious trade issue from time to time. The guilty parties generally seem to be individual branches of major bookshop groups or individual non-specialist booksellers who have bought their stock in bulk from a wholesaler. The cause of early selling seems usually to be ignorance either of the publication date or of its significance; though it must be admitted that a certain amount of deliberate flouting also goes on.

SPECIAL ORDERS

However well you anticipate demand in general, there will always be customers asking for books you haven't got. Keep a record of these enquiries, even if the customer doesn't go on to place a special order. By reviewing your list of enquiries from time to time, you might see how your stockholding policy could be adjusted to bring it more into line with customer demands.

However, your first task when you get a request for an unstocked book is to establish the book's existence: you can see from the *Lost Book Sales* figures that 22 per cent of the Definites who bought nothing were wanting a book that couldn't be traced. The starting point of any search must always be the customer's often inadequate information; but it is your skilled use of up-to-date bibliographical material (see pages 21–34) that can make all the difference. Skilful bibliographical search not only helps you to secure a particular sale, it also impresses customers with your professionalism and expertise – qualities which dispose them to return to your shop for their future purchases.

It is worth noting that bibliographical tools can be impressive in themselves. Don't hide your microfiche reader or CD-ROM monitor away in the office. Have it out in the shop, and position it if possible so that the customer can see the screen and co-operate in the search. You're paying good money for this technological wizardry: exploit it to the full.

The economics of special orders. Taking special orders for unstocked books is one of the specialist bookseller's traditional services; indeed, members of the Charter Group pledge themselves to obtain books to special order *whenever economically feasible* – and that of course goes to the heart of the matter.

Economic feasibility often depends upon how easily a special order can be slotted into a stock order. If the required title is on your wholesaler's list, it will be very little trouble to you, and no extra expense, to add it to your next stock order. But often enough the title won't be on your wholesaler's list; and the publisher may be one with whom you have no routine dealings and who imposes punitive small order surcharges.

Take a typical example – neither especially easy nor especially awkward. A customer places an order for a book costing £4 net. The book has just been published and you know it to be available because you have seen it reviewed in the papers and have noticed recent advertising in the trade press. You have an account with the publisher concerned but place stock orders with him only once every three months – much too long to keep your customer waiting – so you place a special order for the book now, posting it direct to the publisher in the first class post. You receive the book ten days later, discounted at 25 per cent plus 50p small order surcharge, and you settle the bill the following month as part of your BCH cheque. Meanwhile, you drop your customer a card saying that the book is ready for collection.

Now compare the probable cost to you of this transaction – postage, stationery, etc – with the total income it produces:

Mailing the order	£0.20	Payment from customer	£4.00
Payment to publisher	£3.50		
Card to customer	£0.15		
Total paid out	£3.85	Total received	£4.00

All your time, effort and expertise have earned you 15p – provided, of course, that all goes smoothly. If it doesn't – if, for example, you have to chase up the order – you'll almost certainly lose money. Such an order, then, is of doubtful economic feasibility. Should you have accepted it?

If you refuse special orders, you have no right to consider yourself a specialist bookseller; more to the commercial point, you risk losing the goodwill of customers who at other times may buy stock off your shelves. And, rather surprisingly, quite a few special orders may be regarded as *more* profitable than typical sales from stock. While a stock book may be on your shelves for four months, say, before it sells, and for three months after you have had to pay for it, a specially ordered book passes through your hands very quickly, your customer often paying you before you pay the supplier. So no matter how low the discount or high the surcharge, provided income exceeds cost, such a transaction comes near to producing the infinite return on a zero investment already remarked upon in Book Token selling.

You cannot expect customers to distinguish between special orders that are profitable to you and those that are not; they will find it arbitrary and unreasonable if you accept some but refuse others. In practice, only a policy of accepting all special orders or refusing all is likely to be workable without causing yourself unnecessary difficulties or your customers unnecessary offence.

Service charges for special orders. One way of ensuring that all special orders at least cover their cost is to ask the customer to pay a service charge. When the *Lost Book Sales* researchers sought customers' views on this, only one person in three agreed with the idea. One might guess that in practice any attempt to impose a service charge – however fair and reasonable from the bookseller's point of view – would lead to fewer special orders and more customers traipsing from shop to shop in the hope of discovering the book on service-free shelves, possibly losing their enthusiasm for any purchase at all long before finding the book. So it may be that the service charge is a non-starter; but it is still worth thinking about, and possibly trying out, because it is really the only way to make commercial sense of some special orders.

Routines when accepting special orders. It's a sensible precaution to ask the customer for a deposit when accepting a special order. Without it, you may have all the work of processing the order, and then finish up with an unsaleable book obtained for a customer who never comes back to buy it, or who returns only to say he doesn't want it.

To give yourself some protection against possible legal action, you should always make clear to the customer that you cannot guarantee that the supplier will supply the book, nor can you guarantee its price or delivery date: these are matters in the hands of the supplier, and you have no control over them. Indicate also whether you will require the customer to pay any special order charges – either your own, or those that may be imposed by the supplier. To avoid having to make a dispiriting speech to every customer placing a special order, it is a good idea to have your Conditions of Sale, covering such matters as those above, prominently displayed at the point where special orders are taken, and also clearly and noticeably set out on any receipt you give. Consult your solicitor about the precise wording to use. Draw customers' attention to these Conditions of Sale when taking special orders.

If you do it, do it whole-heartedly. If you decide that the advantages of offering a special order service outweigh the disadvantages

– and you probably will – make sure that customers know about the service. Suggest it when appropriate, mention it in your advertising, sign the service prominently in the shop (see, for example, Services Promotion Kit on page 91). Customers sometimes fail to find the book they're looking even though it's there on the shelves, and they may only tell you what they want if they believe you welcome special orders. From time to time you'll have the satisfaction of being able to surprise them by pulling the book off your shelves.

Selling to the Possibles

Except that they are not looking for specific titles, Possibles are much like Definites and probably similarly motivated. A popular television series on archaeology, for example, leads Definites to seek the book of the programme, and Possibles to seek archaeology books in general. While a percentage of Definites decide against an intended purchase on the grounds of price, for the Possibles price is only one factor to be weighed in the title selection process; a high price which turns a Definite off completely only causes a Possible to shift attention to an alternative title – if there is one. The stock implication of this is that you need books at *a range of prices* within each subject section of the shop.

HELP AND ADVICE

An interesting figure in *Lost Book Sales* reveals that only one Possible in five seeks help from bookshop staff. This touches on the tricky matter of how far customers should be left to browse – possibly aimlessly – and how far positive guidance should be offered. Clear and prominent signs should help customers find their way round unaided, and an 'Enquiries' notice at the cash desk or some other manned position, may encourage the diffident to ask for help, but active bookselling intervention at some stage may make the difference between a sale and no sale.

It must be a mistake to bear down on customers as soon as they come into the shop; that not only makes it difficult for them to browse – and remember that 45 per cent of buyers make impulse purchases – it also means that they may be less inclined to come in to browse next time. Over-zealous attention is a way of losing customers. "Can I help you?" is one of the classic turn-offs of the retail trade. The question, demanding an answer, only makes the customer feel cornered. Prefer something like "Please ask if you need any help" – a permissive formula, allowing the customer to browse or to enquire at will.

Waiting till the non-purchasing customer is on the way out

before making your approach is also a mistake, and again may inhibit future visits; the bookseller who seems to be saying 'You'd better have a good excuse before I let you get out of here' is unlikely to win a customer either this time or next.

Even if you have used the permissive formula, and used it in good time, not everyone who needs help or would benefit from it actually asks for it: that one-in-five figure is very low. The best solution is for you and your staff to be always on hand and approachable, ready to intercept customers' enquiring glances as they look round for help. Whatever task you're engaged in at the time, keep a discreet eye on everyone in the shop and avoid behaving in the sort of way that wordlessly sends out the message 'For heaven's sake don't interrupt me – can't you see I'm doing something important?'

Selling to the Browsers

All Browsers who buy are by definition making impulse purchases, as are a substantial number of Definites and Possibles. Impulse purchases account for over 40 per cent by value of shop sales – a substantial part of your business. And while impulse purchasing is experienced as a chance event by the customer, it results from deliberate planning by the bookseller.

One person's impulse purchase is another person's planned purchase. Many a book is picked up and examined by Browsers who notice a title they've heard about recently: like everyone else, Browsers respond to publisher's hype and media coverage. Most books, however, get very little of either and yet may be attractive and appealing books in the bookshop. The bookseller's task is to plan the book displays so as to maximise the chance that customers will come upon interesting books – whether they have previously heard of them or not – beyond the ones they are specifically looking for.

There's a layout problem here. On the one hand, you want your shelves to be clearly signposted so that customers can easily find the sections that interest them. On the other hand, you would prefer that customers didn't home in on their chosen sections too speedily and directly without allowing the rest of your stock the chance of attracting their attention. The ideal layout is the one that channels customers past the largest number of books.

Books displayed face forward are obviously more noticeable than those shelved spine out, and face-forward books at eye-level are most noticeable of all. Make sure that those books you believe to have the greatest impulse-purchase appeal – the ones getting high profile coverage in the media, and others with attractive covers and interesting titles – are displayed face forward on shelves, at eye-level if possible, or face up on tables. However purposefully customers may be heading to their chosen sections of the bookshop, they will by this means be exposed to a number of possible impulse-purchase titles on the way.

A favourite location for possible impulse purchases is at the cash desk. Attractive and low-priced books displayed here will often be added by customers almost incidentally to their purchases even while you're ringing their other books up on the till. In time, you'll discover other particular locations in your own shop which, because of its general layout, turn out to be prime spots for impulse displays. It's not a good idea to use these prime selling spots to try to shift slow-moving stock. Always compound the advantages: put the bestsellers in the best positions. A 50 per cent increase in the sales of a £10 bestseller from 20 copies to 30 copies produces an extra £100 in revenue; on the other hand, even doubling the sales of a £10 slow seller from one copy to two copies gives you only an extra £10.

MOVE STOCK AROUND

Just as you need to change your window frequently to make an impact on passers-by, so you need to vary the location of different subject sections in the shop from time to time so that regular customers have a sense of the shop's liveliness: they never quite know what they'll find next time. It's no bad thing if old customers feel *slightly* disorientated because you've switched things around. In the process of finding what's where again, they may happen upon books they would otherwise have missed.

On the principle of compounding advantages, move sections of seasonal interest into prime selling positions at the appropriate time. Use prime positions for gift books at Christmas, for school aids – dictionaries and so on – at the start of the school year, gardening books in the early spring, and so on.

Try to evaluate the effect on section sales of moving stock to different locations. You may discover – without ever understanding why – that certain sections do particularly well in certain locations. Don't assume you know the answers: keep experimenting.

It is surprising how merely moving books to a different set of shelves can freshen up a display. Perhaps the psychological effect upon you and your staff is as significant as the direct effect upon your customers. Your pleasure and excitement in the way things look contributes subtly to the welcoming atmosphere of the shop. If you're feeling jaded, try moving the stock around.

SELLING BOOKS BY MAIL

Most mail order bookselling is done by publishers direct selling their own titles, and by book clubs selling a limited range of titles to a captive market of members committed to taking a minimum number of club books each year (see page 54).

For the average small bookshop, mail order is likely to be more trouble than it's worth unless there is a subject speciality in which you stock a good range of titles not normally stocked by other booksellers. Even with such a subject speciality, the cost of preparing catalogues and lists, and mailing them to your customers, can very easily use up in advance the gross profit that results from the sales you make. A certain amount of mail order business comes unsolicited to most bookshops in the course of time from old customers who have moved away. Try to encourage such customers to order stock titles – send them the *Books for Giving* Christmas catalogue for example – so as to avoid an excess of special orders.

The trouble is that for the general bookseller 'mail order' tends to be 'special order'. People typically purchase by mail only when it offers advantages not available to them by personal shopping. Because of the NBA, the mail order bookseller cannot compete on price. If you were to take advertising space in a national paper, extolling the merits of a particular book and inviting mail orders for it, there would be no reason why people impressed by your advertisement should not obtain the book from their local bookshop at exactly the same price as you are asking – and save themselves the cost of post and packing into the bargain. And if you offer to supply post free, you will probably be giving away a large chunk of your gross profit, and still have no competitive advantage over the local bookshop.

The only way to avoid putting business the way of other booksellers is to promote books only to your own known loyal customers – but they come into your shop anyway, mail order service or no. What it comes to is this: a mail order bookselling service attracts customers only when it offers books not readily available in local bookshops. That necessarily excludes all the popular titles, and means that you must either offer a subject speciality or be prepared to accept special orders.

A few special orders among a mass of orders you could supply from stock might not worry you too much. But would it be just a few? If you avoid promoting specific titles in order not to put business the way of other bookshops, you will, in effect, be offering to supply any book in print. Unfortunately, such advertising tends to produce orders only for books that people have not been able to find in their local bookshops – often enough because the book is OP or because they have inadequate or incorrect bibliographical information. Either way, you are likely to find yourself knee-deep in special order problems. And even if a book is untraceable or unobtainable, you still have the cost of mailing that negative information to the customer.

Mail order bookselling on any scale is more difficult than it looks. As a small independent bookseller, you should consider it only if (a) you have a well-maintained stock of not easily obtainable titles of specialist interest to people who may be reached by advertising in specialist journals or by mailing to specialist lists, or (2) you have a loyal list of out-of-town customers to whom you can send occasional lists, such as *Books for Giving* or catalogues you compile yourself, and can rely on them to place their orders with you.

SELLING BOOKS BY PHONE

If you are in the main credit card schemes (see page 188), taking orders by phone for delivery by post is well worth doing. Strictly speaking, it's a form of mail order, but you can deal with enquiries immediately without incurring the expense of written replies, and you have complete security of payment as soon as you accept the customer's order.

Mention the service in your advertising and on any give-away booklists, bookmarks, and so on. Try a semi-display advertisement in your local Yellow Pages inviting telephoned credit card orders. If your advertisement copy tells customers to phone and ask, say, for your mail order department, you will be able to identify the callers produced by the ad and so be able to evaluate its success. If it works, think of running the ad in other phone books. The catchment area for mail and telephone selling is the entire country.

LOOK TO THE FUTURE

While the first objective when dealing with customers is to sell to them, the second objective is to ensure that they come back in the future; and that second objective is by no means secondary. Your long-term success depends not merely upon winning customers but keeping them. By publicity and advertising you continuously trawl for prospects and hope to turn them into new customers, but it's when the old customers keep coming back that you know you have an established business.

Customers are retained by the totality of what your shop offers: convenient location, ambience, stock range, helpful but not intrusive service and so on. Sheer habit plays its part too. But it's worth considering how to nudge your customers into even more frequent visits.

Many bookshops put the shop's name and a sales message on the paper bags into which customers' purchases are slipped, and it is certainly a good idea to miss no opportunity to promote your shop. But paper bags are typically thrown away once the customers get home, so the amount of promotional work they do is limited. Far better to put your name on something with a longer life. Bookmarks fit the bill admirably: they are useful, relate perfectly to the product you're selling, are frequently handled by the reader, and have a very long life indeed. Put one in each book or bag of books you sell.

Other give-aways include booklists and catalogues. For example, a copy of something like *Books* – a monthly book review published for free distribution in bookshops – can be popped into the customer's bag and may well lead to further sales. A free monthly allowance of 250 copies of *Books* goes to all qualifying bookshops – mainly Charter Group members and those judged to have good enough stock and staff – and further copies are available at a very low price. Get details from Gradegate Ltd, the publishers.

Above all, you have to remember that every meeting point between the shop and the customer is a marketing contact which – by however small an amount – does its bit to influence the customer to buy or not to buy, to come back in the future or to look elsewhere. Everything from untidy displays to inadequate lighting, from the Saturday girl's smile to the shine on your shoes – *everything* shows up in the end on the bottom line of the accounts. If today's customers are to return as tomorrow's customers, the arts of marketing and salesmanship must be practised at every turn.

Success in bookselling means success in selling books. It may not be easy but it *can* be done. And although bookselling is a commercial and not a literary activity, those who succeed commercially – and, if you put your mind to it, you could be one of them – find that beyond the financial rewards, there is the satisfaction that comes from playing one's part in the furtherance of literature and literacy, and in working, day by day, among such pleasing products as books, and alongside such congenial colleagues as the men and women of the book trade.

NET BOOK AGREEMENT 1957

We the undersigned several firms of publishers, being desirous that in so far as we publish books at net prices (as to which each publisher is free to make his own decisions), those net prices shall normally be the prices at which such books are sold to the public as hereinafter defined, and in order to avoid disorganisation in the book trade and to ensure that the public may be informed of and able uniformly to take advantage of the conditions under which net books may be sold at less than the net prices, hereby agree to adopt and each of us does hereby adopt the following standard sale conditions for the net books published by us within the United Kingdom:

STANDARD CONDITIONS OF SALE OF NET BOOKS

(i) Except as provided in clauses (ii) to (iv) hereof and except as we may otherwise direct net books shall not be sold or offered for sale or caused or permitted to be sold or offered for sale to the public at less than the net published prices.

(ii) A net book may be sold or offered for sale to the public at less than the net published price if
- (a) it has been held in stock by the bookseller for a period of more than twelve months from the date of the latest purchase by him of any copy thereof and
- (b) it has been offered to the publisher at cost price or at the proposed reduced price whichever shall be the lower and such offer has been refused by the publisher.

(iii) A net book may be sold or offered for sale to the public at less than the net published price if it is second-hand and six months have elapsed since its date of publication.

(iv) A net book may be sold at a discount to such libraries, book agents (including Service Unit libraries), quantity buyers and institutions as are from time to time authorised by the Council of The Publishers Association of such amount and on such conditions as are laid down in the instrument of authorisation. Such amount and conditions shall not initially be less or less favourable than those prevailing at the date of this Agreement.

(v) For the purposes of clause (i) hereof a book shall be considered as sold at less than the net published price if the bookseller
- (a) offers or gives any consideration in cash to any purchaser

except under licence from the Council of The Publishers Association or

(b) offers or gives any consideration in kind (e.g. card indexing, stamping, reinforced bindings, etc., at less than the actual cost thereof to the bookseller).

(vi) For the purposes of this Agreement and of these Standard Conditions:

Net book shall mean a book, pamphlet, map or other similar printed matter published at a net price. *Net price* and *net published price* shall mean the price fixed from time to time by the publisher below which the net book shall not be sold to the public.

Public shall be deemed to include schools, libraries, institutions and other non-trading bodies.

Person shall include any company, firm, corporation, club, institution, organisation, association or other body.

(vii) The above conditions shall apply to all sales executed in the United Kingdom and the Republic of Ireland whether effected by wholesaler or retailer when the publisher's immediate trade customer, whether wholesaler or retailer, or the wholesaler's immediate trade customer, is in the United Kingdom or the Republic of Ireland.

We the undersigned several firms of publishers further agree to appoint and each of us does hereby appoint the Council of The Publishers Association to act as our agent in the collection of information concerning breaches of contract by persons selling or offering for sale net books, and in keeping each individual publisher informed of breaches in respect of such net books as are published by him and we further hereby undertake and agree that we will each enforce our contractual rights and our rights under the Restrictive Trade Practices Act 1956 if called upon to do so by the Council of The Publishers Association, and provided that we shall be indemnified by The Publishers Association if so requested by us in respect of any costs of such action incurred by us or by the Council of The Publishers Association on our behalf.

NATIONAL BOOK SALE

CONDITIONS TO BE OBSERVED BY ALL PARTICIPATING PUBLISHERS, WHOLESALERS AND RETAIL BOOKSELLERS

1 The Sale shall not begin before [*date*] nor end after [*date*], both dates inclusive. This period is referred to in the following conditions as the Sale Period.

BOOKSELLERS' OVERSTOCKS

2 Subject to the right of a publisher to exclude his list from the Sale (see Condition 3) licensed Retail Booksellers shall be permitted, during the Sale period, to offer at any price not exceeding two-thirds of the published price (ie at a discount of 33⅓ per cent or more off published price) any title of which they have not ordered a copy during the last twelve months. On conclusion of the Sale such books shall revert to published price unless reduced in accordance with provisions of Clause (ii) of the Standard Conditions of Sale of Net Books.

3 Any publisher shall have the right to stipulate that all his titles shall be excluded from the Sale, except where they have been reduced in price in accordance with the provisions of Clause (ii) of the Standard Conditions of Sale of Net Books, but no publisher shall exclude selected titles only.

PUBLISHERS' OVERSTOCKS

4 Publishers taking part shall send to the Publishers Association by [*date*] 1,000 copies of their lists of any overstocks they wish to offer for disposal during the Sale for co-operative mailing to licensed booksellers.

5 Publishers' overstocks shall be offered on the following terms:- at 50 per cent off the Sale price, the Sale price being fixed by the publisher. Sale prices shall not be more than half the published price. Not less than three copies may be ordered of books of a Sale price of 50p or less.

6 During the last two days of the Sale it shall be permissible for a licensed bookseller to fix his own price on such publishers' overstocks as may still be in his possession, provided always that no announcement of any kind of reduction in the Sale price is made by the bookseller prior to those days.

7 Publishers' overstocks bought by booksellers for disposal during the Sale but which have not been sold shall revert to full price on conclusion of the Sale until they are remaindered by the publishers (see Condition 9) or, alternatively, reduced in accordance with the provisions of Clause (ii) of the Standard Conditions of Sale of Net Books. Booksellers shall be permitted to dispose of such stocks in any subsequent officially recognised national sale at any price without reference to the publishers of the books in question.

8 Titles offered by a publisher at a reduced price for the Sale Period shall not, within six months of the end of the Sale Period, be remaindered or issued by him at a price lower than that obtaining immediately before the Sale. No title shall be offered by a publisher until twelve months after publication.

9 Booksellers taking part shall not accept at a reduced price for the Sale the publications of a non-participating publisher unless such publications have been remaindered in accordance with trade regulations.

10 Reduction in price for the Sale Period shall not entitle booksellers to claim allowances.

11 Wholesale Booksellers taking part shall be permitted to handle publishers' overstocks subject to their agreeing terms of business with the publishers and to their supplying booksellers on the same terms and conditions, as set out below, as do publishers.

WHOLESALE BOOKSELLERS' OVERSTOCKS

12 Wholesale Booksellers taking part shall be permitted to offer to participating booksellers, for the period of the Sale only:-

a) any title in their stocks, of which no copy has been ordered or otherwise added to their stock during the previous twelve months and which has not been excluded from the Sale by the publishers thereof (see Condition 3), and
b) any title in their stock, which is being offered as an overstock by the publishers thereof to licensed booksellers for the Sale Period.

13 Wholesale Booksellers shall themselves determine the discounts at which their overstocks shall be offered to licensed booksellers, but the Sale price, which shall be fixed by the wholesaler, shall not be more than half the published price. Conditions 6 and 7 above shall apply also to wholesale booksellers' overstocks supplied to booksellers for the Sale Period.

GENERAL

14 Books offered to the general public at Sale bargain prices shall not be offered at such prices by advertisement or otherwise more than twenty-one days before the Sale.

LIBRARY LICENCE

TERMS AND CONDITIONS

This Licence is issued by authority of the Council of the Publishers Association in accordance with Condition (iv) of the Standard Conditions of Sale of Net Books set out in the Net Book Agreement, 1957, to permit the Bookseller named overleaf ("the Bookseller") to supply the Library named overleaf ("the Library") with net books, solely for the use of the Library but not for resale, at a discount not exceeding ten per cent of their net published prices, subject to the following conditions:

1 Discount on net books may be allowed only in return for prompt settlement of invoices.
2 Discount may not be allowed on net books on which the Bookseller receives a discount of less than sixteen and two-thirds per cent plus five per cent.
3 Discount may be allowed only so long as the Library's total annual purchases of net books solely for the use of the Library is not less than £100.
4 No consideration in cash or in kind, other than the granting of a discount permitted under this Licence, shall be offered or given by the Bookseller or sought or accepted by the Library in respect of or in connection with the supply of net books by the Bookseller to the Library.
5 Without prejudice to the generality of the last foregoing Condition, supplementary services (such as card-indexing, stamping, reinforcement of binding, the supply and fitting of plastic jackets etc.), if provided by or on behalf of the Bookseller to the Library, shall be charged and paid for at not less than the actual cost thereof to the Bookseller.
6 Books purchased under this Licence shall be purchased solely for the use of the Library and not for resale.
7 This Licence is revocable by the Council of the Publishers Association at any time but, unless revoked on account of a breach of the Standard Conditions of Sale referred to above, not less than three months previous notice shall be given.

Any breach of these terms and conditions constitutes a breach of the Standard Conditions of Sale of Net Books referred to above and will render this Licence liable to immediate revocation.

NOTE: This Licence is valid only in respect of the Bookseller and the Library named overleaf and subject to the endorsement of their names being authorised by signature on behalf of the Publishers Association.

BOOK AGENT'S LICENCE

[*Name*], [*address*], having applied for recognition as a Book Agent, and having given the undertaking printed on the back of this Licence [*see below*], is hereby authorised to purchase new books: for resale to the public at the full published price, from the following bookseller, viz., [*bookseller*], these books being for recreational reading, entirely for resale at full published prices to individual purchasers (i.e. not for class or scholastic or library use) and the said bookseller is hereby authorised to allow the said book agent an allowance not exceeding fifty per centum of the retail discount given to the bookseller by the publisher in respect of each new book supplied to the book agent, BUT ONLY during the period for which this Licence is valid, and so long as the Licensee observes the conditions of his undertaking.

It is a condition of the granting of this Licence that it may be revoked at any time by the Publishers Association upon reason being given and upon its giving written notice by the hand of its Secretary to the parties named herein. But unless revoked on account of any action which the Publishers Association or the Joint Advisory Committee consider to be a breach of its terms and/or conditions three months' notice shall be given to the licensee.

UNDERTAKING

This Licence is granted in consideration of an undertaking by the Licensee:

(i) not to offer for sale or to sell any new net book or books at less than the full net published price, either directly or indirectly or by way of settlement discount;

(ii) not to ask for or accept any allowance upon new net books except from the Bookseller named upon this Licence or upon any endorsement thereof.

QUANTITY BOOK BUYING SCHEME (Revised November 1954)

BEING A SCHEME DESIGNED TO EXTEND THE LARGE SCALE PURCHASE OF NET BOOKS BY INDUSTRIAL, COMMERCIAL AND PHILANTHROPIC ENTERPRISES

1 The Quantity Book Buying Scheme, which was introduced by the Publishers Association and the Booksellers Association in 1937, was simplified in 1951 to provide for a discount to be given to those who *as an exceptional matter* ordered 12 or more copies of a title or titles, of which the total value was not less than £25. The scheme has now been amended and extended to cover large single orders for net books of an aggregate value of £250 or more, regardless of the number of copies of any one title contained in the order.

2 CONDITIONS OF LICENSING
Licences for the grant of discount in accordance with the scale set out below will be issued by the Publishers Association under the Quantity Book Buying Scheme on the following conditions:-

(a) The books must be required for gift or presentation in connection with the purchaser's business, or for philanthropic or propaganda purposes. The provision of a library, whether recreational or educational, for use by the purchaser's own employees, free of charge, would qualify.

(b) The books are not to be offered for sale by the purchaser, nor is their use or distribution to be made subject by him to any charge or other consideration.

(c) The order will be delivered in one consignment and paid for in cash on receipt.

(d) No discount shall be allowable on books on which the bookseller himself does not receive from the publisher a discount of at least 25 per cent. The value of any such books shall be deducted from the total value of any order coming under this scheme before application is made for discount to be allowed.

(e) Licences issued by the Publishers Association under this scheme shall apply to one order only and shall not be valid for repeat orders (although application may be made for fresh licences in respect of repeat orders that qualify on their own account).

3 The scale of discount allowable shall be as follows:-

(a) For an order for assorted titles worth £250 or more:

Value of order	*Discount*
£250–£349	5%
£350–£449	6%
£450–£549	7%
£550–£649	8%
£650–£749	9%
£750 and over	10%

(b) For an order for a large quantity of one title (minimum 12), to a total value of £25 or more:-

A flat 10 per cent discount

REGULATIONS FOR CONDUCT OF BOOK CLUBS

INTRODUCTION

COMMENCEMENT AND ENFORCEMENT OF REGULATIONS

1 The present Regulations shall come into force on 1 April 1985, and replace the *Simultaneous* and *Reprint* Regulations which were brought into force on 1 December 1975 and 1 December 1974 respectively. The Council of The Publishers Association recommends publishers of net books to license such books only to book clubs which are on the Association's register as having signed and agreed to the Regulations currently in force.

OBJECT AND INTERPRETATION OF THE REGULATIONS

2 Recognising at the same time

(a) that book clubs have a valuable function to perform in the publication and distribution of books and

(b) that some regulation of their operations is required to promote and safeguard the interests of the public

(i) in the overall efficiency and good and orderly working of the book trade (including book clubs themselves), and,

(ii) in the wide availability of a variety of books through all channels of distribution, of which stockholding booksellers are of special importance, as well as through book clubs themselves,

the object of these Regulations is to provide such regulation to the minimum degree required for the purpose. The Regulations shall at all times be interpreted in the light of the foregoing.

DEFINITIONS

3 In these Regulations, except where the context otherwise requires, the following expressions shall have the following meanings:-

(a) 'book club' shall mean an organisation that sells books to its registered members;

(b) 'book club choice' shall mean a title offered by a book club as a main or alternative choice;

(c) 'premium' shall mean a title offered by a book club as an inducement to join.

SCOPE OF REGULATIONS

APPLICATION TO ALL BOOK CLUB OFFERS

4 These Regulations shall apply to all offers of books made by book clubs as a book club choice or a premium, or through a catalogue or otherwise.

APPLICATION TO UNITED KINGDOM ONLY

5 These Regulations shall apply to, and only to, book club operations within the United Kingdom.

APPLICABILITY TO NET BOOKS ONLY

6 These Regulations shall apply to, and only to, titles the trade editions of which are published as net books. They shall not apply to the sale of net books at not less than the net price.

REGISTRATION OF BOOK CLUBS

7 (a) The Publishers Association shall maintain a register of book clubs eligible and accepted for registration by the Council of The Publishers Association. The register shall contain the name and address and the name of the proprietor of each club.

(b) A book club shall be eligible for registration if it undertakes in writing to comply, and continue to comply, with these Regulations, and to furnish to the Association the particulars referred to above, and any changes in such particulars as may from time to time occur.

(c) A book club shall be removed from the register if it fails to conform with these Regulations (unless it remedies the matter within 14 days of being asked to do so by the Publishers Association), or on the expiry of three months' notice to the Publishers Association of its intention to withdraw its signature to the Regulations.

AUTHORISATION OF EXCEPTIONS TO REGULATIONS

8 Exceptions may be made to these Regulations only with the written approval of the Council of the Publishers Association.

BOOK CLUB MEMBERSHIP AND RULES

9 Every book club shall maintain a register of its members for the time being and shall keep records of the names and addresses of its membership for at least the preceding twelve months.

10 The rules and conditions of membership of book clubs shall be clearly understandable by members.

PURCHASE REQUIREMENTS

11 Book clubs shall lay down a minimum period of membership which shall be not less than six months and members shall be required to purchase not less than three book club choices (excluding premiums) within the first year of membership, (or such shorter period as may be appropriate).

SUPPLY ONLY TO MEMBERS

12 Book clubs shall supply book club choices only to registered members, and premiums only to persons applying to become members.

DISPOSAL OF SURPLUS STOCK

13 Book clubs shall not dispose of surplus stock of a title as remainders except with the consent of the licensing publisher.

NOTIFICATIONS TO TRADE

14 At least four months before offering a title, book clubs shall send to the Publishers Association a list of all their forthcoming titles which the Publishers Association shall cause to be published forthwith in the trade press. This notification shall include the following details: (a) title; (b) author; (c) licensing publisher.

ANNOUNCEMENTS TO PUBLIC

15 Book clubs shall not make any announcement to the public or to members that a title is to be offered as a book club choice or as a premium until three months before the intended date of issue of the book club choice or of the premium as the case may be.

PREMIUMS

16 A title shall not be offered as a premium until at least six months after its first issue as a trade edition.

IDENTIFICATION OF BOOK CLUB EDITION

17 Every book offered by a book club shall always have its own imprint or a crest, or legend, indicating that the book is a book club edition, on the title page, on the jacket and on the binding; save that

(a) in exceptional cases where there proves to be an inadequate supply of such copies bearing the book club imprint the trade edition may be used up to a maximum number of copies equivalent to 20 per cent of the order for the copies bearing the book club imprint;

(b) when a book club does not have exclusive book club rights to a title, the licensing publisher may permit the use by book clubs of not more than a total of 5,000 copies of the trade edition or 50 per cent of the licensing publisher's print order (whichever is the lower).

ADVERTISING

18 (a) In advertising book club choices or premiums, any comparison with the price of the trade edition issued by the licensing publisher shall be only in the following form:

Publisher's price	£x
(Book Club) price	£y

(b) Advertisements and publicity material relating to the offer of a book club choice or premium shall not suggest or indicate in any way, in particular by the showing of an imprint, that the copies to be supplied by the club are physically identical with the trade edition.

COMPLIANCE WITH RULES

19 In the event of alleged non-compliance with these Regulations, the records of a book club shall be available for inspection by authorised representatives of the Publishers Association who have no direct personal interest in book clubs or in concerns supplying or licensing book clubs or, at the request of the book club and at its own expense, by The Publishers Association's Auditors.

20 If any doubt shall arise as to whether a book club has complied with these Regulations and that doubt cannot be resolved by discussion between the book club and the Publishers Association, then the parties to the dispute shall agree to refer the matter to a confidential Disputes Panel convened by the Publishers Association, or, should the parties not agree to such a procedure, to formal arbitration, with the arbitrator responsible for allocating the costs of the arbitration between the parties.

ADDRESSES

Access
The Joint Credit Card Co Ltd, Chartwell House, 365 Chartwell Square, Southend-on-Sea, SS2 5ST *Tel* 0702 352266
AND Software Ltd
4 Forest Drive, Theydon Bois, Essex, CM16 7EY *Tel* 037881 4655
Antiquarian Booksellers Association
Suite 2, 26 Charing Cross Road, London, WC2H 0DG *Tel* 01-379 3041
Applitek Books
Felgate House, 6 Studland Street, London, W6 0JS *Tel* 01-741 5411
Barclaycard Visa
Dept SE, Northampton, NN1 1SG *Tel* 0604 252801
J. Barnicoat (Falmouth) Ltd
PO Box 11, Falmouth, Cornwall, TR10 9EN *Tel* 0326 72628
Bertram Books Ltd
The Nest, Rosary Road, Norwich, NR1 1TF *Tel* 0603 617617
Basil Blackwell
108 Cowley Road, Oxford, OX4 1JF
Book Data Ltd
Northumberland House, 2 King Street, Twickenham, Middx, TW1 3RZ *Tel* 01-892 2272
Book Information Service
Book Trust, Book House, 45 East Hill, Wandsworth, London, SW18 2QZ *Tel* 01-874 8526
Book Publishers' Representatives' Association
3 Carolina Way, Tiptree, Essex, CO5 0DW *Tel* 0621 816710
Book Tokens Ltd
152 Buckingham Palace Road, London, SW1W 9TZ *Tel* 01-730 9258
Book Trade Benevolent Society
Dillon Lodge, The Booksellers Retreat, Kings Langley, Herts, WD4 8LT *Tel* 09277 63128
Book Trade Improvement Ltd
152 Buckingham Palace Road, London, SW1W 9TZ *Tel* 01-730 9258
Book Trust
Book House, 45 East Hill, Wandsworth, London, SW18 2QZ *Tel* 01-870 9055/8
Booksellers Association of Great Britain and Ireland
154 Buckingham Palace Road, London, SW1W 9TZ *Tel* 01-730 8214
Booksellers Association Service House Ltd
154 Buckingham Palace Road, London, SW1W 9TZ *Tel* 01-730 8214
Booksellers Clearing House
152 Buckingham Palace Road, London, SW1W 9TZ *Tel* 01-730 9258

Booksellers Order Distribution
49 Victoria Road, Aldershot, Hants, GU11 1SJ *Tel* 0252 20697
Bookwatch
7-Up Sycamore Place, Hill Avenue, Amersham, Bucks, HP6 5BG *Tel* 0494 728232
R.R. Bowker (UK) Ltd
Borough Green, Sevenoaks, Kent, TN15 8PH *Tel* 0732 884567
British Council
65 Davies Street, London, W1Y 2AA *Tel* 01-930 8466
British Library
Bibliographic Services, 2 Sheraton Street, London, W1V 4BH *Tel* 01-323 7077
BUPA Ltd
Kett House, Station Road, Cambridge, CB1 2JP *Tel* 0223 316613
Byas, Mosley & Co. Ltd
William Byas House, 14-18 St Clare Street, London, EC3N 1JX *Tel* 01-481 0101
Celesa
C/Justiniano 9, 28004 Madrid, Spain
Christian Booksellers Association
41 Whitehall, London, SW1A 4BH *Tel* 01-839 5297
The Clique Ltd
7 Pulleyn Drive, York, YO2 2DY *Tel* 0904 31752
Copyright Receipt Office
2 Sheraton Street, London, W1V 4BH *Tel* 01-323 7077
Diamond Epos Systems
20 Tithebarn Street, Liverpool, L2 2DT *Tel* 051-236 2558
Diamond Publishing Group Ltd
43/45 St Mary's Road, Ealing, London, W5 5RQ *Tel* 01-579 1082
Euromonitor Publications Ltd
87-88 Turnmill Street, London, EC1M 5QU *Tel* 01-251 8024
Federation of Radical Booksellers
c/o Housmans Bookshop, 5 Caledonian Road, London, N1 9DX
Gardners Books Ltd
Providence Way, Eastwood Road, Bexhill-on-Sea, East Sussex, TN39 3PT *Tel* 0424 224777
Gradegate Ltd
43 Museum Street, London, WC1A 1LY *Tel* 01-404 0304
Hammick's Wholesale
Albany Park, Frimley, Surrey, GU15 2PW *Tel* 0276 686286
Heathcote Books
Hawkes Drive, Heathcote Estate, Warwick, CV34 6LX *Tel* 0926 451555

Hinton Hill Life & Pensions Consultants Ltd
Manor House, 1 The Crescent, Leatherhead, Surrey, KT22 8DH
Tel 0372 377811
IBIS
Orders Clearing, Waterside, Lowbell Lane, London Colney, St Albans, Herts, AL2 1DX *Tel* 0727 25209
ICC Information Group Ltd
28-42 Banner Street, London, EC1Y 8QE *Tel* 01-253 3906
Independent Publishers Guild
147-149 Gloucester Terrace, London, W2 6DX *Tel* 01-723 7328
Informedia
5 High Street, Beckenham, Kent, BR3 1AZ *Tel* 01-658 0286
Insight Design Services
6 Mundells Court, Welwyn Garden City, Herts, AL7 1EN
Tel 0707 322930
International Book Distributors Ltd
66 Wood Lane, Hemel Hempstead, Herts, HP2 4RG *Tel* 0442 231555
International Booksellers Federation
Grünangergasse 4, A-1010 Wien, Austria *Tel* 0222-512 1535
Library Association
7 Ridgmount Street, London, WC1E 7AE *Tel* 01-636 7543
LRB Ltd
Tavistock House South, Tavistock Square, London, WC1H 9JZ
Tel 01-388 6751
Microphax Ltd
36 Nuffield Way, Abingdon, Oxon, OX14 1TF *Tel* 0235 25695
Midland Bank plc
Marketing Dept, 120 Cannon Street, London, EC4 6AB *Tel* 01-260 6382
National Girobank
Bootle, Merseyside, GIR 0AA *Tel* 051-928 8112
Post Office Marketing Department
Postal Headquarters, 33 Grosvenor Place, London, SW1X 1EE
Tel 01-245 7277
Prestel
British Telecom, Telephone House, Temple Avenue, London, EC4
Tel 01-822 1122
Public Lending Right
Bayheath House, Prince Regent Street, Stockton-on-Tees, Cleveland, TS18 1DF *Tel* 0642 604699
Publishers Association
19 Bedford Square, London, WC1B 3HJ *Tel* 01-580 6321/5
K.G. Saur Ltd
Shropshire House, 2-10 Capper Street, London, WC1E 6JA
Tel 01-637 1571

Society of Authors
84 Drayton Gardens, London, SW10 9SB *Tel* 01-373 6642
Standard Book Numbering Agency Ltd
12 Dyott Street, London, WC1A 1DF *Tel* 01-836 8911
Teleordering Ltd
Wellington House, 61-73 Staines Road West, Sunbury-on-Thames, Middx, TW16 7AH *Tel* 0932 781266
Thomas Skinner Directories
Windsor Court, East Grinstead House, East Grinstead, West Sussex, RH19 1XE *Tel* 0342 26972
Thompson Henry Ltd
London Road, Sunningdale, Berks, SL5 0EP
Tel 0990 24615/22639
Times Newspapers Ltd
Priory House, St. John's Lane, London, EC1M 4BX *Tel* 01-253 3000
UBS Publishers' Distributors Ltd
40 Bowling Green Lane, Clerkenwell, London, EC1R 0NE
Tel 01-278 0333
Visa see **Barclaycard Visa**
Volumatic Ltd
Taurus House, Endemere Road, Coventry, CV6 5PY *Tel* 0203 684217
J. Whitaker & Sons Ltd
12 Dyott Street, London, WC1A 1DF *Tel* 01-836 8911
Wildwood Distribution Services
Unit 3, Lower Farnham Road, Aldershot, Hants, GU12 4DY
Tel 0252 331551
Wordstock Software Ltd
22-24 Corsham Street, London, N1 6DR *Tel* 01-251 4312

BIBLIOGRAPHY

ABC for Book Collectors 6th EDITION 1980 John Carter with corrections and additions by Nicolas Barker (Granada Publishing) ISBN 0 246 11352 9

Arthur Young report SEE ***Book Retailing in the 1990s***

Australian Books in Print ANNUALLY (D.W. Thorpe: distributed in the UK by Whitaker)

Book and Magazine Collector MONTHLY (Diamond Publishing Group)

Book Publishers' Representatives' Handbook ANNUALLY (BPRA: distributed by the Booksellers Association)

Book Report BIENNIALLY (Euromonitor)

Book Retailing in the 1990s 1987 Arthur Young Management Consultants (Booksellers Association) ISBN 0 907972 20 9

Book Trade Year Book ANNUALLY (Publishers Association)

Bookbank MONTHLY ON CD-ROM (Whitaker)

Booknews QUARTERLY (Book Trust)

Books MONTHLY (Gradegate)

Books 1976-88 Now OP – on microfiche ANNUALLY (Whitaker)

Books are Different 1966 edited by R.E. Barker and G.R. Davies (Macmillan)

Books in English BI-MONTHLY ON MICROFICHE (British Library) Each issue cumulates the year's titles to date.

Books in Print (American) ANNUALLY (Bowker)

Books in Print Plus (American) MONTHLY ON CD-ROM (Bowker)

Books in the Media WEEKLY (Bookwatch)

The Bookseller WEEKLY (Whitaker)

Booksellers and Stationers in the 1980s 1987 (Euromonitor) ISBN 0 86338 260 6

Bookselling News FIVE TIMES A YEAR (Booksellers Association)

Bookshop Computer Guide 1988 (Booksellers Association) ISBN 0 907972 40 3

British Book News MONTHLY (British Council: distributed by Basil Blackwell)

British National Bibliography WEEKLY (British Library). The weekly issues are cumulated every four months and there is an annual volume (also available on microfiche) for the complete calendar year.

The Business of Books 1984 Eric de Bellaigue (Hutchinson) ISBN 0 09 158211 3

Business Ratio Report: Book Publishers ANNUALLY (ICC)

Business Ratio Report: Booksellers ANNUALLY (ICC)

Buying a Shop 3rd EDITION 1986 A. St J. Price (Kogan Page) ISBN 1 85091 108 8

Canadian Books in Print ANNUALLY (University of Toronto Press: distributed in the UK by International Book Distributors)

Catalogo dei Libri in Commercio (Italian books in print) ANNUALLY (Editrice Bibliografica: distributed in the UK by Wildwood)

Charter Group Economic Survey ANNUALLY (Booksellers Association)

Children's Books in Print ANNUALLY (Whitaker)

Credo Planning 1988 (Midland Bank)

Cumulative Book Index MONTHLY EXCEPT AUGUST (H.W. Wilson: distributed in the UK by Thompson Henry). The monthly issues are cumulated quarterly and there is an annual volume for the complete calendar year.

Directory of Book Publishers and Wholesalers ANNUALLY (Booksellers Association)

Directory of Members ANNUALLY (Booksellers Association)

Discovering Book Collecting 1982 John Chidley (Shire Publications) ISBN 0 85263 588 5

Financial Management for the Small Business 2nd EDITION 1988 Colin Barrow (Kogan Page) ISBN 1 85091 566 0

French Books in Print SEE ***Les Livres Disponibles***

German Books in Print SEE ***Verzeichnis lieferbarer Bücher***

The Guardian Guide to Running a Small Business 7th EDITION 1988 edited by Clive Woodcock (Kogan Page) ISBN 1 85091 604 7

Guide to Literary Prizes, Grants & Awards 5th EDITION 1988 (Book Trust) ISBN 0 85353 418 7

How to Start and Run Your Own Shop 1985 P. Levene (Graham & Trotman) ISBN 0 86010 718 3

The IBF Economic Survey ANNUALLY (International Booksellers Federation)

Indian Books in Print TRIENNIALLY (Indian Bibliographic Bureau: distributed in the UK by UBS Publishers' Distributors)

International Books in Print ANNUALLY (Saur)

International Standard Book Numbering 6th REVISED EDITION, REPRINTED WITH MINOR CORRECTIONS 1988 (Standard Book Numbering Agency) ISBN 0 949999 06 7

International Standard Book Numbers Listing – on microfiche TWICE YEARLY (Whitaker)

Italian Books in Print SEE ***Catalogo dei Libri in Commercio***

Key Note Report: Book Publishing ANNUALLY (ICC)

Key Note Report: Booksellers ANNUALLY (ICC)

Libros Españoles en Venta (Spanish books in print) ANNUALLY (Agencia Española ISBN: distributed by Celesa)

Les Livres Disponibles (French books in print) ANNUALLY (Le Cercle de la Librarie: distributed in the UK by Informedia)

London Review of Books WEEKLY (LRB)

Lost Book Sales 1980 (Booksellers Association and Publishers Association) ISBN 0 901690 68 6

The New Small Business Guide DUE 1989 Colin Barrow (BBC)
Note: this title replaces *The Small Business Guide* which was still in print in 1988.

New Zealand Books in Print ANNUALLY (D.W. Thorpe: distributed in the UK by Whitaker)

Publishers in the United Kingdom and their Addresses ANNUALLY (Whitaker)

Publishing News WEEKLY (Gradegate)

Religious Books in Print ANNUALLY (Whitaker)

Spanish Books in Print SEE ***Libros Españoles en Venta***

Starting a Bookshop 1984 (Federation of Radical Booksellers) ISBN 0 9508739 1 8

Starting a Successful Small Business 1985 M.J. Morris (Kogan Page) ISBN 0 85038 953 4

Stock Control in Bookselling 1965 Gerald Bartlett (Hutchinson)

Teach Yourself Bookselling DUE 1988 edited by John Cheshire (Hodder & Stoughton) ISBN 0 340 42876 7

The Times Literary Supplement WEEKLY (Times Newspapers)

Verzeichnis lieferbarer Bücher (German books in print) ANNUALLY (Saur)

Whitaker's Book List ANNUALLY (Whitaker)

Whitaker's Books in Print ANNUALLY (Whitaker)

Whitaker's Books in Print – on microfiche MONTHLY (Whitaker)

Whitaker's Books of the Month and Books to Come MONTHLY (Whitaker)

Whitaker's Classified Monthly Booklist MONTHLY (Whitaker)

Willing's Press Guide ANNUALLY (Thomas Skinner Directories)

Working for Booksellers 1984 (Booksellers Association)

The World Book Industry 1986 Peter Curwen (Euromonitor) ISBN 0 86338 093 X

Writers' & Artists' Yearbook ANNUALLY (A & C Black)

INDEX